T0326216

A Special Issue of
Language and Cognitive Processes

Language Production

Edited by

F.-Xavier Alario
Université de Provence, France

Albert Costa
Universitat de Barcelona, Spain

Martin Pickering
University of Edinburgh, UK

and

Victor Ferreira
University of California in San Diego, USA

Routledge
Taylor & Francis Group
LONDON AND NEW YORK

Published in 2006 by Psychology Press

Published 2014 by Routledge
2 Park Square, Milton Park, Abingdon, Oxfordshire OX14 4RN

Simultaneously published in the USA and Canada by Routledge
711 Third Avenue, New York, NY 10017

Routledge is an imprint of the Taylor & Francis Group, an informa business

British Library Cataloguing in Publication Data
A catalogue record for this book is available from the British Library.

ISBN 978-1-84169-819-9 (hbk)
ISBN 978-1-138-87770-2 (pbk)
ISSN 0169-0965

Cover design by Jim Wilkie
Typeset in the UK by MFK Mendip, Frome, Somerset

Contents*

---

*This book is also a special issue of the journal *Language and Cognitive Processes* and forms issues 7/8 of volume 21 (2006). The page numbers are taken from the journal and so begin with p. 777.

LANGUAGE AND COGNITIVE PROCESSES
2006, 21 (7–8), 777–789

Architectures, representations and processes of language production

F.-Xavier Alario
CNRS & Université de Provence, Marseille, France

Albert Costa
Universitat de Barcelona, Barcelona, Spain

Victor S. Ferreira
University of California in San Diego, San Diego, CA, USA

Martin J. Pickering
Department of Psychology, University of Edinburgh, Edinburgh, UK

We present an overview of recent research conducted in the field of language production based on papers presented at the first edition of the *International Workshop on Language Production* (Marseille, France, September 2004). This article comprises two main parts. In the first part, consisting of three sections, we review the articles that are included in this Special Issue. These three sections deal with three different topics of general interest for models of language production: (A) the general organisational principles of the language production system, (B) several aspects of the lexical selection

---

Correspondence should be sent to F.-Xavier Alario, Laboratoire de Psychologie Cognitive, CNRS UMR 6146, Université de Provence – Centre St Charles, 3 place Victor Hugo (Bât 9, Case D), 13331 Marseille CEDEX 1, France. E-mail: alario@up.univ-mrs.fr

The *International Workshop on Language Production*, organised by the Laboratoire de Psychologie Cognitive (UMR 6146 CNRS and Université de Provence) was held in Marseille (France) in September 2004. The scientific committee was formed by the authors of this article, together with Jonathan Grainger. The organisation of the workshop and the writing of this article were made possible by financial support from the following institutions: *Ville de Marseille, Conseil Général des Bouches du Rhône, Institut Fédératif de Recherche 131: Sciences du Cerveau et de la Cognition, Université de Provence* (BQR grant *Bonus Qualité Recherche*).

---

http://www.psypress.com/lcp   DOI: 10.1080/016909600824112

process and (C) the representations and processes used during syntactic encoding. In the second part, we discuss future directions for research in the field of language production, given the considerable developments that have occurred in recent years.

For many years, language production has been the least prominent member of the 'psycholinguistic trinity' (language comprehension, language acquisition, and language production). To be sure, some research threads within the field have a long history. Research of aphasic deficits in the ability to speak (or write, or both) can be traced back to early studies such as those conducted by Paul Broca (Broca, 1861). Other investigations of deviant performance (in normal speakers) led to the construction of early models of speech production based on speech errors (most prominently by Vicki Fromkin and Merrill Garrett: Fromkin, 1971; Garrett, 1975; see also Dell, 1986). In fact, for many years insights on the processes of language production came almost exclusively from investigations into these deviations from normal performance. However, experimental approaches developed during the 1980s. It is largely because of the publication in 1989 of Willem Levelt's seminal book (*Speaking*, Levelt, 1989) that the field of language production has become a theoretically and methodologically broad area of interdisciplinary investigation. The product of such research activities has been the development of theories and models informed by varied techniques, covering the whole range of cognitive processes required for producing language, from determining (pre-verbal) messages to be expressed, to retrieving words, to configuring them in sequences according to the rules of language, and finally to producing them in speech, sign, or print (e.g., Caramazza, 1997; Dell, 1986; Levelt, 1989; Levelt, Roelofs, & Meyer, 1999).

The articles presented in this special issue stem from talks presented at the *International Workshop on Language Production*, organised by the Laboratoire de Psychologie Cognitive (UMR 6146 CNRS and Université de Provence) in Marseille (France) in September 2004. This workshop was the first of a series of annual meetings. The conferences bring together researchers who specialise on different topics within the field of language production, who work in different disciplines and with different methodologies. Accordingly, the articles presented in this special issue of *Language and Cognitive Processes* cover a broad range of topics. They are organised into three sections: (A) the structure of the language production system, (B) lexical representations and their selection, and (C) syntactic processing. In the following, we provide a brief introduction to each of these areas. We then provide some discussion of possible directions that the investigation of language production might take from where it stands now, and of important issues that are not addressed in this Special Issue.

THE STRUCTURE OF THE LANGUAGE PRODUCTION SYSTEM

The first series of articles deals with general issues about the structure of the language production system. The articles by Vigliocco and Kita (2006) and by Goldrick (2006) present different approaches and models addressing the issue of information propagation in the language production system. Vigliocco and Kita review a series of experiments that exploit cross-linguistic differences among Turkish, Japanese, and English to explore the links between the different levels of representation that are postulated in the system. For example, the authors discuss influences of language-specific lexicalisation patterns (Lehrer & Kittay, 1992) on conceptually driven gesture production (McNeill, 1992). They interpret these findings as evidence of information feedback between the lexical and conceptual levels.

In a complementary approach, Goldrick (2006) reviews studies and experiments conducted in a variety of languages (e.g., Dutch, German, Spanish, English). The goal of his review is to identify universal processes that characterise the propagation of activation in the speech production system, irrespective of the language being spoken. For example, Goldrick discusses in detail one widespread operationalisation of the issue of cascading activation in the lexical system: is there phonological activation and encoding for lexical items that are activated but not produced? Goldrick argues that results across experimental, neuropsychological, and computational studies suggest that activation in the lexical system proceeds interactively and he discusses in detail the quantitative aspects of this hypothesis (see Vigliocco & Hartsuiker, 2002, for similar conclusions; and see Levelt et al., 1999, for different conclusions).

Finally, Hartsuiker (2006) discusses an aspect of the architecture of language production which has received relatively less attention, namely the monitoring system – the processes by which language production is checked for accuracy and adequacy (Baars, Motley, & Mackay, 1975; Postma, 2000). His discussion directly relates to the two previous articles, because the monitoring system is often invoked as an alternative explanation of effects that appear to imply the existence of feedback within the production system (Levelt et al., 1999). Hartsuiker provides a thorough discussion about whether the monitor is a plausible theoretical construct to account for certain features of speech error patterns. He argues that the currently available evidence does not allow drawing strong conclusions on this issue, but his discussion clarifies the relationship between monitoring and the 'central' language production system.

LEXICAL REPRESENTATIONS AND THEIR
SELECTION

A second series of articles deals with how the message to be expressed is formed and how the corresponding word representations are selected. Nearly all models hypothesise that language production involves a mechanism that constructs a message and a mechanism that selects lexical representations appropriate for the message through some form of competitive process (for a discussion of alternative selection mechanisms, see Goldrick, in press). The articles by Kuipers, La Heij, and Costa (2006), Gumnior, Bölte, and Zwitserlood (2006), and Schiller and Caramazza (2006) are all empirical reports that address issues of lexical competition.

Kuipers et al. (2006) compare models that differ by the level – lexical or pre-lexical – at which they locate the competition process. To do so, they empirically examine various parameters that affect semantic facilitation or interference during word production tasks, including whether speakers name pictures at the basic or at the category level, whether they name pictures or translate words, or whether they name pictures with distractors presenting different types of semantic relationships. They discuss how their pattern of results constrains models of selection that include a conceptualisation stage in which the preverbal message is constructed. Their interpretation challenges a number of assumptions about lexical selection made on the basis of the popular picture-word interference paradigm (e.g., Roelofs, 1992; Costa, Alario, & Caramazza, 2005; Damian & Bowers, 2003).

Gumnior et al. (2006) used a translation task to investigate the representation of morphological information in the language production system. They report the intriguing finding that the semantic interference effect usually produced by distractor words is absent when morphologically complex distractors are used (in their study, German compound words). In fact, identical facilitation effects are reported for a given target (e.g., *Tasche*, 'bag') when transparent (e.g., *Handtasche*, 'hand bag') or opaque words (e.g., *Plaudertasche*, 'chatterbox') are used as distractors (see Dohmes, Zwitserlood, & Bolte, 2004, for similar findings in picture naming). The discussion of these findings provides valuable insights on the representation of morphological information in language production, a topic that has not been extensively investigated to this day (although see Allen & Badecker, 2000, for a review of neuropsychological studies, some of which describe deficits in morphological production).

Finally, Schiller and Caramazza (2006) report an investigation centered on the representation of grammatical gender in the lexical system. Grammatical gender is thought to be a property of lexical items (see

Corbett, 1991, for a linguistic discussion; and see Schriefers & Jescheniak, 1999, for a psycholinguistic discussion). Its investigation is informative about the processes of lexical selection, as well as about the processes of agreement that occur in contexts such as noun phrases (Schriefers, 1993). Schiller and Caramazza address two issues: the representation of grammatical gender for morphologically derived words (namely, Dutch diminutives), and the role played by this representation in the agreement-guided selection of other words in the noun phrase (namely, definite determiners). The authors interpret the results of two picture-word interference experiments as showing that the grammatical gender of base nouns is accessed automatically, without competition, when a derived word is accessed. By contrast, the selection of gender-marked determiner forms appears to be sensitive to interference effects and hence is presumably not automatic. This article extends previous findings bearing on the processes involved in noun phrase production and selection of determiner forms (for an overview, see for example Caramazza, Miozzo, Costa, Schiller, & Alario, 2001).

SYNTACTIC PROCESSING

The last topic area includes two articles that report investigations of syntactic processing, on the basis of the well known phenomenon of syntactic priming. Syntactic priming (sometimes called structural priming or structural/syntactic persistence) refers to speakers' tendency to re-use recently experienced syntactic structures (Bock, 1986), and has provided one of the main ways to investigate the processes of syntactic encoding during sentence production. Articles by Branigan, Pickering, McLean, and Stewart (2006) and by Ferreira and Bock (2006) report investigations addressing different aspects of this phenomenon.

Branigan et al. (2006) investigate a linguistic property of the representations and processes involved in syntactic priming, namely whether these representations are sensitive to the hierarchical or recursive structure of language. They test the degree to which priming is sensitive (or not) to whether primed structures are embedded in longer sentences, in order to determine whether speakers use syntactic rules that are contextually specified or not. They report eight sentence-completion experiments (see Pickering & Branigan, 1998), which suggest that the representations primed in these experiments, which are thought to drive syntactic encoding, are not specified for context. This research contributes to our understanding of syntactic encoding by constraining the linguistic properties of the representations that it engages.

Ferreira and Bock (2006) review explanations of the functional basis of syntactic priming – what priming might be good for in everyday language use (relatively independently of the specific representations or processes that are involved). They review several lines of evidence, including the performance of anterograde amnesic individuals. They conclude that syntactic priming primarily reflects an implicit learning mechanism responsible for learning to talk, but also that the repetition of linguistic features from utterance to utterance serves to promote successful communication.

FUTURE AVENUES IN THE INVESTIGATION OF LANGUAGE PRODUCTION

Like all fields, research on language production operates by integrating past efforts with current innovations. This special issue represents well these traditions and future directions. In this context, we consider how the different research threads published in this volume represent perennial issues and future movements in the field.

We identify two issues of perennial importance to the field of language production, for which continued progress is imperative if we are to improve our understanding of the most fundamental aspects of linguistic and cognitive functioning. The first issue concerns the relationship between formal notions of linguistic structure and the psychological representations they correspond to (e.g., morphological structure, Gumnior et al., 2006; grammatical gender, Schiller & Caramazza, 2006; the context-free nature of syntactic knowledge, Branigan et al., 2006). Current research in language production makes use of ever-more-finely tuned linguistic materials when addressing issues of representation and processing. This continues to be a critical avenue of research, as it promises to synthesise insights from two independent research threads – those from formal linguistics, and those from psycholinguistics. The second issue concerns the dynamics of information flow during processing. The field has moved beyond the original strong dichotomy between 'modular' and 'interactive' distinctions, and has begun to investigate more thoroughly the computational and formal benefits of different patterns of information flow (Goldrick, 2006). This development includes a more sophisticated understanding of speech monitoring, which can be seen as a functionally interactive influence on production (Hartsuiker, 2006).

Recent work on production is characterised by the integration of previously separate research themes. One type of integration is between the systems that underlie language-processing proper and the systems responsible for learning (Ferreira & Bock, 2006), gesture (Vigliocco & Kita, 2006), categorisation and response selection (Kuipers et al., 2006), memory maintenance and retrieval (Martin & Freedman, 2001; Martin, Miller, & Vu, 2004), and eye-movement control (e.g., Griffin & Bock,

2000; Meyer, Sleiderink, & Levelt, 1998). Such integration continues the strong tradition of situating psycholinguistic research within the frameworks of cognitive psychology and cognitive neuroscience. Another type of integration involves the study of different languages and linguistic populations, including many who speak more than one language. The current issue includes work conducted in Belgium, Germany, the Netherlands, Spain, France, the USA, and the UK. This work investigates speakers of Dutch, English, German, Spanish, Japanese, and Turkish. These cross-linguistic and multilingual methodologies provide a powerful source of variation to gain scientific insights; the field of production is at the forefront of such efforts (for a review see Costa, Alario, & Sebastian-Gallés, in press). A third type of integration comes from a stronger recognition of the communicative functions of language production, bringing the domains of pragmatics and social psychology (among others) into contact with psycholinguistics. This is emphasised most in the current work by Hartsuiker's (2006) investigations of monitoring and Ferreira and Bock's (2006) review of structural priming: Monitoring is explicitly about determining the communicative efficacy of an utterance, and Ferreira and Bock discuss the influential alignment framework (Pickering & Garrod, 2004) that portrays structural priming as functioning to coordinate communicated meaning among interlocutors. Related research threads in production include increasing attention to pragmatics and language use (Clark, 1996; Schober & Brennan, 2003), and the possible tight relationship between production patterns and the distribution of information in the environment (a kind of Gibsonian approach to production; Brown-Schmidt & Tanenhaus, 2006).

The articles presented in this Special Issue are also representative of some of the 'biases' that have characterised the field of language production to this day. For example, almost every article in this issue deals with the production of speech, while other important modalities of language production such as the production of written language (spelling) or the production of sign language are not represented (although see Vigliocco & Kita, 2006, for an example of research using sign language to address general issues on language production). Some bias towards researching speech over writing and signing is not unreasonable; speech represents the primary means of linguistic communication, and spoken language users heavily outnumber sign language users. Nonetheless, psycholinguistic investigations should not overlook a valuable opportunity to gain fuller insights about language processing by exploiting these distinct linguistic modes. Interestingly, the bias towards speech is much less pronounced in aphasia research, where the investigation of written output deficits has provided a great number of insights (Tainturier & Rapp, 2001), from the description of mechanisms that are involved in spelling (e.g., the graphemic buffer: Caramazza, Miceli, Villa, & Romani, 1987; Jonsdottir, Shallice, & Wise, 1996; Miceli & Capasso, 2006; Miceli, Silveri, & Caramazza, 1985; Tainturier & Rapp, 2004) to the study of modality-specific dissociations that are informative of the relationship between the speaking and writing systems (Alario & Cohen, 2004; Caramazza & Hillis, 1991; Miceli & Capasso, 1997). A full integration of speaking and writing models with the mechanisms of typical language production should be a high priority for the field (Bonin & Fayol, 2000; Cleland & Pickering, 2006; Hotopf, 1980; Kellog, 1988).

The study of the production of sign language is even more in its infancy than the study of writing. However, a strong programmatic effort investigating the neural and cognitive basis of sign-language production is acquiring increasing prominence, spearheaded by Karen Emmorey (Emmorey, 2002). Sign language production presents a valuable means of probing the nature of language representation and language production, including investigations of the modality dependence and the neural organisation of language, bilingualism (Emmorey et al., 2005; Thompson, Emmorey, & Gollan, 2005), and how atypical patterns of language exposure affect processing (Mayberry, Lock, & Kazmi, 2002).

Another major issue that is not represented in this Special Issue is the study of the neural basis of language production. Of course, the aphasic tradition and more recent studies have provided major insights about this (Kreisler et al., 2000). However, the use of electrophysiology and brain-imaging tools to inform language production models has been noticeably slower to develop than in other areas of psycholinguistic research, such as visual or auditory language perception. This delay could be due to methodological considerations. In principle, producing speech requires movement of the articulators, a constraint that appears to impose limits on the measures of brain activity. However, this methodological consideration should not limit the research. First, it has been found that it is possible to record the activity of speaking brains without major loss of signal to noise ratio, when comparing overt and covert production situations (Barch, Sabb, Carter, Braver, Noll, & Cohen, 1999; Birn, Bandettini, Cox, & Shaker, 1999; Rosen, Ojemann, Ollinger, & Petersen, 2000). Also, alternative production situations that avoid articulation have been used. For example, participants are sometimes asked to provide manual responses based on lexical access induced by pictures or other non-verbal stimuli or to produce verbal responses in a delayed fashion, etc. (e.g., Jescheniak, Schriefers, Garrett, & Friederici, 2002; van Turennout, Hagoort, & Brown, 1998). Furthermore, the area of language production can benefit greatly from a number of investigations whose main purpose was not the investigation of language production per se, but that used tasks recruiting some or all of the stages of language production (Indefrey &

Levelt, 2004). In recent years, investigations aimed directly at addressing the neural correlates of language production have become more and more common. Importantly, these investigations cover a wide range of language production processes: from syntactic processing (e.g., Heim, Opitz, & Friederici, 2002; Indefrey et al., 2001) to lexical selection (e.g., Damasio, Grabowski, Tranel, Hichwa, & Damasio, 1996; Maess, Friederici, Damian, Meyer, & Levelt, 2002) and issues of phonological encoding and articulation (e.g., Alario, Chainay, Lehericy, & Cohen, 2006; Riecker et al., 2000). Clearly, the integration and development of the existing research on spelling and signing, as well as the neurophysiology of producing language are central topics for the years to come.

CONCLUSIONS

In closing, we note that the field of language production promises valuable and unprecedented insights into both the structure and the processing of linguistic systems more broadly. These insights stem from a number of features specific to production. First, to know a language is to speak it; this implies that real understanding of language acquisition and the nature of linguistic competence more generally must necessarily account for how we produce linguistic forms. Second, language comprehension of course takes as its subject of investigation exactly the products of language production; increasingly, theories of comprehension will need to account for how production works to explain how comprehension works. Finally, language production permits near-direct observation of the products of a language-processing system: What speakers say is necessarily a result of the operations of their production mechanisms, whereas how comprehenders press buttons, answer questions, or move their eyes only indirectly results from how they understand language. Investigations of language processing that exploit these features that are inherent to production will necessarily advance the field. Our aim with this special issue is to promote that advancement.

REFERENCES

Alario, F.-X., Chainay, H., Lehericy, S., & Cohen, L. (2006). The role of the supplementary motor area in word production. *Brain Research, 1076*, 129–143.

Alario, F.-X., & Cohen, L. (2004). Closed-class words in sentence production: Evidence from a modality-specific dissociation. *Cognitive Neuropsychology, 21* (8), 787–819.

Allen, M., & Badecker, W. (2000). Morphology: The internal structure of words. In B. Rapp (Ed.), *The handbook of cognitive neuropsychology: What deficits reveal about the human mind* (pp. 211–232). Hove, UK: Psychology Press.

Baars, B. J., Motley, M. T., & Mackay, D. G. (1975). Output editing for lexical status in artificially elicited slips of tongue. *Journal of Verbal Learning and Verbal Behavior, 14* (4), 382–391.

Barch, D. M., Sabb, F. W., Carter, C. S., Braver, T. S., Noll, D. C., & Cohen, J. D. (1999). Overt verbal responding during fMRI scanning: empirical investigations of problems and potential solutions. *Neuroimage, 10* (6), 642–657.

Birn, R. M., Bandettini, P. A., Cox, R. W., & Shaker, R. (1999). Event-related fMRI of tasks involving brief motion. *Human Brain Mapping, 7* (2), 106–114.

Bock, J. K. (1986). Syntactic persistence in language production. *Cognitive Psychology, 18,* 355–387.

Bonin, P., & Fayol, M. (2000). Writing words from pictures: What representations are activated and when? *Memory and Cognition, 28,* 677–689.

Branigan, H. P., Pickering, M. J., McLean, J. F., & Stewart, A. J. (2006). The role of local and global syntactic structure in language production: Evidence from syntactic priming. *Language and Cognitive Processes, 21,* 974–1010.

Broca, P. (1861). Remarques sur le siège de la faculté du langage articulé; suivies d'une observation d'aphemie [Remarks on the seat of the faculty of articulate language, followed by an observation of aphemia]. *Bulletins de la Société Anatomique de Paris, XXXVI,* 330–357.

Brown-Schmidt, S., & Tanenhaus, M. K. (2006). Watching the eyes when talking about size: An investigation of message formulation and utterance planning. *Journal of Memory and Language, 54,* 592–609.

Caramazza, A. (1997). How many levels of processing are there in lexical access? *Cognitive Neuropsychology, 14,* 177–208.

Caramazza, A., & Hillis, A. E. (1991). Lexical organization of nouns and verbs in the brain. *Nature, 349,* 788–790.

Caramazza, A., Miceli, G., Villa, G., & Romani, C. (1987). The role of the graphemic buffer in spelling: evidence from a case of acquired dysgraphia. *Cognition, 26* (1), 59–85.

Caramazza, A., Miozzo, M., Costa, A., Schiller, N. O., & Alario, F. X. (2001). A crosslinguistic investigation of determiner production. In E. Dupoux (Ed.), *Language, brain, and cognitive development: Essays in honor of Jacques Mehler* (pp. 209–226). Cambridge, MA: The MIT Press.

Clark, H. H. (1996). *Using language.* Cambridge,UK: Cambridge University Press.

Cleland, A. A., & Pickering, M. J. (2006). Do writing and speaking employ the same syntactic representations? *Journal of Memory and Language, 54,* 185–198.

Corbett, G. (1991). *Gender.* Cambridge, UK: Cambridge University Press.

Costa, A., Alario, F. X., & Caramazza, A. (2005). On the categorical nature of the semantic interference effect in the picture-word interference paradigm. *Psychonomic Bulletin and Review, 12* (1), 125–131.

Costa, A., Alario, F.-X., & Sebastian-Gallés, N. (in press). Cross-linguistic research on language production. In G. Altmann, P. Bloom, A. Caramazza, & W. J. M. Levelt (Eds.), *Handbook of psycholinguistics.* Oxford, UK: Oxford University Press.

Damasio, H., Grabowski, T. J., Tranel, D., Hichwa, R. D., & Damasio, A. R. (1996). A neural basis for lexical retrieval. *Nature, 380* (6574), 499–505.

Damian, M. F., & Bowers, J. S. (2003). Locus of semantic interference in picture-word interference tasks. *Psychonomic Bulletin and Review, 10* (1), 111–117.

Dell, G. S. (1986). A spreading activation theory of retrieval in sentence production. *Psychological Review, 93,* 283–321.

Dohmes, P., Zwitserlood, P., & Bolte, J. (2004). The impact of semantic transparency of morphologically complex words on picture naming. *Brain and Language, 90* (1–3), 203–212.

Emmorey, K. (2002). *Language, cognition, and the brain: Insights from sign language research.* Mahwah, NJ: Lawrence Erlbaum and Associates.

Emmorey, K., Grabowski, T. J., McCullough, S., Ponto, L., Hichwa, R., & Damasio, H. (2005). The neural correlates of spatial language in English and American Sign Language: A PET study with hearing bilinguals. *NeuroImage, 24*, 832–840.

Ferreira, V. S., & Bock, K. (2006). The functions of structural priming. *Language and Cognitive Processes, 21*, 1011–1029.

Fromkin, V. A. (1971). The non-anomalous nature of anomalous utterances. *Language, 47*, 27–52.

Garrett, M. F. (1975). The analysis of sentence production. In G. Bower (Ed.), *Psychology of learning and motivation* (Vol. 9). New York: Academic Press.

Goldrick, M. (2006). Limited interaction in speech production: Chronometric, speech error, and neuropsychological evidence. *Language and Cognitive Processes, 21*, 817–855.

Goldrick, M. (in press). Connectionist approaches to language production. In G. Altmann, P. Bloom, A. Caramazza, & W. J. M. Levelt (Eds.), *The Oxford handbook of psycholinguistics*. Oxford, UK: Oxford University Press.

Griffin, Z. M., & Bock, K. (2000). What the eyes say about speaking. *Psychological Science, 11* (4), 274–279.

Gumnior, H., Bölte, J., & Zwitserlood, P. (2006). A chatterbox is a box: Morphology in German word production. *Language and Cognitive Processes, 21*, 920–944.

Hartsuiker, R. J. (2006). Are speech error patterns affected by a monitoring bias? *Language and Cognitive Processes, 21*, 856–891.

Heim, S., Opitz, B., & Friederici, A. D. (2002). Broca's area in the human brain is involved in the selection of grammatical gender for language production: evidence from event-related functional magnetic resonance imaging. *Neuroscience Letters, 328* (2), 101–104.

Hotopf, W. H. N. (1980). Slips of the pen. In U. Frith (Ed.), *Cognitive processes in spelling* (pp. 287–307). New York: Academic Press.

Indefrey, P., Brown, C. M., Hellwig, F., Amunts, K., Herzog, H., Seitz, R. J., et al. (2001). A neural correlate of syntactic encoding during speech production. *Proceedings of the National Academy of Sciences, USA, 98* (10), 5933–5936.

Indefrey, P., & Levelt, W. J. (2004). The spatial and temporal signatures of word production components. *Cognition, 92* (1-2), 101–144.

Jescheniak, J. D., Schriefers, H., Garrett, M. F., & Friederici, A. D. (2002). Exploring the activation of semantic and phonological codes during speech planning with event-related brain potentials. *Journal of Cognitive Neuroscience, 14* (6), 951–964.

Jonsdottir, M. K., Shallice, T., & Wise, R. (1996). Phonological mediation and the graphemic buffer disorder in spelling: cross-language differences? *Cognition, 59* (2), 169–197.

Kellog, R. T. (1988). Attentional overload and writing performances: effects of rough draft and outline strategies. *Journal of Experimental Psychology: Learning, Memory, and Cognition, 14*, 355–365.

Kreisler, A., Godefroy, O., Delmaire, C. et al. (2000). The anatomy of aphasia revisited. *Neurology, 54* (5), 1117–1123.

Kuipers, J.-R., La Heij, W., & Costa, A. (2006). A further look at semantic context effects in language production: The role of response congruency. *Language and Cognitive Processes, 21*, 892–919.

Lehrer, A., & Kittay, E. F. (1992). *Frames, fields, and contrasts: New essays in semantic and lexical organization*. Hilsdale, NJ: Lawrence Erlbaum Associates Inc.

Levelt, W. J. M. (1989). *Speaking: From intention to articulation*. Cambridge, MA: MIT Press.

Levelt, W. J. M., Roelofs, A., & Meyer, A. (1999). A theory of lexical access in speech production. *Behavioral and Brain Sciences, 22*, 1–75.

Maess, B., Friederici, A. D., Damian, M., Meyer, A. S., & Levelt, W. J. (2002). Semantic category interference in overt picture naming: sharpening current density localization by PCA. *Journal of Cognitive Neuroscience, 14* (3), 455–462.

Martin, R. C., & Freedman, M. L. (2001). Short-term retention of lexical-semantic representations: Implications for speech production. *Memory*, *9*, 261–280.

Martin, R. C., Miller, M., & Vu, H. (2004). Working memory and sentence production: Evidence for a phrasal scope of planning at a lexical-semantic level. *Cognitive Neuropsychology*, *21*, 625–644.

Mayberry, R. I., Lock, E., & Kazmi, H. (2002). Linguistic ability and early language exposure. *Nature*, *417* (6884), 38.

McNeill, D. (1992). *Hand and mind*. Chicago, IL: University of Chicago Press.

Meyer, A. S., Sleiderink, A. M., & Levelt, W. J. M. (1998). Viewing and naming objects: eye movements during noun phrase production. *Cognition*, *66* (2), B25–B33.

Miceli, G., & Capasso, R. (1997). Semantic errors as neuropsychological evidence for the independence and the interaction of orthographic and phonological word forms. *Language and Cognitive Processes*, *12* (5–6), 733–764.

Miceli, G., & Capasso, R. (2006). Spelling and dysgraphia. *Cognitive Neuropsychology*, *23* (1), 110–134.

Miceli, G., Silveri, M. C., & Caramazza, A. (1985). Cognitive analysis of a case of pure dysgraphia. *Brain Language*, *25* (2), 187–212.

Pickering, M. J., & Branigan, H. P. (1998). The representation of verbs: Evidence from syntactic priming in language production. *Journal of Memory and Language*, *39*, 633–651.

Pickering, M. J., & Garrod, S. (2004). Toward a mechanistic psychology of dialogue. *Behavioral and Brain Sciences*, *27* (2), 169–190.

Postma, A. (2000). Detection of errors during speech production: A review of speech monitoring models. *Cognition*, *77* (2), 97–132.

Riecker, A., Ackermann, H., Wildgruber, D. et al. (2000). Articulatory/phonetic sequencing at the level of the anterior perisylvian cortex: A functional magnetic resonance imaging (fMRI) study. *Brain and Language*, *75* (2), 259–276.

Roelofs, A. (1992). A spreading activation theory of lemma retrieval in speaking. *Cognition*, *42*, 107–142.

Rosen, H. J., Ojemann, J. G., Ollinger, J. M., & Petersen, S. E. (2000). Comparison of brain activation during word retrieval done silently and aloud using fMRI. *Brain and Cognition*, *42* (2), 201–217.

Schiller, N. O., & Caramazza, A. (2006). Grammatical gender selection and the representation of morphemes: The production of Dutch diminutives. *Language and Cognitive Processes*, *21*, 945–973.

Schober, M. F., & Brennan, S. E. (2003). Processes of interactive spoken discourse: The role of the partner. In A. C. Graesser & M. A. Gernsbacher (Eds.), *Handbook of discourse processes* (pp. 123–164). Mahwah, NJ: Lawrence Erlbaum Associates.

Schriefers, H. (1993). Syntactic processes in the production of noun phrases. *Journal of Experimental Psychology: Learning, Memory, and Cognition*, *19*, 841–850.

Schriefers, H., & Jescheniak, J. D. (1999). Representation and production of grammatical gender in language production: A review. *Journal of Psycholinguistic Research*, *28*, 575–600.

Tainturier, M. J., & Rapp, B. (2001). The spelling process. In B. Rapp (Ed.), *The handbook of cognitive neuropsychology: What deficits reveal about the human mind* (pp. 263–289). Philadelphia, PA: Psychology Press.

Tainturier, M. J., & Rapp, B. C. (2004). Complex graphemes as functional spelling units: evidence from acquired dysgraphia. *Neurocase*, *10* (2), 122–131.

Thompson, R., Emmorey, K., & Gollan, T. (2005). Tip-of-the-fingers experiences by ASL signers: Insights into the organization of a sign-based lexicon. *Psychological Science*, *16*, 856–860.

van Turennout, M., Hagoort, P., & Brown, C. M. (1998). Brain activity during speaking: From syntax to phonology in 40 milliseconds. *Science, 280* (5363), 572–574.

Vigliocco, G., & Hartsuiker, R. J. (2002). The interplay of meaning, sound, and syntax in sentence production. *Psychological Bulletin, 128* (3), 442–472.

Vigliocco, G., & Kita, S. (2006). Language-specific properties of the lexicon: Implications for learning and processing. *Language and Cognitive Processes, 21*, 790–816.

LANGUAGE AND COGNITIVE PROCESSES
2006, 21 (7–8), 790–816

Ψ Psychology Press
Taylor & Francis Group

Language-specific properties of the lexicon: Implications for learning and processing

Gabriella Vigliocco
University College London, London, UK

Sotaro Kita
University of Bristol, Bristol, UK

This paper presents a discussion of the constraints imposed on lexicalisation during production by language-specific patterns, such as whether words exist in a language to describe a given event and whether language-specific syntactic and phonological information correlates with semantic properties. First, we introduce in broad strokes relevant architectural assumptions concerning the levels of representation consulted in lexicalising concepts and we discuss how cross-linguistic research can inform both architectural and processing assumptions. We then assess whether information at one level can affect processing at other levels. In particular we address issues of separability and information flow between lexico-semantic information, on one hand, and conceptual, syntactic, and phonological information on the other hand. Our aim is not to provide a new theory of lexicalisation and lexical retrieval in production, but to discuss the consequences of language-specific effects on lexicalisation for the architecture of the production system, the processes engaged during word-learning, and the information flow during production.

Word production involves the retrieval of different types of information. For example, in describing a scene, the different objects represented and their relations need to be recognised first, that is, mapped into the speaker's conceptual knowledge. Then words corresponding to the

Correspondence should be addressed to Gabriella Vigliocco, Department of Psychology, University College London, 26 Bedford Way, London WC1, UK.
E-mail: g.vigliocco@ucl.ac.uk
The work reported here was supported by a ESRC research grant to Gabriella Vigliocco (RES000230038). We would like to thank Stavroula Kousta, Padraig O'Seaghdha, and David Vinson for their comments on previous versions of the manuscript.

http://www.psypress.com/lcp   DOI: 10.1080/016909600824070

concepts available in a given language need to be retrieved along with information on how to use these words in sentences (their syntax) and their phonological form. The retrieval of these different types of information is effortless and clearly orchestrated in time in a way that follows the task demands of going from concepts to phonological form that characterises production. Thus, conceptual information drives a semantically driven lexical retrieval process in which a lexical representation is retrieved that specifies the meaning of the intended word but not its phonological form. At this stage, syntactic information is also retrieved. Then, during a second, phonologically driven lexical retrieval step, information concerning the phonological word-form is retrieved and prepared for articulation. The distinction between a semantically driven and a phonologically driven lexical retrieval stage is generally agreed upon and it is supported by a plethora of evidence (see Vigliocco & Hartsuiker, 2002).

Thus, in retrieving words for speaking, at least four different types of information need to be accessed, and their retrieval coordinated in time in the manner discussed above, namely: first conceptual, then lexico-semantic, syntactic, and finally phonological. The goal of this paper is to show how the investigation of idiosyncratic language-specific properties can provide novel and important constraints on the architecture of the lexical system, on how the system is engaged during learning and how it is engaged during on-line production. Regarding the issue of information flow during on-line production, in particular we discuss whether information supposed to be used later constrains information used earlier. There is a large body of literature that has addressed the questions of whether the information flow from one level to the next is strictly serial, whether it cascades, and whether information can feed back from a later to an earlier level (see e.g., Cutting & Ferreira, 1999; Damian & Martin, 1999; Dell, Schwartz, Martin, Saffran, & Gagnon, 1997; Griffin & Bock, 1998; Jescheniak & Schriefers, 1998; Rapp & Goldrick, 2000; Starreveld & LaHeij, 1996). In broad strokes, this literature concerns lexical access in a single language and uses speech errors or naming latencies as data. Vigliocco and Hartsuiker (2002) provide a comprehensive review of this literature concluding that whereas there is substantial evidence supporting the cascading nature of information flow during word production, evidence for feedback of information from one level to another is far less strong because results that have been taken to provide evidence for feedback (e.g., mixed errors, Dell & Reich, 1981), can also be accounted for in a system allowing only cascading of information (see also Rapp & Goldrick, 2000).

Here we take a different approach to the issue of relationship among different types of information in learning and speech production. In particular, we take a cross-linguistic approach in which we consider languages that show interesting differences concerning: (1) how concepts are lexicalised (English vs. Japanese and Turkish), (2) what lexico-syntactic properties are present and how they are correlated with meaning (Italian vs. English), and (3) how phonological properties of certain types of words are correlated with meaning (Japanese vs. English). We suggest that evidence from these cross-linguistic studies, in some cases, are compatible with on-line feedback during speech production, and in other cases, can be best accounted for assuming some degree of cross-talk among information types in the course of child language development.

We do not present novel experimental results, rather we discuss findings from experiments we have reported elsewhere concerning the interplay of gesture and lexicalisation (Kita & Özyürek, 2003); and effects of grammatical gender on semantic errors (Vigliocco, Vinson, Paganelli & Dworzynski, 2005). In addition, we present predictions for words with special phonological properties (i.e., mimetic words) that are found among some, but not other, languages (Kita, 1997, 2001). These previous findings and novel predictions are integrated here in a discussion that highlights the importance of cross-linguistic research, in particular, research that focuses on language-specific properties of the lexicon for the study of language production. We start by presenting and justifying a number of assumptions concerning the architecture of the system in light of cross-linguistic variation.

FROM CONCEPTS TO PHONOLOGY: WHAT ARE THE IMPLICATIONS OF CROSS-LINGUISTIC VARIATION?

As we mentioned above, there is general agreement concerning the fact that lexical access in speech production involves conceptual, lexico-semantic, lexico-syntactic, and phonological information. Theories, how-ever, differ with respect to both how information is represented at these different levels, and in the characterisation of the information flow. Moreover and importantly, with only very few exceptions (Cheng, Dell, & Bock, 2006) models do not extend to taking into account developmental mechanisms. In characterising the architecture of the lexical system, given our focus on conceptual and lexico-semantic information, we follow the proposal by Vigliocco, Vinson, Lewis, and Garrett (2004b). In this proposal, referred to as the *Featural and Unitary Semantic Space (FUSS) Hypothesis* conceptual representations are conceived as distributed featural representations. Lexico-semantic representations bind the dis-tributed conceptual features and provide an interface with syntactic and phonological information (see Vigliocco et al., 2004b for a discussion of behavioural and neuroscientific evidence supporting distributed rather than unitary conceptual representations; see Jackendoff, 2002 for additional arguments from a linguistic perspective).

Thus, lexico-semantic representations are conceived as intermediary representations between conceptual and other linguistic information, namely lexico-syntactic and phonological information. Specifically, in FUSS this level of representation is assumed to develop, during childhood, on the basis of the properties of conceptual featural representations, in particular how salient features are for different concepts, what features are shared among concepts and what features are correlated (see also McRae, de Sa, & Seidenberg, 1997; Cree & McRae, 2003). The assumption of an intermediate level of representation between concepts and word-forms is shared with all models of language production (e.g., Butterworth, 1989; Caramazza, 1997; Garrett, 1984; Levelt, 1989; Levelt, Roelofs, & Meyer, 1999). Models differ with respect to whether this level is considered to be 'semantic' (e.g., Butterworth, 1989; Levelt, 1989) or 'post-semantic' (e.g., Caramazza, 1997). In FUSS, this level is considered as semantic because its organisation is dictated by conceptual properties.

Among the reasons for assuming this intermediate level of representation between concepts and linguistic information such as syntax and phonology, the most relevant here is that it provides a way to account for cross-linguistic differences (Levinson, 2003; Vigliocco & Filipovic Kleiner, 2004). Let us elaborate on this point as it clearly highlights the implications of cross-linguistic variation for assumptions concerning how information about meaning is represented. Gentner and Goldin-Meadow (2003) describe the dominant position within cognitive psychology for the last few decades as one in which: (a) human conceptual structure is relatively constant in its core features across cultures, and (b) conceptual structure and semantic structure are closely coupled. Levinson (2003) terms one version of such position 'Simple Nativism', according to which 'language is essentially innate' and 'linguistic categories are a direct projection of universal concepts that are native to species' (p. 26). Universality of conceptual structures coupled with isomorphism of conceptual and (lexico) semantic information is also represented in cognitive neuroscience (e.g., Pulvermuller, 1999).

However, languages map conceptual domains into lexical domains in different manners (see Lehrer & Kittay, 1992). To take very simple examples, English has two words corresponding to the concepts of *foot* and *leg*, but Japanese has just one word corresponding to 'that part of the body that includes foot and leg'. English has multiple words corresponding to different manners of *jumping* (e.g., *bound, vault, leapfrog*), but Spanish and Italian have not. Surely, Japanese speakers can differently conceptualise *foot* and *leg*, and there do not appear to be obvious cultural reasons (independent of language) for why Spanish or Italian speakers have fewer verbs to describe manner of motion. To consider a further example, spatial categories (from which most universals have been expected to come, given the universality of human spatial abilities) differ across even closely related languages such as Dutch and English (Bowerman & Choi, 2001). If semantic and conceptual structures are not decoupled, conceptual knowledge cannot be universal. That is, if people have different semantic structures in their languages they also have different conceptual structures and therefore a 'Simple Nativism' view cannot be correct. Thus, cross-linguistic variability has important consequences to the assumption of universal conceptual structures.

According to Levinson (2003), this implication applies in particular to theories of conceptual knowledge according to which there is a one-to-one mapping between lexical and conceptual representations (non-decompositional views, Fodor, Garrett, Walker, & Parkes, 1980; Fodor, 1998). These views implicitly assume that conceptual structures differ across languages and therefore are incompatible with claims of universality of conceptual structures, unless conceptual structures are conceived to encompass every possible concept that is lexicalised (or lexicalisable) in every possible language. Assuming decomposed conceptual representations (as in FUSS) does not necessarily imply assuming universality of conceptual representations. It allows, however, for at least certain putative conceptual (universal) primitives (such as those grounded in our direct perceptual and motoric experience) to be bound in somewhat different manners in different languages.

Thus a model like FUSS differs from non-decompositional proposals such as the one put forward by Fodor and colleagues because FUSS assumes at least some (e.g., those directly linked to our perceptual and motoric experience) primitive conceptual features that could be universal, whereas lexico-semantic representations are language-specific. The assumption of compositionality is shared with other models of language production (Dell, 1986) and models of conceptual representation (e.g., Barsalou, Simmons, Barbey, & Wilson, 2003; Hinton & Shallice, 1991; McRae et al., 1997; Rogers et al., 2004). FUSS differs from a model of lexical retrieval during speaking such as WEAVER++ because in FUSS lexico-semantic representations are the only linguistic representations interfacing between nonlinguistic conceptual structures and syntax and phonology whereas in WEAVER++, two levels are postulated: lexical concepts and lemmas. Our lexico-semantic representations are closer to the lexical concepts in Levelt et al.'s proposal as their organisation is dictated primarily by the conceptual properties that are bound into lexico-semantic representations, whereas lemmas in Levelt et al.'s (1999) model are not considered to be grounded in conceptual knowledge but provide a link between lexical concepts on the one hand, and syntactic properties and word-forms[1] on the other hand.

In the specific implementation of FUSS presented in Vigliocco et al. (2004b) and Vinson and Vigliocco (2002), the organisation of the lexico-semantic space is developed solely on the basis of the properties of conceptual featural information without taking lexico-syntactic and phonological information into account. Regarding lexico-syntactic information, although across the world's languages, lexico-syntactic properties such as grammatical class; count-mass in English; classifiers in Japanese are often highly correlated to semantic distinctions (e.g., objects vs. events vs. properties for grammatical class; entities vs. stuff, for count-mass in English and physical properties of referents for the classifiers in Japanese), because of the existence of cases in which the mapping between conceptual and lexico-syntactic properties is not transparent (e.g., grammatical gender of nouns referring to objects in Romance languages), most researchers in language production have argued that lexico-syntactic information is represented separately from lexico-semantics (e.g., grammatical class or gender nodes; Caramazza & Miozzo, 1997; Levelt et al., 1999).

Regarding phonological information, in the vast majority of spoken languages there is no clear correlation between properties of word-forms and properties of concepts (at least when we consider morphologically simple words), thus, because of the arbitrariness in the mapping, phonological properties would not come to affect the organisation of the lexico-semantic space.[2]

It is, however, the case that language-specific syntactic and phonological information when clearly correlated with conceptual features may also play a role in shaping the lexico-semantic representations along with conceptual information during development. In standard connectionist models, our lexico-semantic representations could be conceived as hidden units that develop an organisation on the basis of the properties and correlations between input (conceptual features) and output (syntax and phonology). The importance of input-output correlations in shaping the organisation of a hidden unit layer has been shown, for example, in recent work by Gonnermann and colleagues who have demonstrated that morphology may, at least to some extent, be considered as an emergent property of hidden units that develop on the basis of phonology (input)

---

[1] In this paper, we use the term 'word-form' just to refer to phonological properties of words. We remain agnostic as to whether 'word-forms' constitute a level of representation of its own that bundles phonemes.

[2] This is not to say that there are no statistical semantics-phonology correlations beyond onomatopoeias at all in these languages (e.g., Rapp & Goldrick, 2000).

and semantics (output) (Plaut & Gonnerman, 2000; Seidenberg & Gonnerman, 2000).

Regarding lexico-syntactic information, it is important to note that even in cases in which the mapping between conceptual and lexico-syntactic features is opaque (as for gender of nouns) there usually is a core conceptual foundation (gender of nouns referring to humans is transparently related to the sex of the referent in Romance languages). The existence of this core transparent mapping between conceptual (sex) and lexico-syntactic (gender of nouns) properties must be reflected at the lexico-semantic level for these words, and may also have repercussions for other words for which the mapping is less (or not) transparent. Such a possibility has been defended in Linguistic Relativity circles (e.g., Boroditsky, 2001; Sera, Elieff, Forbes, Burch, Rodriguez, & Dubois, 2002) and it is compatible with the hypothesis that children may bootstrap properties of meaning on the basis of syntactic information (e.g., Bates & MacWhinney, 1989; Fisher, 1994; Fisher, Gleitman, & Gleitman, 1991; see discussion in Vigliocco et al., 2005).

Regarding phonology, although it is certainly the case that for Indo-European languages the mapping between meaning and form is largely arbitrary (with the exception of a few onomatopoeias) this is less clear in some other languages: sign languages embed a high degree of more transparent mappings between conceptual properties and phonological properties (iconicity), and also, as we will see below, some spoken languages have a large inventory of words with a far greater degree of correlation between meaning and form.

Here we discuss the hypothesis that syntactic and phonological information may have some role in shaping the lexico-semantic space when there is at least a core systematic correlation between these types of information and conceptual features. How important this role may be crucially depends on the strength of these correlations, in particular languages. Note here that there are two caveats to this argument. First, the presence of a correlation between language-specific syntactic/phonological properties and semantics might have a historic origin and may not be relevant to on-line processing or language acquisition. Second, although we favour a view in which these idiosyncratic properties of the lexicon affect semantic representation, any behavioural effect could arise post-semantically during word-form retrieval. We will return to these two caveats in the discussion, after we have introduced the phenomena we are interested in and the relevant evidence.

INTERACTION BETWEEN THREE LEVELS OF REPRESENTATION

Given these general assumptions and the potential for cross-linguistic variability to affect how representations develop and how they are used in on-line retrieval during production, we turn our attention to three cases in which interactions between different levels of representation may be found: the interface between concepts and lexico-semantic representations, the interface between lexico-semantic and lexico-syntactic information, and the interface between lexico-semantic and phonological information. For each of these cases we ask whether language-specific properties at a specific level may constrain the organisation and processing at a preceding higher level. For the first two interfaces, we present the results of experiments we have carried out and reported elsewhere (Kita and Özyurek, 2003; Vigliocco et al., 2005) in this novel light. For the last interface, however, we limit ourselves to presenting a case for possible effects on the basis of some special properties of Japanese (also discussed in Kita, 1997, 2001).

Note here that the interfaces at which we look for interactions are defined on the basis of the assumptions underlying FUSS. These interfaces are shared with some (Dell, 1986; Dell et al., 1997; Garrett, 1984) but not other (Levelt et al., 1999) theories of lexical retrieval in speaking.

The mapping between concepts and lexico-semantic representations

What concepts are lexicalised differs across languages. The question is whether cross-linguistic differences in lexicalisation can affect any nonlinguistic conceptual processes associated with speaking. Kita and Özyürek (2003) reported evidence in favour of such effect. They showed that cross-linguistic differences in lexicalisation patterns are reflected in *nonlinguistic* representations that are generated at the moment of speaking, such as those that underlie gestures that spontaneously accompany speech.

Their investigation focused on so-called representational gestures, which convey spatio-motoric properties of a referent based on iconicity and deixis (i.e., pointing). These gestures are considered to be generated on the basis of a type of imagery (McNeill, 1992), therefore they must be generated by a cognitive system that has access to non-linguistic spatio-motoric information. They are also tightly coordinated with speaking as, for example, they systematically precede or are synchronised with co-expressive speech (McNeill, 1992; Morrel-Samuels & Krauss, 1992).

In Kita and Özyürek's (2003) experiment, gestures produced by Turkish, Japanese, and English speakers were compared. The participants were presented with animated cartoons depicting motion events and were asked to describe the events. In the critical event, a cat (Sylvester), one of the main protagonists of the cartoon, swung on a rope like Tarzan from one building to another to catch a bird (Tweetie Bird), another main protagonist (see Figure 1). Crucially, it is straightforward for English speakers to verbally describe the arc trajectory in the change of location event, as English has an intransitive verb *swing*, whereas it is very difficult for Turkish and Japanese speakers to encode the arc trajectory as the two languages do not have any intransitive verb equivalent to English *swing*. Japanese and Turkish speakers described the swinging event, using expressions that do not entail an arc trajectory, such as *jump/fly*, *go*, and *sneak in*.

Gestures produced by the speakers of the three languages showed a difference that mirrors the linguistic difference. In particular, there was a cross-linguistic difference in how often the following two types of gestures were used to depict the swinging event: arc gestures depicting the event with the arc trajectory, and straight gestures depicting the event as a pure change of location with the trajectory shape stripped out. Percentages of English, Turkish, and Japanese speakers producing arc and straight gestures are given in Figure 2. Far more English speakers produced arc gestures when describing the swinging event than Turkish and Japanese speakers. In contrast, Turkish and Japanese speakers produced straight gestures more often than English speakers. Thus, nonlinguistic gestural representations are influenced by lexicalisation patterns that differ cross-linguistically.

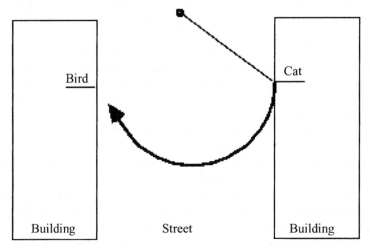

Figure 1. The schematic representation of the Swing Event in the Stimulus (reproduced from Kita & Özyürek, 2003, permission pending).

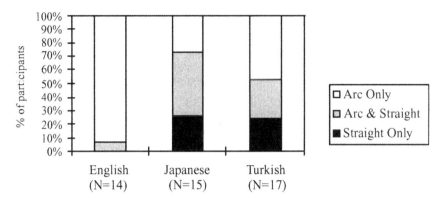

Figure 2. Percentage of participants with the three patterns of arc, straight and arc+straight gestures (reproduced from Kita & Özyürek, 2003, permission pending)

Kita and Özyürek argued that this linguistic effect on gesture indicates that lexicalisation patterns at least partially shape conceptual representations, which are to a large extent independent from the linguistic system. However, there is an alternative account that would make the linguistic effect rather trivial. Namely, representational gestures might have been generated from the lexico-semantic representation of the words that have already been retrieved. If this were the case, then gestures should not systematically encode any information that is not lexically encoded. Kita and Özyürek, however, provided two pieces of evidence against this alternative interpretation. First, it is not the case that Turkish and Japanese speakers did not express the arc trajectory at all in their gestures. They, in fact, often produced multiple gestures to represent the event: an arc gesture and a straight gesture. Second, the gestures systematically encoded spatial details that were never verbally expressed. The lateral direction of the swinging movement (i.e., rightward or leftward) was never verbally expressed, but was very accurately reflected in gestures (90–100%, well above the chance level of 50%). Crucially, the Japanese and Turkish straight gestures encoded the lateral direction very accurately, suggesting that gestures are *simultaneously* shaped by lexicalisation and nonlinguistic spatial representation of the event. These findings make it very unlikely that gestural representations are mere motoric translations of lexico-semantic representations.

Thus, these findings strongly suggest that representational gestures are generated from nonlinguistic spatial-motoric representations, but they also reflect what aspects of the event are lexicalised in the specific language. In other words, lexicalisation patterns affect nonlinguistic conceptual representations generated for gestures at the moment of speaking. The question to ask next is how this effect may come about.

This effect of lexicalisation on gesture production may come about in two ways. First, the effect may be a consequence of language-specific tuning of conceptual systems in the course of development. For example, during language development those conceptual properties that can be more easily encoded in a language might become salient and therefore easier to activate (a similar idea was proposed, for example, in Levelt, 1989). This type of explanation is especially plausible when there is a lexicon-wide tendency to readily encode certain conceptual properties. The second explanation for the lexicalisation effect on gesture production is that there is on-line feedback from the process that selects lexico-semantic representations to the nonlinguistic conceptual representation that drives gestures and speech.

There are two reasons for which we favour the second possibility. First, the lexical gap in Japanese and Turkish is idiosyncratic. For example, Japanese has a transitive verb of swinging (*furu*, 'to swing something') and a non-agentive intransitive verb of swinging (*fureru*, 'something (e.g., pendulum) swings non-agentively'). However, there is no agentive intransitive verb of swinging, which would have been appropriate for the swinging event. It seems unlikely that such details of the lexicon are reflected in the organisation of conceptual representation through developmental tuning, unless one takes a very strong linguistic relativity view that semantic idiosyncrasy of each word in the lexicon is mirrored in conceptual representation. Second, it is not possible to attribute the lexicalisation effect on gesture to more general properties of the English, Japanese, and Turkish lexicons. For example, it is known that manner of motion is lexicalised in verbs less often in Japanese and Turkish than in English (Talmy, 1985). One could assume that the arc trajectory is a type of manner of motion. Furthermore, one could hypothesise that Japanese and Turkish speakers are in general less likely to encode manner in gesture because their conceptual representation of manner is not as accessible, reflecting the tendency in their lexicons. However, Kita and Özyürek found in the analysis of another motion event (a cat rolling down a slope) for which Japanese and Turkish have a readily accessible manner verb that Japanese and Turkish speakers gesturally expressed manner to the same extent and in the same manner as English speakers. Thus, it is difficult to attribute the lack of an arc trajectory in Japanese and Turkish speakers' 'swinging' gestures to a general lack of gestural expression of manner in the languages.

A further question can be raised to the interpretation that the cross-linguistic difference in lexicalisation caused the gestural difference since Kita and Özyürek demonstrated merely a correlation between lexicalisation patterns and gestural patterns. This interpretation, however, is made more plausible by Kita and colleagues' (2006) recent study, which experimentally manipulated how people linguistically encoded events. They manipulated whether English speakers described manner and path of a motion event with one clause (e.g., 'he spun down the hill') or multiple clauses (e.g., 'he span as he went down the hill'). They found that gestural representation of manner and path changed in such a way that it was isomorphic to the linguistic representation. Namely, manner and path tended to be simultaneously expressed in a single gesture when the speaker used a single clause expression. In contrast, manner and path tended to be expressed in two separate gestures when the speakers used a multi-clause expression.

Taken together, the most straightforward way to account for how gestures reflect idiosyncrasies of the lexicon is to assume on-line feedback from the process that selects lexico-semantic representations to the process that generates the nonlinguistic conceptual representations underlying gestures, as Kita and Özyürek (2003) argued.[3] This relates to Slobin's (Slobin, 1987, 1996) notion of 'thinking for speaking'. Slobin proposes that when a speaker generates a message to be verbalised, he or she has to take into account what is necessary or desirable for the language being spoken. For example, the content of the message has to contain information necessary for obligatory morphological marking (Slobin, 1987) and it has to be compatible with lexical and constructional resources of the language (Slobin, 1996). Slobin's thinking for speaking concerns propositional representation of a message for verbalisation. Kita and Özyürek's above finding extends Slobin's notion to the spatio-motoric representations for gesturing (see also McNeill & Duncan, 2000).

The mapping between syntactic and lexico-semantic representations

The possibility that lexico-syntactic and lexico-semantic information are strictly linked is suggested by the existence, in spontaneously occurring slips of the tongue, of the *grammatical category constraint* (i.e., the fact that in semantically related substitution errors, the target and intruding words are from the same grammatical class, e.g., Garrett, 1984). However, there are multiple possible interpretations of this constraint. The constraint may reflect direct effects of grammatical class (as a lexico-semantic property) on lexico-semantic representations, such that words that share the same syntactic properties are semantically more similar than words that do not

---

[3] As an anonymous reviewer suggested, a possible alternative is that the linguistic effect on gesture is 'direct', namely, at the level of gesture-specific planning representation. According to this proposal, the linguistic effect is not mediated by general conceptual representations that can provide information to various output modalities, including gesture and speech.

share the same syntactic properties. Alternatively, the tendency of targets and intruders to share the same syntactic properties may reflect the triggering of syntactic frames during production: the syntactic congruency effects on semantic substitutions described above have been reported during connected speech in which lexical retrieval and syntactic frame building cannot be teased apart. Finally, it cannot be excluded that the congruency effect arises during phonological encoding, along lines similar to the 'mixed error' effect mentioned above. It is, in fact the case that there are phonological correlates to syntactic properties. For example, in English whereas disyllabic nouns tend to be stressed on the first syllable, disyllabic verbs tend to be stressed on the second syllable (e.g., Kelly, 1992). In addition to a grammatical category constraint, a *gender congruency effect* (i.e., the fact that, in semantically related errors, the intruding word tends to preserve the gender of the target word, in gendered languages such as German or Italian) has also been reported for spontaneously occurring semantically related substitution errors (Marx, 1999; Paganelli, Vigliocco, Vinson, & Cappa, 2003). Our focus here is on the gender congruency effect. In particular, the question we ask is whether a language-specific syntactic property such as *grammatical* gender of Italian nouns (which is not correlated in any transparent manner to semantic properties such as sex of referents for words that do not refer to humans) is nonetheless reflected in the organisation of the lexico-semantic space (i.e., words that share the same gender are semantically more similar) and thus more likely to be erroneously selected during the semantically driven retrieval process. As we discussed above, in FUSS lexico-semantic representations bound conceptual features (and thus their organisation is semantic in nature) and provide an interface with phonological information. In order to assess whether gender can affect lexico-semantic representations, and therefore, in order to exclude the possibility that any putative effect can be accounted for in terms of triggering syntactic frames, the experiments described below required speakers to produce words in isolation.

Vigliocco and colleagues (Vigliocco et al., 2005) addressed this question in a series of two experiments in Italian targeting words referring to animals and words referring to artifacts. In Italian all nouns are gender-marked: either masculine or feminine. For nouns referring to humans and a few animals, the gender of the noun transparently reflects the sex of the referent. This transparent relation is realised by the use of different word forms to refer to humans of different sexes and different morphologically derived forms (just like in English: e.g., *man/woman*; *actor/actress*), but also by inflectional processes that apply to the masculine form to change it into feminine (e.g., *ragazz-o/ragazz-a*; boy/girl). For all other nouns, however, there is no clear transparent relation between gender of nouns and sex of referents. Nonetheless speakers need to know the gender of a noun in order to correctly realise syntactic dependencies such as agreement.

In the study by Vigliocco et al., speakers of Italian and English were presented with blocks of pictures (either land animals or artifacts) to name in quick succession in a continuous manner. Of interest were the lexical errors made by the participants while naming the pictures. These lexical errors were primarily semantically related errors and almost always involved other items from our experimental set. The critical question was whether, under these conditions, the intruders produced by Italian participants tended to preserve the grammatical gender of the target in the semantically related errors once other factors that could contribute to the errors, such as visual similarity among pictures, degree of semantic similarity between the items (Vigliocco et al., 2004b) and phonological overlap (Dell & Reich, 1981) were taken into account. In order to exclude a role for these other factors, first, the errors by Italian speakers were compared with the errors, made in the same experiment, by English speakers. This comparison allowed us to exclude influences from visual and language-general semantic similarity to any putative effect of gender given that effects of these other variables should be the same for English and Italian speakers. Second, in order to exclude that the effect could be mediated by greater phonological overlap between Italian words sharing gender than between words that did not share gender, in a crucial analysis, all 'mixed errors' (Dell & Reich, 1981) were excluded.[4] Results from this analysis are reported in Figure 3 in terms of percentages of cases in which target and intruder words shared the same gender. For English, the percentages refer to our classification of the words according to the gender of Italian translational equivalents. As we can see from the Figure, Italian speakers' errors tended to preserve gender more often than the same errors by English speakers even when only semantic errors that did not share phonological resemblance were included in the analysis. Crucially, however, this result was significant for words referring to animals, but not for words referring to artifacts.

We argue that the observed effects of gender on the lexico-semantic retrieval process arises during the semantically driven lexical retrieval step and thus they are genuinely semantic in nature. The fact that such effect is present only for animals and not for artifacts suggests important constraints on the organisation of the lexical system and on the learning

---

[4] We excluded from analyses all errors which exhibited the greatest phonological similarity to the targets, that is those sharing 33% or more of the target word's phonemes in either language. This value was determined by setting a threshold at the mean, plus one standard deviation, of the phonological similarity proportion of all targets and errors in a given category; comparable thresholds were obtained for animal and tool categories even though they were separately analysed.

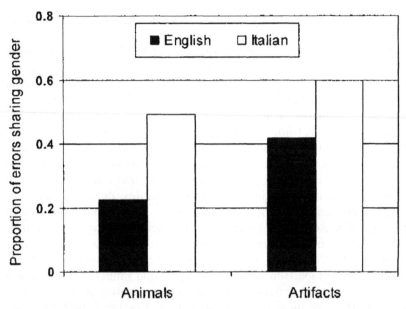

Figure 3. Percentage of errors in which the Italian gender of the intruder was the same as the gender of the target for trials involving naming of animals and tools (from Vigliocco et al., 2005, permission pending).

process. Before discussing what these constraints are, let us address alternative accounts according to which the effect could arise post-semantically. First, the effect could come about as the results of feedback from a syntactic frame (or node) marked for gender instead of during the semantically driven lexical retrieval step. We believe this alternative possibility is unlikely. Nouns referring to animals and artifacts are both marked for grammatical gender, hence they should both trigger activation of their syntactic properties, however, the effect was only observed for nouns referring to animals and not for words referring to artifacts.

Second, it could be argued that the congruency effect comes about as a consequence of greater phonological overlap between words sharing the same gender (i.e., a form of a mixed error effect). Our conservative analysis of the errors that excluded all those instances of likely mixed influence renders this alternative account also quite unlikely. Interestingly, among the items used if anything a greater degree of phonological overlap was present among the tools than among the animals, nonetheless gender preservation was observed for the animals and not for the tools.

How can these effects of gender on the semantically driven lexical retrieval process come about? Vigliocco and colleagues proposed a developmental account of their results. In particular, they discuss how the observed results go against a plausible and general hypothesis according to which any effect of grammatical gender on substitution errors would arise as a byproduct of a very general learning mechanism used by children to bootstrap aspects of meaning from the linguistic input (Fisher, 1994; Fisher, Gleitman, & Gleitman, 1991; Landauer & Dumais, 1997). The basic idea is that words which are similar in their syntactic and morphophonological properties also tend to be similar in their meanings. Nouns that share the same gender are used in the same sentential contexts (i.e., with the same determiners, pronouns etc.), different from the context in which nouns of different gender are used. In this view, gender effects would not depend upon establishing associations between grammatical gender of nouns and sex of referents and therefore this view would not predict a difference between animals and artifacts. Importantly, in this hypothesis lexico-syntactic properties such as gender would have a direct effect on the organisation of lexico-semantics as a whole: all nouns that share the same gender would be semantically more similar. However, this is not what we found. These results suggest a more sophisticated and constrained mechanism of generalisation, one that is mediated by the existence of reliable and strong associations between sex of human referents and gender of nouns referring to sexuated entities. More precisely, children who learn a gendered language like Italian in which gender of nouns (masculine or feminine) for *human* referents almost always coincides with the sex of the referent should notice this correspondence. They could then generalise the correspondence between genders of nouns and male- or female-like aspects of meaning, to encompass other nouns for which there is no direct correspondence but that nonetheless possess male or female conceptual features (i.e., referring to animals). This generalisation would have consequences for the organisation of the lexico-semantic space: words referring to animals but not words referring to other entities of the same gender would be more similar among themselves than words of different gender by virtue of sharing male- or female-like conceptual properties. In other words, an association would first be established between the gender of nouns referring to humans and the sex of referents due to the co-occurrence of the linguistic features (gender: masculine or feminine) and the conceptual features (sex: male or female). Once this association is established it is generalised to other cases in which both features are present: activation of one of the two features (gender of nouns) will also activate the other (sex of referents), thus affecting the development of the lexico-semantic level of representation. This mechanism, does not predict an effect of gender for artifacts, and also does not predict an effect of gender in gendered languages in which the association between gender of nouns and sex of human referents is not strong. Compatible with this prediction, Vigliocco, Vinson, Indefrey, Levelt, & Hellwig (2004a) reported that gender did not constrain errors for words referring to animals for German speakers.

Importantly, for this mechanism to give rise to the effects of gender we observed, the system involved must include feature (decomposition) conceptual representations in order to allow for an association between the conceptual feature (male or female sex) and the linguistic feature (masculine or feminine gender) to be established in the first place. Therefore, these results impose constraints on the architecture of the system. Moreover, they are compatible with the idea that lexico-semantic representations become organised under the joint influence of conceptual and linguistic properties (as we have discussed above), where lexico-syntactic properties for which a core conceptual motivation (like gender) exists may play a role beyond the core cases in which the mapping between conceptual and syntactic properties is transparent (for human referents in Italian).

The mapping between phonological and lexico-semantic representations

Lexico-semantic representations are linked to syntactic but also phonological information. In a manner that is parallel to our discussion of whether grammatical gender of nouns can affect the retrieval of lexico-semantic representations, we can ask whether phonological properties of nouns can affect lexico-semantic retrieval. Most previous studies have addressed this question in one of two ways. Interactivity between semantically driven and phonologically driven retrieval processes has been argued on the basis of the finding that semantically related substitution errors also tend to show phonological relatedness (e.g., saying *oyster* when *lobster* is intended: the mixed error effect also introduced in the previous section; Dell, 1986; Dell & Reich, 1981; Martin, Weisberg, & Saffran, 1989). However, as mentioned above and discussed in Rapp & Goldrick (2000) and Vigliocco and Hartsuiker (2002), these results do not univocally require feedback from phonology to semantics as they can be accounted for in terms of phonologically related errors which show semantic influence: a fact that can be accommodated in a system which includes cascading of information from one level to the next, but no feedback. Interactivity has also been argued on the basis of the results of studies investigating the time course of lexicalisation (e.g., Cutting & Ferreira, 1999; Damian & Martin, 1999; Starreveld & LaHeij, 1996). However, again, these results do not univocally require feedback to be explained.

Here we take a very different approach to the issue of whether phonological properties can affect semantic representation and processing. We propose to consider a very special type of words: *mimetic* or *sound-*

symbolic words that can be found in languages such as Japanese (Kita, 1997, 2001).

Mimetic words show consistent correlations between properties of their phonology and properties of their meaning, somewhat similarly to onomatopoeias (e.g., *bang*) in languages such as English. Just like onomatopoeias in English, or iconic signs in British Sign Language, mimetic words are conventionalised, which is evident from the existence of dictionaries (Asano, 1978; Atoda & Hoshino, 1995; Chang, 1990; Ono, 1994). Even in the sound domain, these words are conventionalised and thus constrained, for example, by the phonological repertoire of the language.

Nonetheless, it is possible that such phonology-meaning correlations cause mimetic words to be produced differently from other words with arbitrary form-meaning correspondence. Moreover, the existence of such words may have implications for the processing of other words in the lexicon. That is, just as in the case of grammatical gender of Italian nouns, the existence of a core set of words for which there is a consistent and transparent mapping between properties of the form and conceptual properties may have consequences for other words for which the mapping is not consistent. Because to our knowledge no experimental study to date has investigated the spoken production of such words, below we first describe some properties of sound-symbolic or mimetic words in Japanese, and then we present predictions concerning their production.

Mimetic words show some systematic relation between specific sounds in the word and aspects of meaning (Hamano, 1998). Examples of such systematic mapping are presented in Table 1. Such form-meaning relationships are not always fully productive, but they are shared among many mimetic words.

TABLE 1

Examples of systematic correspondences between sound-meaning in Japanese mimetic words

Mimetic words	Meaning
Voicing of initial consonant indicates the size of the object involved	
goro	'a heavy object rolling'
koro	'a light object rolling'
poto	'thin/little liquid hitting a solid surface'
boto	'thick/much liquid hitting a solid surface'
Reduplication indicates repetition	
gorogoro	'a heavy object rolling repeatedly'
korokoro	'a light object rolling repeatedly'

Mimetic words can refer to many different types of events and states. Some of the mimetic words refer to sounds. For example, dogs bark *wanwan*. This type of mimetic word expressing sound is a relatively small set. The majority of mimetic words refer to other type of events or states in which sound is not essential. Mimetic words can refer to sensory experiences in non-auditory modalities. For example, *nurunuru* refers to tactile sensation caused by slimy substance, and *pika* to a flash of light. Mimetic words can refer to various types of motion events. For example, *baan* refers to intensive collision of heavy objects, *pyon* to a swift jump, *gorogoro* to continuous rolling of a heavy object, and *yochiyochi* to the manner of walking typical for infants. Mimetic words can also refer to physiological and psychological states. For example, *kutakuta* refers to the state of fatigue, and *sowasowa* to restlessness due to anxiety before an important event.

Japanese has a large inventory of mimetic words. One mimetic word dictionary (Atoda & Hoshino, 1995) lists more than 1,700 entries. Therefore, these words cannot be considered as an isolated phenomenon (as one may argue regarding onomatopoeias in languages such as English or Italian). Mimetic words participate in sentential syntax. Some mimetic words are used as adverbial, predicative nominals, and a component of derived verbs. They are used very frequently in everyday conversation, and they are also used in many different forms of verbal arts (Schourup, 1993), from comic books to novels by Nobel-Prize winning authors. Finally, they are among the first words to be acquired (Maeda & Maeda, 1983).

Japanese is not unique in this respect among the world's languages (cf. Hinton, Nichols, & Ohala, 1994; Nuckolls, 1999; Voeltz & Kilian-Hatz, 2001). Languages for which a large sound symbolic lexicon has been reported include virtually all sub-Saharan African languages (Childs, 1994), some of the Australian Aboriginal languages (Alpher, 2001; McGregor, 2001; Shultze-Berdnt 2001), Korean, Southeast Asian languages (Diffloth, 1972; Watson, 2001), indigenous languages of South America (Nuckolls, 1996), and Balto-Finnic languages (Mikone, 2001). Thus, a number of unrelated languages from diverse geographic areas have a large repertoire of mimetic words.

How could studies of mimetics relate to the question of whether form information can affect the retrieval of lexico-semantic information? Assuming that the system uses the consistent mappings between form and meaning provided by mimetic words in some ways, we can make the following predictions that await empirical scrutiny. First, for a mimetic word, the lexico-semantic representation is, to a certain extent, predictable from the phonological representation, and vice versa; thus, it can be hypothesised that the lexico-semantic and phonological representations may directly co-activate each other. Consequently, the time-course of activating semantic and phonological representations may differ in retrieval of mimetic and nonmimetic words. Namely, for mimetic words activation of these two types of information should overlap to a greater extent than for nonmimetic words.

Second, the existence of mimetic words in a language may affect the retrieval of other words. The correlation between certain conceptual properties and phonological properties (e.g., 'big' <=> [+voiced] in the initial consonant) may influence retrieval of nonmimetic words and lead, for example, to certain phonological regularities in semantic errors. More specifically, we predict that when the target nonmimetic word has the lexico-semantic feature, 'big', then the intruder in the semantic error should tend to have a [+voiced] initial consonant. This is precisely parallel to our discussion of gender effects in Italian where we explained the gender congruency constraint for nouns with grammatical gender but referring to animals as arising from co-activation of the conceptual (sex) and syntactic (gender) feature.

How might such effects come about? Assuming that the predictions presented above are, in fact, borne out in empirical testing, the mechanism that gives rise to such effects could be analogous to those we have hypothesised to account for the effect of grammatical gender of Italian nouns. This is because both grammatical gender and sound symbolism in mimetic words involve correlation between conceptual features and linguistic properties. More specifically for mimetic words, during language learning, correlated conceptual and phonological properties (e.g., 'big' and [+voicing]) could become strongly associated such that activation of one would induce co-activation of the other. This association would, then, be reflected in the emerging organisation of the lexico-semantic space. Thus, intruders in semantic errors due to the shared meaning (e.g., 'big') should tend to have the corresponding phonological property (e.g., [+voicing]), even when neither the target nor the intruder is a mimetic word.

Just as we discussed for the effect of grammatical gender, establishing an association of this type requires a system in which conceptual properties such as 'big' or 'wet' are separately represented, and each of these conceptual properties can become associated with phonological properties such as [+voicing] during the development of the system.

Note also that Kita (1997, 2001) has also raised the possibility that the representation of at least some mimetic words involves a direct mapping between conceptual features and word-form. Namely, for such mimetic words, there would not be any intermediate lexico-semantic representation (see Kita, 1997 for an extensive discussion which is beyond the scope of this paper).

To conclude, for languages such as Japanese with a large inventory of mimetics, one cannot ignore systematic mapping between lexico-semantic and phonological representations. We have explored possible processing implications of such mapping. It has to be acknowledged, however, that the mapping might be just a historical vestige. We await future studies, which may reveal interaction of semantic and phonological representation in acquisition and processing of language. Such findings would force us to reconsider our architectural assumption that there is no direct processing link between lexico-semantic and phonological representations.

SUMMARY AND CONCLUSIONS

The goal of this paper was to discuss how idiosyncratic properties of languages can be revealing concerning the architecture of the production system and the mechanisms underlying on-line production and acquisition of a specific language. In particular we have considered idiosyncrasies in the lexicon as to whether words exist for given concepts, and lexico-syntactic and phonological properties that are correlated with meaning.

These different types of idiosyncrasies in the lexicon bear on three different interfaces: the mapping between conceptual and lexico-semantic information, the one between lexico-semantic and syntactic information and, finally, the one between lexico-semantic and phonological information.

The effects (or predicted effects) of these different idiosyncrasies cannot be accounted for on the basis of just one general process (e.g., on-line feedback during production) or learning mechanism (e.g., establishing associations between conceptual and linguistic features). Rather, they provide a range of distinct constraints on the architecture of the production system in addition to constraints on processing and learning mechanisms. Let us briefly summarise the implications of these findings and predictions.

First, the work by Kita and Özyürek (2003) strongly suggests that the idiosyncratic nature of lexicalisation patterns at the lexico-semantic level can affect via on-line feedback conceptual representations, in particular the conceptual (spatio-motoric) representations that generate gestures on the fly. Because gestures are generated and coordinated with speaking and because a recent study (Kita et al., 2006) showed a causal link from linguistic encoding patterns to gestural representations, these effects can be best captured in terms of on-line feedback from lexico-semantic to conceptual representations. These effects cannot easily be accounted for by the hypothesis that gestural representations are motoric translations of lexico-semantic representations of already retrieved words or by the hypothesis that frequent lexicalisation of manner of motion in English as compared to Japanese and Turkish modified the conceptual representations in the three languages in the course of language acquisition. It has to be acknowledged, however, that the effects are also compatible with a strong linguistic relativity position of word-by-word shaping of conceptual representation, in which case on-line feedback is not necessary.

Second, the work by Vigliocco and colleagues (Vigliocco et al., 2005) concerning semantic effects of grammatical gender of Italian nouns and our predictions concerning semantic effects of mimetic words in Japanese suggest further constraints. In particular, we have argued that in order to accommodate such effects the production system needs to be sensitive to meaning to syntax and meaning to form correlations during language development. Moreover, because these correlations are correlations between linguistic features (masculine or feminine gender of Italian nouns; + or – voiced phoneme for Japanese mimetic words) and conceptual *features* (male or female; big or small) these phenomena further suggest that conceptual properties are available to the language production system, at least during development, and therefore the existence of such effects argues in favour of decompositionality in conceptual representation (Bierwisch & Schreuder, 1992; Jackendoff, 2002; Vigliocco et al., 2004b).

In the section 'From Concepts to Phonology: What are the Implications of Cross-Linguistic Variation' we have introduced two caveats to our interpretation of syntactic and phonological effects in terms of their effects on the lexical-semantic information. First, the correlations observed in a language between conceptual features and syntactic or phonological properties of words may have an historic origin and therefore to show that a correlation exists, does not allow to draw any conclusion concerning whether such correlation affects on-line processing. Although it is possible that these correlations are rooted in the historical development of the language, with respect to gender, at least, the findings we have discussed here (reported in detail in Vigliocco et al., 2005) show that these correlations affect on-line lexical retrieval. With respect to the correlations between conceptual and phonological properties, behavioural effects still remain to be demonstrated and we cannot exclude that these correlations are not taken into account by the system. Second, although we have favoured a view in which these idiosyncratic properties of the lexicon affect semantic retrieval, the effects could arise post-semantically. This possibility is not likely for the gender effects we have described. In particular, the finding of an effect of gender for the category of animals but not for the category of tools is difficult to account for as occurring post-semantically. This is because phonological cues to gender are common across the two categories; however, the conceptual property sex is only relevant for the animals. Again, we can only offer speculations with respect to phonological effects given the lack of empirical data. For both caveats, we have decided here to present a parallel interpretation for syntactic and phonological properties for the sake of parsimony. Whether these predictions will hold empirical scrutiny or not, such investigations will nonetheless provide important constraints on lexical retrieval processes.

Although in this paper we presented only a very limited number of cross-linguistic phenomena, we have shown how even from this small repertoire of demonstrated or possible language-specific effects novel and potentially important constraints can be derived concerning the architecture and the mechanisms subserving learning and processing in adulthood. A cross-linguistic approach to psycholinguistics was crucial in investigating such issues. Importantly, because it is generally assumed that the conceptual and lexico-semantic representations consulted during language production are also consulted during language comprehension (Levelt, 1989; Vigliocco et al., 2004b) the language-specific effects we have discussed here have also implications for models of word recognition. Further systematic investigation of language-specific properties of the lexicon of the type described here bear the promise to reveal aspects of the speech production system that would be impossible to discover in investigations confined to a single language or a few closely related languages.

REFERENCES

Apher, B. (2001). Ideophones in interaction with intonation and the expression of new information in some indigenous languages of Australia. In F. K. E. Voeltz & C. Kilian-Hatz (Eds.), *Ideophones* (pp. 9–24). Amsterdam: John Benjamins.

Asano, T. (1978). Giongo gitaigo jiten [Dictionary of sound/manner mimetics]. Tokyo: Kadokawa.

Atoda, T., & Hoshino, K. (1995). Giongo gitaigo tsukaikata jiten [Usage dictionary of sound/manner mimetics]. Tokyo: Sotakusha.

Barsalou, L. W., Simmons, W. K., Barbey, A. K., & Wilson, C. D. (2003). Grounding conceptual knowledge in modality-specific systems. *Trends in Cognitive Science*, 7, 84–91.

Bates, E., & MacWhinney, B. (1989). Functionalism and the competition model. In B. MacWhinney & E. Bates (Eds.), *The crosslinguistic study of sentence processing* (pp. 10–75). Cambridge: Cambridge University Press.

Bierwisch, M. & Schreuder, R. (1992). From concepts to lexical items. *Cognition, 42*, 23–60.

Boroditsky, L. (2001). Does language shape thought? Mandarin and English speakers' conception of time. *Cognitive Psychology*, 43, 1–22.

Bowerman, M. & Choi, S. (2001). Shaping meanings from language: Universal and language-specific in the acquisition of spatial semantic categories. In M. Bowerman and S. C. Levinson (Eds.), *Language acquisition and conceptual development* (pp. 475–511). Cambridge: Cambridge University Press.

Butterworth, B. (1989). Lexical access and representation in speech production. In W. Maslen-Wilson (Ed.), *Lexical representation and process*. Cambridge, MA: MIT Press.

Caramazza, A. (1997). How many levels of processing are there in lexical access? *Cognitive Neuropsychology, 14*, 177–208.

Caramazza, A., & Miozzo, M. (1997). The relation between syntactic and phonological knowledge in lexical access: Evidence from the 'tip-of-the-tongue' phenomenon. *Cognition, 64*, 309–343.

Chang, A. (1990). *A thesaurus of Japanese mimesis and onomatopoeia: Usage by categories*. Tokyo: Taishukan.

Chen, F., Dell, G. S., & Bock, K. (2006). Becoming syntactic. *Psychological Review, 113*, 234–272.

Childs, G. T. (1994). African ideophones. In L. Hinton, J. Nichols, & J. J. Ohara (Eds.), *Sound symbolism* (pp. 178–206). Cambridge: Cambridge University Press.

Cree, G. S., & McRae, K. (2003). Analyzing the factors underlying the structure and computation of the meaning of *chipmunk, cherry, chisel, cheese* and *cello* (and many other such concrete nouns). *Journal of Experimental Psychology: General, 132*, 163–201.

Cutting, J. C., & Ferreira, V. S. (1999). Semantic and phonological information flow in the production lexicon. *Journal of experimental Psychology: Learning, Memory, & Cognition, 25*, 318–344.

Damian, M. F., & Martin, R. M. (1999). Semantic and phonological codes interact in single word production. *Journal of Experimental Psychology: Learning, Memory, and Cognition, 25*, 345–361.

Dell, G. S. (1986). A spreading-activation theory of retrieval in sentence production. *Psychological Review, 93*, 283–321.

Dell, G. S., & Reich, P. A. (1981). Stages in sentence production: An analysis of speech error data. *Journal of Verbal Learning and Verbal Behavior, 20*, 611–629.

Dell, G. S., Schwartz, M., Martin, M., Saffran, E. M., & Gagnon, D. A. (1997). Lexical access in aphasic and nonaphasic speakers. *Psychological Review, 104*, 801–838.

Diffloth, G. (1972). The notes on expressive meaning. P. M. Peranteau, J. N. Levi, & G. C. Phares (Eds.), *Papers from the eighth regional meeting of Chicago Linguistic Society* (pp. 440–447). Chicago: Chicago Linguistic Society.

Fisher, C. (1994). Structure and meaning in the verb lexicon: Input for a syntax-aided verb learning procedure. *Language and Cognitive Processes, 9*, 473–517.

Fisher, C., Gleitman, L. R., & Gleitman, H. (1991). On the semantic content of subcategorization frames. *Cognitive Psychology, 23*, 331–392.

Fodor, J. A. (1998). *Concepts: Where cognitive science went wrong*. Oxford: Oxford University Press.

Fodor, J. A., Garrett, M. F., Walker, E. C. T., & Parkes, C. H. (1980). Against definitions. *Cognition, 8*, 263–367.

Garrett, M. F. (1984). The organization of processing structure for language production: Application to aphasic speech. In D. Caplan, A. R. Lecours, & A. Smith (Eds.), *Biological perspectives on language*. Cambridge, MA: MIT Press.

Gentner, D., & Goldin-Meadow, S. (2003). Whither Whorf. In D. Gentner & S. Goldin-Meadow (Eds.), *Language in mind. Advances in the study of language and thought* (pp. 3–14). Cambridge: MA: MIT Press.

Griffin, Z. M., & Bock, K. (1998). Constraint, word frequency, and the relationship between lexical processing levels in spoken word production. *Journal of Memory and Language, 38*, 313–338.

Jackendoff, R. (2002). *Foundations of language*. Oxford: Oxford University Press.

Jescheniak, J. D., & Schriefers, H. (1998). Discrete serial versus cascaded processing in lexical access in speech production: Further evidence from the co-activation of near synonyms. *Journal of Experimental Psychology: Learning, Memory and Cognition, 24*, 1256–1274.

Hamano, S. (1998). *The sound-symbolic system of Japanese*. Stanford, CA & Tokyo: CSLI & Kuroshio.

Hinton, G. E., & Shallice, T. (1991). Lesioning an attractor network: Investigations of acquired dyslexia. *Psychological Review*, *98*, 74–95.

Hinton, L., Nichols, J., & Ohala, J. J. (1994). *Sound symbolism*. Cambridge: Cambridge University Press.

Kelly, M. H. (1992). Using sound to solve syntactic problems: The role of phonology in grammatical category assignments. *Psychological Review*, *99*, 349–364.

Kita, S. (1997). Two-dimensional semantic analysis of Japanese mimetics. *Linguistics*, *35*, 379–415.

Kita, S. (2001). Semantic schism and interpretive integration in Japanese sentences with a mimetic: A reply to Tsujimura. *Linguistics*, *39*, 419–436.

Kita, S., & Özyürek, A. (2003). What does cross-linguistic variation in semantic coordination of speech and gesture reveal?: Evidence for an interface representation of spatial thinking and speaking. *Journal of Memory and Language*, *48*, 16–32.

Kita, S., Özyürek, A., Allen, S., Brown, A., Furman, R., & Ishizuka, T. (2006). *Relation between syntactic encoding and co-speech gestures: Implications for a model of speech-gesture production*. Manuscript submitted for publication.

Landauer, T. K., & Dumais, S. T. (1997). A solution to Plato's problem: The Latent Semantic Analysis theory of acquisition, induction and representation of knowledge. *Psychological Review*, *104*, 211–240.

Lehrer, A., & Kittay, E. F. (1992). *Frames, fields, and contrasts: New essays in semantic and lexical organization*. Hillsdale, NJ: Lawrence Erlbaum Associates Inc.

Levelt, W. J. M. (1989). *Speaking*. Cambridge, MA: MIT Press.

Levelt, W. J. M., Roelofs, A., & Meyer, A. S. (1999). A theory of lexical access in speech production. *Behavioral and Brain Sciences*, *22*, 1–75.

Levinson, S. C. (2003). Language and mind: Let's get the issues straight! In D. Gentner and S. Goldin-Meadow (Eds.), *Language in mind. Advances in the study of language and thought* (pp. 25–46). Cambridge: MA: MIT Press.

Maeda, T., & Maeda, K. (1983). Yoji no goihattatsu no kenkyu [Investigation of a child's lexical development]. Tokyo: Musashino Shoin.

Martin, N., Weisberg, R. W., & Saffran, E. M. (1989). Variables influencing the occurrence of naming errors: Implications for models of lexical retrieval. *Journal of Memory and Language*, *28*, 462–485.

Marx, E. (1999). Gender processing in speech production: Evidence from German speech errors. *Journal of Psycholinguistic Research*, *28*, 601–621.

McGregor, W. (2001). Ideophones as the source of verb in Northern Australian languages. In F. K. E. Voeltz & C. Kilian-Hatz (Eds.), *Ideophones* (pp. 205–211). Amsterdam: John Benjamins.

McNeill, D. (1992). *Hand and mind*. Chicago: University of Chicago Press.

McNeill, D., & Duncan, S. (2000). Growth point in thinking-for-speaking. In D. McNeill (Ed.), *Language and thought* (pp. 141–161). Cambridge: Cambridge University Press.

McRae, K., de Sa, V., & Seidenberg, M. C. (1997). On the nature and scope of featural representations of word meaning. *Journal of Experimental Psychology: General*, *126*, 99–130.

Mikone, E. (2001). Ideophones in the Balto-Finnic languages. In F. K. E. Voeltz & C. Kilian-Hatz (Eds.), *Ideophones* (pp. 223–233). Amsterdam: John Benjamins.

Morrel-Samuels, P., & Krauss, R. M. (1992). Word familiarity predicts temporal asynchrony of hand gestures and speech. *Journal of Experimental Psychology: Learning, Memory, and Cognition*, *18*, 615–622.

Nuckolls, J. (1996). *Sounds like life*. New York: Oxford University Press.

Nuckolls, J. B. (1999). The case for sound symbolism. *Annual Review of Anthropology*, *28*, 225–252.

Ono, S. (1994). Nichiei giongo-gitaigo katsuyo jiten [Japanese-English mimetics usage dictonary]. Tokyo: Hokuseido.

Plaut, D. C., & Gonnerman, L. M. (2000). Are non-semantic morphological effects incompatible with a distributed connectionist approach to lexical processing? *Language and Cognitive Processes, 15*, 445–485.

Paganelli, F., Vigliocco, G., Vinson, D. P., Siri, S., & Cappa, S. (2003). An investigation of semantic errors in unimpaired and Alzheimer's speakers of Italian. *Cortex, 39,* 419–439.

Pulvermüller, F. (1999). Words in the brain's language. *Behavioral and Brain Sciences, 22,* 253 336.

Rapp, B., & Goldrick, M. (2000). Discreteness and interactivity in spoken word production. *Psychological Review, 107*, 460–499.

Rogers, T. T., Ralph, M. A. L., Garrard, P., Bozeat, S., McClelland, J. L., Hodges, J. R., & Patterson, K. (2004). Structure and deterioration of semantic memory: A neuropsychological and computational investigation. *Psychological Review, 111*, 205–235.

Schourup, L. (1993). Nihongo no kakikotoba-hanashikotoba ni okeru onomatope no bunpu ni tsuite [On distribution of onomatopoeias in spoken and written Japanese]. In H. Kakehi & I. Tamori (Eds.), *Onomatopia: Giongo-gitaigo no rakuen [Onomatopoeia: Paradise of mimetics].* Tokyo: Keiso Shobo.

Schultz-Berndt, E. (2001). Ideophone-like characteristics of uninflected predicates in Jaminjung (Australia). In F. K. E. Voeltz & C. Kilian-Hatz (Eds.), *Ideophones* (pp. 355–373). Amsterdam: John Benjamins.

Seidenberg, M. S., & Gonnerman, L. M. (2000). Explaining derivational morphology as the convergence of codes. *Trends in Cognitive Science, 4*, 353–361.

Sera, M. D., Elieff, C., Forbes, J., Burch, M. C., Rodriguez, W., & Dubois, D. P. (2002). When language affects cognition and when it does not: An analysis of grammatical gender and classification. *Journal of Experimental Psychology: General, 131*, 377–397.

Slobin, D. I. (1987). *Thinking for speaking.* The proceedings of the thirteenth annual meeting of Berkeley Linguistics Society.

Slobin, D. I. (1996). From 'thought and language' to 'thinking for speaking'. In J. J. Gumperz & S. C. L. Levinson (Eds.), *Rethinking linguistic relativity.* Cambridge: Cambridge University Press.

Starreveld, P. A., & LaHeij, W. (1996). Time-course analysis of semantic and orthographic context effects in picture naming. *Journal of Experimental Psychology: Learning, Memory and Cognition, 22*, 896–918.

Talmy, L. (1985). Lexicalization patterns: semantic structure in lexical forms. In T. Shopen (Ed.), *Grammatical categories and the lexicon* (Vol. III, pp. 57–149). Cambridge: Cambridge University Press.

Vigliocco, G., & Filopovic Kleiner, L. (2004). From mind in the mouth to language in mind. *Trends in Cognitive Science, 8*, 5–7.

Vigliocco, G., & Hartsuiker, R. (2002). The interplay of meaning, sound, and syntax in sentence production. *Psychological Bulletin, 128*, 442–472.

Vigliocco, G., Vinson, D., Indefrey, P., Levelt, W., & Hellwig, F. (2004a). The interplay between meaning and syntax in language production. *Journal of Experimental Psychology: Learning, Memory & Cognition, 30*, 483–497.

Vigliocco, G., Vinson, D. P., Lewis, W., & Garrett, M. F. (2004b). Representing the meanings of object and action words: The featural and unitary semantic space hypothesis. *Cognitive Psychology, 48*, 422–488.

Vigliocco, G., Vinson, D. P., Paganelli F., & Dworzynski, K. (2005). Grammatical gender effects on cognition: Implications for language learning and language use. *Journal of Experimental Psychology: General, 134*, 501–520.

Vinson, D. P., & Vigliocco, G. (2002). A semantic analysis of noun-verb dissociations in aphasia. *Journal of Neurolinguistics, 15*, 317–351.

Voeltz, F. K. E., & Kilian-Hatz, C. (Eds.). (2001). *Ideophones*. Amsterdam: John Benjamins.

Watson, R. L. (2001). A comparison of some Southeast Asian ideophones with some African ideophones. In F. K. E. Voeltz & C. Kilian-Hatz (Eds.), *Ideophones* (pp. 385–405). Amsterdam: John Benjamins.

LANGUAGE AND COGNITIVE PROCESSES
2006, 21 (7–8), 817–855

Limited interaction in speech production: Chronometric, speech error, and neuropsychological evidence

Matthew Goldrick

Northwestern University, Evanston, IL, USA

Results from chronometric and speech errors studies provide convergent evidence for both lower and upper bounds on interaction within the speech production system. Some degree of cascading activation is required to account for patterns of speech errors in neurologically intact and impaired speakers as well as the results of recent chronometric studies. However, the strength of this form of interaction must be limited to account for the occurrence of selective deficits in the production system and restrictions on the conditions under which interactive effects influence reaction times. Similarly, some amount of feedback from phonological to word-level representations is necessary to account for patterns of speech errors in neurologically intact and impaired individuals as well as the influence of phonological neighbours on response latency. This interactive mechanism must also be limited to account for restrictions on the types of speech errors produced following selective deficits within the production system. Results from a variety of empirical traditions therefore converge on the same conclusion: interaction is present, but it must be crucially limited.

Historically, research into single word production has been conducted within two distinct empirical traditions (Levelt, 1999).[1] One has focused on

---

[1] More recent studies (see Indefrey & Levelt, 2004, for a recent review) have utilised neuroimaging techniques to examine word production. This review, however, is limited to speech error and chronometric data (for discussion of neuroimaging evidence specifically concerning the interaction between speech production processes, see deZubicaray, Wilson, McMahon, & Muthiah, 2001).

Correspondence should be addressed to Matthew Goldrick, Department of Linguistics, Northwestern University, Evanston, IL, 60208, USA. E-mail: goldrick@ling.northwestern.edu

Preparation of this paper was supported in part by National Institute of Health grants R01 MH-64733, R01 HD21011, and R01 MH66089, and National Science Foundation grant BCS 0213270.

http://www.psypress.com/lcp   DOI: 10.1080/01690960600824112

speech errors from a variety of sources. Within this tradition, early theories (e.g., Garrett, 1980) claimed that spoken production processes were highly discrete. The various subprocesses underlying speech production were assumed to be highly independent and non-overlapping. During the 1980s, it became clear that such theories were unable to account for the full range of speech error data, leading to the introduction of (localist connectionist) interactive-activation theories (e.g., Dell, 1986; Stemberger, 1985). These theories incorporated the mechanisms of cascading activation and feedback to allow spoken production processes to interact. A parallel empirical tradition focuses not on errors but on reaction time – the latency of speech production behaviour. In contrast to research in errors, extensive work by Levelt, Roelofs, Meyer, and their colleagues (see Levelt, Roelofs, & Meyer, 1999, for a review) has found that theories assuming a discrete relationship between semantic and phonological processes provide an impressive qualitative and quantitative fit to much of the existing latency data.

Why is there disagreement between these two approaches? If speech production is an interactive process, why is a system with substantial discreteness so successful at modeling chronometric data? If it is discrete, why do speech errors require the presence of interaction? This review argues that the first step towards resolving this conflict is recognizing the presence of *limited* interactivity – that is, the presence of not just lower but also upper bounds on the strength of both cascading activation and feedback.

After laying out a generic processing framework for spoken word production, evidence supporting limited interaction is reviewed. A broad array of results – from speech errors in neurologically intact and impaired speakers, as well as chronometric and accuracy studies of production – converges on the conclusion that although interactive mechanisms are present, they must be crucially limited. Specifically, the results support three features for the adult speech production system:

1. Significant cascading activation from word-level to phonological representations is present, but its strength must be limited.

2. Significant feedback from phonological to word-level representations is present, but its strength must be limited.

3. Feedback from word-level to lexical semantic representations is either absent or functionally insignificant.

New simulation data are provided to reinforce these claims. The discussion concludes with open questions and future directions for research.

REPRESENTATIONAL AND PROCESSING ASSUMPTIONS

Scope of the review

This review concerns the question of interaction among processes that map from lexical semantic representations (e.g., the concept of a furry four-legged feline {CAT}) to phonological representations stored in long-term memory (e.g., the phonemes /k/ /ae/ /t/). Two broad clarifications are in order. First, since the review concerns speech production, interactions from other perceptual domains (e.g., object recognition) will not be discussed. Second, this review focuses on lexical access of single, morphologically simple words. Since full discussion of the influence of syntactic information would require broadening the discussion to include sentence production and other connected speech tasks, the role of syntactic features is also omitted (see Vigliocco & Hartsuiker, 2002, for a review).

Representational assumptions

Lexical semantic representations.   Lexical semantic representations are amodal representations (common to all sensory and production modalities) of the meaning of lexical items in a particular language (e.g., the feature set {furry four-legged feline} for lexical concept {CAT}; see the top of Figure 1A–D). These representations codify the message the speaker intends to communicate in a language-specific way, allowing more general (non-linguistic) conceptual processes to interface with those that specify linguistic form. For the purposes of this discussion, lexical semantic representations are depicted as sets of distributed semantic features (following, e.g., Caramazza, 1997; Dell, Schwartz, Martin, Saffran, & Gagnon, 1997), although the findings are also consistent with theories assuming unitary semantic representations (e.g., Levelt et al., 1999).

Phonological representations.   Phonological representations are stored, sublexical representations of the spoken form of lexical items (e.g., /k/ /ae/ /t/; see the bottom of Figure 1A–D). For the purposes of discussion, these have been depicted as segments (following Dell et al., 1997), although the results are also consistent with the storage of additional aspects of phonological structure (e.g., metrical structure; Levelt et al., 1999).

L-level representations.   As shown in Figure 1, theories of speech production generally assume a third level of representation mediating the mapping between semantic and phonological representations – a lexical, or word-level, level of representation (e.g., <CAT>). There is widespread disagreement as to whether a single lexical level is sufficient (see Caramazza, 1997; Levelt et al., 1999, for discussion) and whether lexical representations are amodal or modality specific (see Caramazza, 1997; Dell et al., 1997; Levelt et al., 1999, for discussion). To emphasise the common properties of this theories, this discussion follows Rapp & Goldrick (2000) by assuming a single 'L-level' of lexical representation (which may or may not be modality specific). With the exception of homophonic primes[2] and the influence of feedback across multiple representational levels (see the general discussion for further details), adopting this assumption does not impact the interpretation of the majority of the findings reviewed here.

Processing stages

Most theories of speech production assume that the mapping from lexical semantic to L-level then phonological representations is accomplished through a series of processing stages (stemming from Garrett's, 1980, 'two-stage' theory of speech production). Here, three broad stages of processing – corresponding to a selection of a representation at each of the three levels discussed above – are assumed to be involved in lexical access in speech production.

Stage 0: Lexical semantic processing. Processing begins with the selection or generation of a message that the speaker wishes to express, and ends with the selection of a lexical semantic representation specifying a lexicalised concept within the speaker's language. This corresponds to selecting a concept from one's language to express a pre-verbal message.

Stage 1: L-level processing. Processing begins with the selection of a lexical semantic representation corresponding to a particular concept, and ends with the selection of an L-level unit. This corresponds to the selection of a particular word or lexical item to express a concept.

Stage 2: Phonological processing. Processing begins with the selection of an L-level unit and ends with the selection of a phonological

---

[2] Assuming a single level of lexical representation leads one to attribute the effects of *homophonic primes* to overlapping phonological, not lexical, representations. It is generally assumed that homophones have distinct lexical representations at some level in the processing system (Bonin & Fayol, 2002; Caramazza, Bi, Costa, & Miozzo, 2004; Caramazza, Costa, Miozzo, & Bi, 2001; Dell, 1990; Jescheniak & Levelt, 1994; Jescheniak, Meyer, & Levelt, 2003; Levelt et al., 1999). Assuming a single lexical level means that homophones share no lexical representation; their only overlap is at the phonological level.

representation. This corresponds to retrieving the phonological components of a word from long-term memory.

Note that during Stages 1 and 2, the units of representation are words; errors at these levels are therefore restricted to words. During Stage 3, sublexical representations are selected; at this level, both word and nonword errors can occur.

As seen above, each stage begins with the selection of a representation at one level (e.g., lexical semantics) and ends with the selection of a representation at the next level in the processing stream (e.g., the L-level). In this context, selection refers to those mechanisms that allow one or more representations[3] to dominate subsequent processing. For example, many authors (e.g., Roelofs, 1992) have argued that during L-level selection multiple semantically related words are activated (e.g., in addition to target <CAT>, <DOG> may be partially activated). In spite of this partial activation of other words, on the vast majority of productions the target is correctly produced. Selection mechanisms are what allow the target, rather than its competitors, to determine the form that is ultimately produced.

In speech production theories, a variety of mechanisms accomplish this by singling out the most active contextually appropriate representation and enhance its activation relative to that of competitors: either by boosting the selected representation's activation (e.g., Dell, 1986; Dell et al., 1997; Rapp & Goldrick, 2000); inhibiting less active competitors (Berg & Schade, 1992; Cutting & Ferreira, 1999; Dell & O'Seaghdha, 1994; Harley, 1993; Meyer & Gordon, 1985; Schade & Berg, 1992; Stemberger, 1985); or restricting the activation flow from competitors (Laine, Tikkala, & Juhola, 1998; Levelt et al., 1999). The term 'selection strength' will be used to refer to the degree to which selected representations are enhanced. In systems with strong selection points, selected representations will be much more active than competitors (due to very large boosts in activation, very strong inhibition, or very strong restrictions on competitors' activation flow). Weakening selection points will decrease the activation advantage of the selected representation (due to smaller boosts in activation, weaker inhibition, or weakened restrictions on competitors' activation flow).

Mechanisms for increasing interaction

A discrete system is defined by three characteristics: one, processing involving one representational level is not initiated until selection has

---

[3] It is possible that errors such as blends reflect the simultaneous selection of multiple representations (e.g., Levelt et al., 1999).

occurred at the previous level; two, selection strength is extremely high, such that only selected representations are allowed to pass on activation to other processing levels; and three, activation flows in a strictly feed-forward manner. These properties have several notable consequences. First, due to the strength of selection in discrete systems, subsequent processing stages only receive information about the representations selected at prior levels (e.g., phonological processing occurs for the selected L-level representation alone). Second, due to the staged, feed-forward nature of processing, later stages cannot influence processing at higher levels in the system (e.g., phonological processing cannot influence L-level processing). There are two widely used mechanisms for increasing interaction beyond this discrete endpoint: cascading activation and feedback.

Cascading activation. In contrast to discrete systems, those with cascading activation reject the assumption that representations can pass on activation only after they have been selected. This claim leads to the weakening of the first two characteristics of discrete systems. Representations can pass on activation before selection has occurred, such that processing at subsequent stages is initiated prior to selection (e.g., L-level processing can begin prior to the completion of lexical semantic processing). De-linking activation flow from selection points also leads to a decrease in selection strength. Typically, cascading activation systems allow nonselected representations to pass on activation to subsequent processing stages both prior to and after selection has occurred (e.g., in processing target 'cat', the partially activated lexical concept {DOG} activates its corresponding L-level representation <DOG>).

All current theories of speech production assume that cascading activation is present between lexical semantic and L-level representations (Caramazza, 1997; Dell et al., 1997; Levelt et al., 1999; Rapp & Goldrick, 2000). During lexical semantic processing, multiple (semantically related) concepts are activated [via connections linking related concepts (Levelt et al., 1999) or overlapping distributed representations (e.g., Dell et al., 1997)]. Cascading activation allows these multiple concepts to activate the L-level representation of words semantically related to the target.

Feedback. Systems with feedback relax the third assumption of discrete systems and allow later stages to influence processing at higher levels in the system. This creates a number of different effects, discussed in more detail below. The discussion here remains agnostic as to whether these effects are driven by mechanisms entirely internal to the production system (e.g., reciprocal connections between representational levels; Dell, 1986) or indirectly, via speech perception mechanisms (e.g., monitoring systems; Levelt et al., 1999; see Roelofs, 2004a, 2004b, Rapp & Goldrick, 2004, for further discussion).

What degree of interaction do speech production theories require?

The following sections consider the consequences of incremental increases in interaction between adjacent representational levels in the production system. As interaction is increased, two questions are examined:

1. Does this increased amount of interaction explain results that cannot be accounted for by a system lacking this type of interaction? This provides a lower bound on the strength of this form of interaction.
2. Do the data suggest any limitations to the strength of this type of interaction? This provides an upper bound on the strength of interaction.

Figure 1A depicts the most discrete system considered here. The consequences of increasing cascading activation by allowing nonselected L-level units to activate phonological representations (Figure 1B) are examined first. Feedback interactions are then examined, moving upward through the processing system (considering feedback from phonological to L-level units, as shown in Figure 1C, then from the L-level to lexical semantics, as in 1D).

EVIDENCE SUPPORTING LIMITED CASCADING ACTIVATION

Limited cascading activation: Speech error evidence

The mixed error effect.   Probably the most widely cited piece of evidence for interaction in the spoken production system is the mixed error effect. This refers to the observation that in a variety of contexts mixed errors (e.g., 'cat' → 'rat') occur more often than predicted based on the rates of purely semantic (e.g., 'cat' → 'dog') or purely phonological (e.g., 'cat' → 'cab') errors (for more detailed discussion of how predicted rates have been calculated, see Goldrick & Rapp, 2002). A system with cascading activation predicts that such an effect can be generated at the phonological level. For example, as shown in Figure 1B, cascading activation from <RAT> activates /r/. In contrast, /b/ receives no support from the purely phonologically related <CAB>. This activation difference makes 'rat' a more likely phonological error than 'cab,' meaning that in a cascading activation system the rate of mixed errors will exceed the simple sum of purely semantic and purely phonological errors. Such an effect

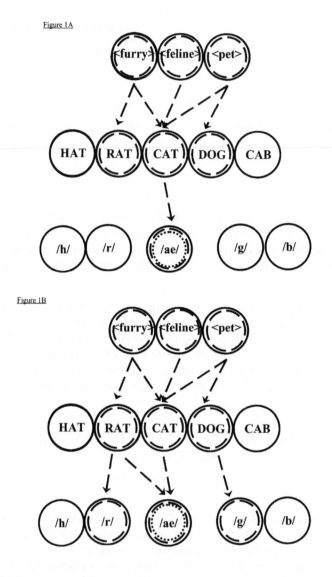

Figure 1 (above and opposite). Schematic depictions of four theoretical positions regarding interaction within the speech production system. The first set of units denotes lexical semantic representations (amodal representations of the meaning of lexicalised concepts). The second denote L-level units (word representations mediating the mapping between the other two representational levels). The third set denotes phonological representations (sublexical representations of word form). Note that each representational level is only partially depicted (e.g., onset /k/ and coda /t/ from 'cat' are not shown). To show the consequences of different types of interaction on the activation of each unit, as well as the flow of activation between units, semantic activation driven by the target is depicted with long dashes; phonological activation driven by the target is depicted with square dots.

824

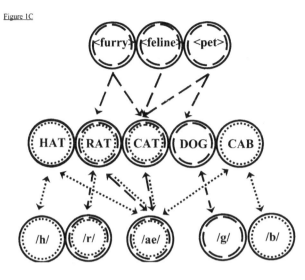

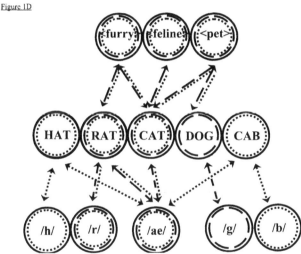

A. Theory with no cascading activation or feedback. Multiple semantic competitors are activated at the L-level, but only the target activates its phonological representation.

B. Theory with cascading activation from the L-level to phonological representations. Semantic competitors activate their phonological representations.

C. Theory with feedback from phonological representations to the L-level. Phonological neighbours of the target are activated at the L-level; through cascading activation, these phonological neighbours activate their phonological representations.

D. Theory with feedback from the L-level to semantics. Activation differences based on L-level and/or phonological distinctions are transmitted back to semantic representations.

cannot be produced in a discrete system. As shown in Figure 1A, in such systems /r/ is no more active than /b/ – 'rat' is therefore no more likely to occur as a phonological error than 'cab'.

Consistent with cascading activation, many empirical reports of mixed error effects can plausibly be attributed to the phonological level. Many studies of spontaneous speech errors have shown mixed error effects (Dell & Reich, 1981; Harley, 1984; Harley & MacAndrew, 1995, 2001; Martin, Gagnon, Schwartz, Dell, & Saffran, 1996; but see del Viso, Igoa, & García-Albea, 1991[4] and Igoa, 1996, for null results). Given that it is unclear at what level(s) of the processing system spontaneous speech errors arise, these effects can be plausibly attributed to the phonological level. Similarly, mixed error effects in experimentally induced speech errors (Brédart & Valentine, 1992; Martin, Weisberg, & Saffran, 1989; but see Levelt, 1983, for a null result) can be plausibly attributed to the phonological level. Finally, the mixed error effects observed in the production errors of many aphasic individuals (Blanken, 1998; Dell et al., 1997; Kulke & Blanken, 2001; Martin et al., 1996; Rapp & Goldrick, 2000; but see Best, 1996 and Nickels, 1995, for null results) can also be attributed to phonological processing.

Two caveats are warranted. As discussed in more detail below, mixed error effects are also predicted to occur at the L-level in systems incorporating feedback. However, the data discussed in this section do not require this increase in interactivity; they can be parsimoniously explained by a minimal increase in interaction over a discrete system (i.e., by the incremental addition of cascading activation). Second, some authors have attributed the mixed error bias to the influence of perceptual monitoring systems. We return to this alternative account following the discussion of chronometric evidence supporting cascade.

Homophone priming of semantically related word substitution errors.
Ferreira and Griffin (2003; see Burke, Locantore, Austin, & Chae, 2004, for related speed and accuracy findings) had participants name pictures following visual presentation of cloze sentence fragment. These cloze sentence fragments primed participants to make a large number of semantic word substitution errors relative to conditions when an unrelated

---

[4] As noted by Vigliocco and Hartsuiker (2002: footnote 8), del Viso et al.'s (1991) claim that their data do not show a mixed error bias is debatable. del Viso et al. did find a significant mixed error effect in their overall corpus. However, the effect was carried by a small subset of highly similar items; when these were excluded no significant mixed error effect was found. Although this subset analysis is justifiable (the mixed error effect should not be carried by only a few items), it may in fact be too conservative (obscuring a true mixed error effect).

word was primed[5] (e.g., 'The woman went to a convent to become a . . .', primed participants to misname a picture of a priest 'nun'). With respect to interaction, a significant number of errors were also induced when cloze sentences primed homophones of semantic neighbours (e.g., 'I thought that there would be some cookies left, but there were . . .' primed participants to produce 'none' for a picture of a priest). The errors in the homophone priming condition can be plausibly accounted for by cascading activation. Homophone primes serve to pre-activate the phonological representation of semantic neighbours (e.g., /n/ /•/ /n/). During processing of the target picture, cascading activation from L-level representations of semantic neighbours (e.g., <NUN>) serves to drive these representations over threshold, leading to substitution errors.

Evidence for limits on cascading activation to phonology.   Although a significant degree of cascading activation is clearly required, other evidence supports upper bounds on its strength. Simulation results show that systems with very strong cascade activation predict patterns inconsistent with the empirical data.

Figure 2 reports new simulation results documenting how systems with very strong cascading activation predict that phonological processing will be indirectly disrupted following damage localised to the L-level (see Rapp & Goldrick, 2000, for implementation details).[6] Following simulated L-level damage (activation noise 0.7), the rate of nonword errors was used to index the disruption of phonological processing. Such errors can only be produced during phonological selection (at the L-level, the representational units are words). The extent of cascade was manipulated by altering selection strength here, the predetermined high level to which a selected representation's activation is boosted over that of competitors ('jolt' strength). Note that weaker L-level selection entails a greater amount of cascading activation. As shown in Figure 2, the rate of nonword errors in the simulation is related to the strength of L-level selection; significant numbers of nonword errors are found when selection strength is weakened. This shows that in systems with strong cascading activation phonological processing can be indirectly disrupted when L-level selection strength is too weak. Similar results have been observed in a variety of systems with weak selection points (e.g., when feedback is incorporated or

---

[5] To guard against strategic effects, Ferreira & Griffin discouraged participants from covertly completing each sentence by including a condition where pictures were never an appropriate sentence completion (Experiment 3). Effects of similar magnitude were observed here, arguing against a strategic basis for the findings.

[6] The 'Cascading Feedforward Account' simulation of Rapp & Goldrick (2000) was used. With the exception of the L-level jolt (which was varied as described above), parameters were set at the default levels described in that paper.

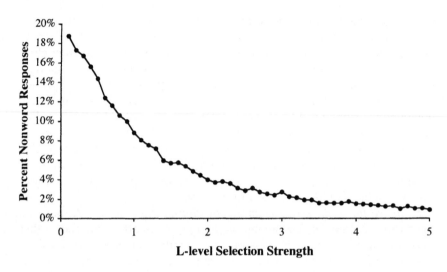

Figure 2.   Indirect disruption to phonological processing due to decreases in L-level selection strength (jolt size). Results show percentage of nonword responses over 10,000 simulated naming attempts in a system with cascading activation. L-level noise was fixed at 0.7.

in attractor-based distributed connectionist systems; Rapp & Goldrick, 2000; Plaut & Shallice, 1993).

This predicted consequence of systems with strong cascading activation is inconsistent with the empirical data; individuals with deficits localised to the L-level do not produce nonword errors. A number of studies have documented speakers with modality-specific impairments to speech production that produce only semantic errors (Basso, Taborelli, & Vignolo, 1978; Caramazza & Hillis, 1990; Miceli, Benvegnú, Capasso, & Caramazza, 1997; Nickels, 1992; Rapp, Benzing, & Caramazza, 1997; Rapp & Goldrick, 2000). Rapp and Goldrick (2000; see also Caramazza & Hillis, 1990) argued that this pattern of performance can be best explained by postulating a deficit to selecting the target L-level representation. The possibility that their errors result from a deficit to amodal lexical semantic representations is precluded by the modality-specific nature of their deficits. Furthermore, detailed testing of semantic processing in these individuals has revealed no significant impairment (see, e.g., Goldrick & Rapp, 2002). Second, the production of only semantic errors suggests that the deficit cannot arise at the phonological level. Given that the units of phonological processing are sublexical, it is highly likely that a deficit at this level will result in the production of phonologically related word and nonword errors. For example, in all of the architectures simulated by Rapp & Goldrick (2000), damage to phonological processing *invariably* led to the production of phonologically related word and nonword errors. The most likely locus of their deficit is to L-level processing.

These case studies therefore provide an upper bound on the strength of cascading activation. As shown above, if cascading activation was very strong, individuals with L-level deficits are predicted to produce nonword errors. These case studies show that they do not; their errors are limited to semantic word substitutions.

Limited cascading activation: Chronometric and accuracy evidence

Facilitation of words phonologically related to semantically activated items. A number of studies have shown phonological facilitation (reflected by reduced naming latency and/or higher accuracy) for words that overlap in form with lexical items that have been semantically activated (e.g., semantic neighbours of the target). Each of these studies provides evidence for cascading activation from L-level to phonological representations. In each experiment, a nontarget L-level representation is activated via semantic processes. Activation from this L-level unit cascades to phonological representations, facilitating production of words that overlap with its phonological representation. Without cascading activation, no pre-activation would be present, and no facilitation would be observed.

To consider a specific example, in Peterson and Savoy's (1998) paradigm, near-synonyms of a target picture name become activated at the lexical semantic level (e.g., for target 'couch', {SOFA}). These conceptual representations activate their corresponding L-level representations (e.g.,), and, via cascade, their phonological representations (e.g., /s/ /oU/ /f/ /'/). In their cued-response paradigm, this facilitates production of visually presented words related to the near-synonym (e.g., 'soda') relative to phonologically unrelated controls (e.g., 'horse').

These studies are summarised in Table 1. The first column lists the citation. The second column briefly describes the paradigm. The third column lists the (nontarget) lexical item that is claimed to be activated via semantic processes. Finally, the fourth column describes the word phonologically related to the semantically activated lexical item that shows evidence of facilitation.

Interference for words phonologically unrelated to semantically activated items. Several studies have shown the complementary effect to those above: increased reaction times for targets that are phonological *dissimilar* to semantically activated words. Cascading activation provides a plausible mechanism for this effect. Activation from semantically related words enhances the activation of nontarget phonological representations; this

TABLE 1

Studies showing phonological facilitation by semantically activated nontarget words

Experiment(s)	Task	Semantically activated lexical item:	Phonological facilitation observed in:
Peterson & Savoy (1998)	Cued response: After picture presentation, either name the picture or a visually presented word	Near-synonym of picture name (e.g., 'sofa' for 'couch').	Naming latency of visually presented word phonologically related to near synonym of picture name (e.g., naming of target 'soda', similar to 'sofa').
Cutting & Ferreira (1999); Taylor & Burke (2002)	Picture naming during auditory picture-word interference	Semantic associate of distractor (e.g., 'ball,' a formal dance, for distractor 'dance').	Picture naming latency of homophone of semantic associate of distractor (e.g., target 'ball', a toy, is a homophone of 'ball,' a formal dance).
Damian & Martin (1999); Starreveld & La Heij (1995, 1999); Taylor & Burke (2002)	Picture naming during auditory or orthographic picture word interference	Mixed (semantic-phonological) neighbor of picture target (e.g., 'calf' for target 'camel').	Picture naming latency of target[1] (Damian & Martin, 1999; Starreveld & La Heij, 1995; Taylor & Burke, 2002); target accuracy (Starreveld & La Heij, 1999).
Costa, Caramazza, & Sebastián-Gallés (2000); Gollan & Acenas (2004)	Picture naming	Cognate (phonologically similar translation) of target (e.g., for target Spanish 'gato' 'cat,' Catalan cognate 'gat').	Picture naming latency of target (Costa et al.); target accuracy (Gollan & Acenas)
Morsella & Miozzo (2002); Navarrete & Costa (2005)	Picture naming during picture-picture interference	Phonologically related non-target picture (e.g., 'bell' for target 'bed').	Picture naming latency of target[2]

[1] Typically, these findings have been interpreted as reflecting modulation of the activation of L-level representations, not phonological representations (e.g., Damian & Martin, 1999; Roelofs, 2004a; but see Vigliocco & Hartsuiker, 2002, for a cascading activation account of these results). This interpretation is based on the observation that pure phonological distractors in these studies do not exhibit facilitation at the SOAs (stimulus-onset asynchronies) at which interactive effects are observed (Roelofs, 2004a). However, phonological facilitation effects have been observed at a wide range of SOAs (Jescheniak & Schriefers, 2001; Starreveld, 2000). Second, the facilitation of formally related neighbours may simply be too weak to be observed.

[2] Other studies have claimed that nontarget pictures are not activated post-semantically. Interference effects produced by semantically related distractor words in picture naming (Damian & Bowers, 2003; Humphreys, Lloyd-Jones, & Fias, 1995) or word translation (Bloem & La Heij, 2003; Bloem, van den Boogaard, & La Heij, 2004) are absent when pictorial distractors are used. If semantic interference effects arise during lexical selection processes, the absence of interference here suggests that pictorial input does not automatically activate post-semantic representations. However, recent work has challenged the post-semantic account of semantic interference (see Costa, Mahon, Savova, & Caramazza, 2003, for discussion), undermining these claims.

may make retrieval of target phonological representations more difficult (e.g., by increasing the competition for selection at the phonological level).

To consider a specific example, Jescheniak and Schriefers' (1998) paradigm relied on the phonological activation of near-synonyms of a target picture (e.g., for target 'couch', the activation of 'sofa' at the phonological level; see the discussion of Peterson and Savoy, 1998, above). Cascade from the near-synonym increases the activation of the phonological representation of distractor words which are related to it but dissimilar to the target picture name (e.g., the phonological representation of 'soda' – similar to 'sofa' but not 'couch' – will be more active than that of 'horse'). The increased activation of these distractors during the picture/word interference task yields more competition for selection at the phonological level, slowing reaction times in picture naming.

These studies are summarised in Table 2. The first three columns follow the format of Table 1. The fourth column identifies the critical distractor word. In these studies, retrieval of the phonological representation of the picture name was inhibited. This inhibition was attributed to a distractor word (identified in column 4) whose activation was enhanced by its phonological relationship to the semantically activated lexical item.

Evidence for upper limits on cascading activation to phonology. Although the above chronometric studies provide clear evidence for cascading activation, this does not imply that it is unlimited in its power and influence. Across these studies, it appears that cascading activation effects in chronometric studies are only observed in three conditions.

1. *Very strong semantic similarity. Near-synonyms* (Jescheniak & Schriefers, 1998; Peterson & Savoy, 1998) have nearly complete overlap with target semantic representations. A similar situation holds for *translation equivalents* (Costa et al., 2003; Hermans et al., 1998) as well as *alternative target names at different levels of categorisation* (Jescheniak, Hantsch, & Schriefers, 2005).
2. *Very high phonological overlap.* Words cannot be any more phonologically similar than *homophones* (Cutting & Ferreira, 1999; Taylor & Burke, 2002).
3. *Simultaneous overlap with the semantic and phonological structure of the target. Mixed* neighbours simultaneously overlap the target at both levels of structure (Damian & Martin, 1999; Starreveld & La Heij, 1995, 1999; Taylor & Burke, 2002). *Cognates* exhibit very strong, simultaneous overlap at both levels (Costa et al., 2000; Gollan & Acenas, 2004).

With respect to strong semantic or phonological similarity, parallel studies with stimuli that exhibit neither simultaneous overlap at semantic

TABLE 2

Studies showing phonological inhibition by semantically activated nontarget words

Experiment(s)	Task	Semantically activated lexical item:	Target phonologically inhibited by:
Jescheniak & Schriefers (1998)	Picture naming during auditory picture-word interference	Phonologically dissimilar near-synonym of picture name (e.g., 'sofa' for 'couch')	Distractor, dissimilar to target, but phonologically related to near-synonym of picture name (e.g., 'soda', similar to 'sofa' but not target 'couch').
Hermans et al. (1998); Costa et al. (2003)	Picture naming during auditory picture-word interference	Non-cognate translation equivalent (e.g., Dutch 'berm' for English target 'mountain')	Distractor, dissimilar to target, but phonologically related to non-cognate translation equivalent (e.g., 'bench', similar to 'berm' but not target 'mountain').[3]
Jescheniak et al. (2005)	Picture naming during auditory picture-word interference	Phonologically dissimilar basic or subordinate level label for picture (in subordinate or basic level naming context; e.g., 'fish' in context where 'shark' is appropriate)	Distractor, dissimilar to target, but phonologically related to basic or subordinate level label (e.g., 'finger', similar to 'fish' but not target 'shark').

[3] Note that Hermans et al. (1998) interpreted this inhibition as arising at the L-level.

and phonological nor high degrees of overlap at either single level fail to find interactive effects. For semantic associates that are not synonyms (e.g., for target 'sheep', 'goat'), phonological facilitation effects on non-homophones (e.g., 'goal') are either absent (Levelt, Schriefers, Vorberg, Meyer, Pechmann, & Havinga, 1991a; Peterson & Savoy, 1998) or extremely weak (O'Seaghdha & Marin, 1997). With respect to simultaneous overlap, Melinger and Abdel Rahman (2004) utilised a version of the picture-word interference task with two distinct distractor words (e.g., naming a picture of a pig with PILL and SOCK simultaneously superimposed on the picture). When semantic and phonological overlap equivalent to that of a single mixed neighbour was carried by two different distractors, interactive effects are not observed. For example, the naming latency of 'pig' accompanied by both a semantic and a phonological distractor (e.g., BEAR, PILL) reflected a simple additive interaction of semantic interference (from BEAR) and phonological facilitation (from PILL).

These contrasting findings suggest that although cascading activation from L-level to phonological representations is present, it must be limited. Specifically, the divergent results across studies reflects the restriction of chronometric effects due to cascading activation to situations with strong, convergent activation. For example, in most situations, the source of the cascading activation is fairly weak; limited cascading activation from this weak source cannot significantly influence processing at the phonological level. In certain exceptional cases of strong semantic similarity (e.g., near-synonyms, translation equivalents), activation of the nonselected L-level unit is very strong, allowing it to produce interactive effects in spite of weak cascade. With respect to phonological priming, cascading activation usually provides at best partial support for the response. However, in the case of homophones and cognates, virtually the entire response is supported by cascading activation, allowing these stimuli to exhibit an effect.

Why then are effects observed with mixed neighbours (which have neither strong semantic activation nor complete phonological overlap)? Unlike stimuli in the other studies, mixed neighbours do not provide the sole source of activation for the response on which interactive effects are observed. Activation from the mixed neighbour *converges* with that of the (already activated) target (Dell & O'Seaghdha, 1991). In other studies, the phonological representation which is used to indicate the presence of interaction (e.g., 'goal' in Levelt et al., 1991a) receives no activation from the target; weak cascading activation is its only source of support. In contrast, when mixed neighbours are activated, they modulate the activity of representations that are already above threshold. Therefore, although the phonological and L-level representation of mixed neighbours themselves are not highly activated, they can exert an influence on representations that receive other sources of support. This provides a ready account of the lack of interactive effects in Melinger and Abdel Rahman (2004). In this study, activation from the L-level representation of the semantic distractor fails to converge with the phonological representation of the target (e.g., BEAR fails to converge with 'pig'). Since the phonological and semantic distractors fail to converge on the target's phonological representation, they fail to enhance its activation any more than predicted by each individual distractor. Finally, convergent activation also accounts for the positive results of Morsella and Miozzo (2004) and Navarette and Costa (2005); as with mixed distractors, activation from the pictorial distractor converges with that of the already activated target word.

Role of the monitor

Some researchers (e.g., Levelt, 1983; Levelt et al., 1999; Roelofs, 2004a) have questioned some of the evidence for cascading activation. For example, they have attributed mixed error biases solely to the influence of monitoring systems (see Hartsuiker, 2006, for further discussion). As described by Roelofs (2004a), prior to articulation the phonological form of the speaker's utterance is fed back through the comprehension system. The speaker monitors for mismatches between the concept activated by this phonological form and the intended concept. Since mixed neighbours partially activate the intended concept, it is more difficult to detect them compared with purely semantic errors (e.g., mixed error 'calf' will partially activate the target 'cat' within the perceptual system, while pure semantic neighbour 'dog' will not).

There are two major problems with this account. Monitoring theories have remained quite underspecified, making their precise predictions under particular processing conditions rather unclear (see Goldrick & Rapp, 2002; Rapp & Goldrick, 2004, for further discussion). Furthermore, even perception-based monitoring accounts (e.g., Levelt et al., 1999; Roelofs, 2004a) appear to require cascading activation in addition to monitoring to account for phonological effects of pictorial distractors (Morsella & Miozzo, 2002; Navarette & Costa, 2005). In order for distractors or mixed errors to induce monitoring effects, their phonological representations must be activated (if they are not, they cannot engage perceptual processes). However, pictorial distractors can only activate their phonology via semantic and L-level representations (Hillis, 2001). In other words, the monitor requires cascade to be present to account for these data – without it, the phonology of distractors would simply be inactive and the monitor would not be engaged. Given that all accounts require this mechanism, it is more parsimonious to attribute the various effects discussed here to cascading activation.

Implications for the strength of cascading activation

There is abundant evidence from both traditions of speech production research to support the presence of both upper and lower bounds on cascading activation. Note the discussion above is limited to those effects that can be accounted for solely by the presence of cascading activation; namely, phonological effects attributable to semantically activated L-level representations. As discussed below, cascading can also interact with feedback to allow other L-level representations (i.e., formally related words) to influence phonological processing.

Although the data support both upper and lower bounds on cascade, it is unclear how to more precisely formulate these limitations. One concrete proposal that is not consistent with the data is that of Levelt et al. (1999). They claimed the upper bound of cascade is defined by words that are semantically similar and contextually appropriate targets (e.g., synonyms). Empirical data suggest this is too strong a limitation on cascade. With respect to errors, phonological level errors are facilitated for members of the same semantic category (e.g., 'cat' and 'rat'), which are clearly neither synonymic nor contextually appropriate. With respect to chronometric data, effects are also observed for contextually inappropriate items (e.g., cognates or translation equivalents in a monolingual context; alternative target names at inappropriate levels of categorisation; see Jescheniak et al., 2005, for further discussion). It is unclear what alternative formulation would provide a better account of restrictions on cascade. This is in part due to lingering disagreements between chronometric and error data. For example, while direct chronometric effects of cascading activation are only observed under very high degrees of conceptually driven activation (e.g., cognates, near-synonyms), speech error effects are observed in a wider range circumstances (e.g., categorically related semantic associates). This issue is returned to in the general discussion.

EVIDENCE SUPPORTING LIMITED FEEDBACK: PHONOLOGICAL TO L-LEVEL REPRESENTATIONS

As discussed below, adding feedback from phonological to L-level representations (Figure 1C) accounts for a number of interactive effects that cannot be produced by cascading activation. Following the limitation of the discussion to data from speech production, arguments for feedback based on shared representations for production and perception (see Martin & Saffran, 2002, for a review) will not be considered here.

Evidence supporting limited feedback effects on L-level selection

Above, cases of deficits to L-level processing were reviewed. These individuals had modality-specific impairments to speech production that resulted in the production of only semantic errors. Deficits to lexical semantic processing were ruled out, as these individuals did not exhibit comprehension deficits. Phonological impairments were ruled out because they failed to produce purely phonologically related word and nonword errors.

Rapp and Goldrick (2000) examined the performance of two of these individuals (PW and RGB) and found that both exhibited a significant mixed error effect. Specifically, their semantic errors showed greater phonological overlap than predicted by chance (i.e., a higher degree of phonological overlap than randomly paired targets and errors; see Rapp & Goldrick, 2000, for a detailed description of the analysis). This supports the presence of feedback. Feedback from phonological representations serves to facilitate the L-level representation of mixed neighbours relative to those of purely semantic neighbours. This facilitation translates into a greater likelihood of errors, producing the mixed error effect. Note that unlike the mixed error data reviewed above these effects cannot be accounted for by cascading activation. Cascading activation only allows for a mixed error benefit at the phonological level, and in these cases there is independent evidence that their deficit is to L-level processing.

Upper limits on feedback to L-level selection. The many cases of L-level deficits reviewed above also provide an upper bound on the strength of feedback. As described above, despite relatively low accuracy levels (e.g., 28% error in untimed picture naming), these individuals produce only semantic errors. This suggests a limit to the strength of feedback; very strong feedback predicts that these individuals should also produce formally related errors (Rapp & Goldrick, 2000). Figure 3 reports new simulation results that further document the relationship between feedback strength and the production of formal errors following L-level damage. The simulation reported here implements a system with cascading activation and feedback from the phoneme to the L-level (see Rapp &

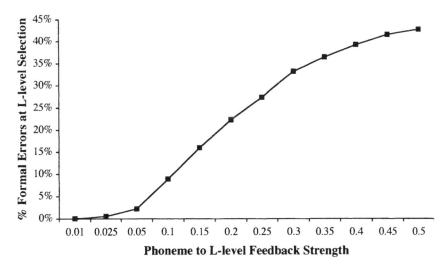

Figure 3. Production of formal errors due to increases in feedback strength. Results show percentage of formal related errors selected at the L-level over 10,000 simulated naming attempts in a system with cascading activation and feedback from the phoneme to L-level. L-level noise was fixed at 0.7.

Goldrick, 2000, for implementation details).[7] Damage to the L-level was simulated by setting L-level noise to a high level (0.7). Feedback strength was set to two very low levels (.01 and .025) and then varied from 0.05 to 0.50 in 0.05 increments. As shown in Figure 3, when feedback strength is limited, formal errors were produced at negligible levels. However, when feedback strength was increased beyond this point, a highly significant number of formal errors occurred at L-level selection. If feedback is not sufficiently limited, theories of speech production cannot account for the production of only semantic errors following L-level damage.[8]

Evidence supporting indirect effects of feedback on phonological processing

The results reviewed above suggest that formally related neighbours are not highly active at the point of L-level selection. However, following L-level selection, feedback can continue to exert an influence on L-level

---

[7] The 'Restricted Interaction Account' simulation of Rapp & Goldrick (2000) was used. Parameter settings that deviated from default settings were: feedforward connections were set to 0.05; L-level jolt was set to 5.0; and feedback connections were varied as specified above.

[8] Limited feedback predicts that some formal errors should be produced with sufficiently high levels of L-level damage. The pattern of performance exhibited by EA (Shelton & Weinrich, 1997) is consistent with this prediction.

representations, allowing phonological related words (e.g., <HAT> for target <CAT>) to grow in activation. If cascading activation is present, these formally related L-level representations will pass on activation to their phonological representations. The positive feedback loops created by this interaction of feedback and cascade allow L-level properties to bias the outcome of phonological processing (Dell, 1986).[9]

Phonologically related error outcomes are biased by lexical proper-ties. To concretely illustrate the influence of positive feedback loops, consider their most well-studied consequence: the lexical bias effect. Suppose that subsequent to L-level selection, phonological processing is randomly disrupted, increasing the activation of a nontarget phoneme that creates a word outcome (e.g,. while naming 'cat', the activation of /h/ in onset is randomly increased, creating the potential word error 'hat'). Via feedback, this nontarget phoneme can pass its increased activation back to the L-level unit corresponding to the word outcome (e.g., <HAT>). This drives up the activation of the L-level unit. Via cascade, this L-level unit then reactivates its constituent phonemes (e.g., /h/). The cycle then repeats, increasing activation levels of both phonological and L-level representa-tions corresponding to this word outcome – hence, a *positive* feedback loop. In contrast, if random disruptions boost the activity of phoneme that creates a nonword outcome (e.g., /z/), it will be unable to enter into such a strong feedback relationship. Since there is no L-level unit corresponding to this outcome (e.g., <ZAT> is not present), this phoneme will be unable to benefit from the influence of strong feedback loops.[10] Phonemes that create word outcomes will therefore be more active than those that create nonword outcomes. This will bias errors at the phonological level to produce more word outcomes than matched nonword outcomes – creating the lexical bias effect. Simulation results consistent with this analysis have been reported in multiple architectures (e.g., Dell, 1986, Rapp & Goldrick, 2000).

Empirically, the lexical bias effect has been reported in studies of spontaneous speech errors (Dell & Reich, 1981; Harley, 1984; Nooteboom, 2005b; Stemberger, 1985; but see del Viso et al., 1991 and Garrett, 1976, for null results), experimentally induced errors (Baars, Motley, & MacKay, 1975; Dell, 1986, 1990; Humphreys, 2002; Hartsuiker, Corley, &

---

[9] Related mechanisms can produce similar effects within attractor-based systems (Plaut & Shallice, 1993).

[10] Of course, the phoneme will enter into feedback loops with some L-level units (e.g., <ZIP>); however, these units are more distant from the target and thus will receive less feedback support from the target (e.g., <HAT> will receive support from the /ae/ and /t/ of target 'cat').

Martensen, 2005; Nooteboom, 2005a), as well as in errors produced by aphasic speakers (Best, 1996; Gagnon, Schwartz, Martin, Dell, & Saffran, 1997; but see Nickels & Howard, 1995, for a null result).

It should be noted that the lexical bias effect may be influenced not only by automatic mechanisms such as feedback, but may also be modulated by mechanisms monitoring the outcome of speech production processes. Current evidence from experimentally induced errors suggests that both mechanisms are required to provide a full account of performance (see Hartsuiker et al., 2005, for discussion).

If cascading activation from the L-level plays a crucial role in the lexical bias effect, the strength of the bias should vary with lexical frequency. Most current theories of speech production (e.g., Dell, 1990; Jescheniak & Levelt, 1994; Miozzo & Caramazza, 2003; Roelofs, 1997), assume that lexical frequency[11] effects are localised to L-level representations (i.e., in their selection thresholds; time required for L-level representations to accumulate activation; verification times for lexical representations). Since the L-level representations of low frequency words are in general more weakly activated than those of high frequency words, they should transmit less cascading activation to the phonological level. This activation difference should cause errors to exhibit a frequency bias (i.e., errors at the phonological level should be more likely to result in high frequency than lower frequency words). The frequency bias has been observed in errors in neurologically intact speakers (see Harley & MacAndrew, 2001, for a review of positive results in spontaneous speech errors; but see Dell, 1990, for a null result in experimentally induced errors), as well as in a number of studies of individuals with acquired neurological impairments (Blanken, 1990, 1998; Gagnon et al., 1997; Goldrick & Rapp, in press; Martin, Dell, Saffran, & Schwartz, 1994; but see Best, 1996, for a null result).

Note that these effects cannot be produced by a system with only cascading activation. In such a system, the only L-level units that are active are semantic neighbours of the target (see Figure 1B). As discussed above, this serves to boost the activation of mixed neighbours at the phonological level. It does not boost the activation of purely phonological neighbours. Thus, in a system with only cascading activation, nontarget phonemes that correspond to word outcomes not semantically related to the target (e.g., 'hat' for 'cat') are no more active than those that correspond to nonword outcomes (e.g., 'zat'). Similarly, with respect to a frequency bias, all formally related outcomes will be equally activated, regardless of their

---

[11] Note that lexical frequency is highly correlated with other lexical properties such as age of acquisition (for recent reviews, see Bonin, Barry, Méot, & Chalard, 2004; Zevin & Seidenberg, 2002).

lexical frequency. Feedback is required to activate purely phonologically related words at the L-level; without it, these lexical effects cannot be produced at the phonological level.

Neighbourhood density effects.   The previous section documented how feedback enhances the representation of nontarget words. It can enhance the phonological representation of the target as well. For example, as shown in Figure 1C, feedback activates <HAT> and , and they enhance the activation of phonological structure they share with the target 'cat' (e.g., /ae/). This facilitatory effect of formal neighbours predicts that words with many neighbours should more quickly and accurately retrieve their phonological representations compared to words with few neighbours (see Dell & Gordon, 2003, for simulation results supporting this prediction).

Several empirical findings are consistent with this claim. With respect to chronometric experiments, picture naming latency for high density words is shorter than that of matched low density words (Vitevitch, 2002; Vitevitch, Armbrüster, & Chu, 2004). These effects are arguably driven by the lexical properties of the stimuli. Density effects on latency are still present when responses are initiated via button press, suggesting that the effects are not attributable to articulatory differences between stimuli (Vitevitch, 2002). Furthermore, the effect is still found when sublexical properties of the stimuli are explicitly controlled (e.g., phonotactic probability; Vitevitch, 2002). With respect to the accuracy of lexical retrieval, words in high density neighbourhoods (i.e., words that are phonologically similar to many other words) are less susceptible to TOT states than low density words (Harley & Bown, 1998; Vitevitch & Sommers, 2003). Experimentally induced (Stemberger, 2004; Vitevitch, 2002) and spontaneous (Vitevitch, 1997) speech errors are more likely to occur on forms in low density neighbourhoods. Finally, individuals with acquired speech production deficits produce more errors on words in low density as compared with those in high density neighbourhoods (Goldrick & Rapp, in press; Gordon, 2002).

Implications for the strength of feedback and cascading activation. Although these lexical effects suggest that both feedback and cascading activation are present, they are also consistent with restrictions on both forms on interaction. Since these effects are due to positive feedback loops that allow activation to build up over time, they can be realised by fairly weak levels of interaction.

Assuming that feedback is weak implies that formally related words will require time to become significantly active at the L-level. This is consistent with the claim that prior to L-level selection formally related words are not strongly active. As processing continues, the positive feedback loops will allow the formally related words to become more active and influence phonological processing. Similarly, assuming weak cascade implies that only strongly activated L-level representations will be able to influence phonological processing. This is consistent with the restrictions on cascade from semantically related items noted in the first section of the paper. With respect to formally related words, weak cascade interacts with weak feedback to gradually boost the activation of their L-level representations, allowing them to influence phonological processing following L-level selection. In contrast, since purely semantically related neighbours do not share the phonology of the target, they are not re-activated by feedback. Their influence therefore decays over time, while formally related neighbours grow in strength.

As an existence proof that limited feedback and cascade can produce the proper mix of interactivity and discreteness, Rapp and Goldrick (2000) presented simulation results from systems where phonological to L-level feedback was set to half the strength of feedforward connections. Cascade was also limited by incorporating a strong L-level selection process. These simulations demonstrated attested effects of interaction (e.g., lexical bias, mixed error effects at the L-level) without resulting in unattested effects (e.g., following L-level damage, there were very few formal errors or nonword errors produced).

EVIDENCE SUPPORTING ABSENT/ FUNCTIONALLY INSIGNIFICANT FEEDBACK FROM L-LEVEL TO LEXICAL SEMANTIC REPRESENTATIONS

Increasing feedback by allowing L-level representations to feed back and activate lexical semantic representations creates the potential for information at lower levels in the production system (e.g., L-level information such as lexical frequency, or phonological information such as phonological overlap) to influence semantic processing. For example, as shown in Figure 1D, feedback from <RAT> transfers its activation (enhanced by phonological overlap with the target) back to the lexical semantic level.[12] Note that following the discussion above, feedback

---

[12] This feedback would have similar consequences in systems with unitary lexical semantic representations and those with distributed feature representations. In the former, the activation of a single unit would be enhanced, making it a stronger competitor for selection at the lexical semantic level. In the latter, a set of semantic features would have their activation enhanced, allowing their corresponding lexical concept to compete more strongly for selection.

motivated by shared representations across production and perception (cf. Roelofs, 2004a, footnote 2) will not be considered.

Lexical frequency does not influence semantic processing

A number of studies have found that when pictures have to be recognised, but not named, lexical frequency effects are not found (see Jescheniak & Levelt, 1994, for a review; for a recent replication of this null result [for items matched for name agreement], see Schatzman & Schiller, 2004).[13] For example, Jescheniak and Levelt (1994: Experiment 1) found a robust effect of lexical frequency on picture naming latency (pictures with high frequency names were named on average 62 milliseconds faster than those with low frequency names). In contrast, in a picture-word matching task (with basic-level word targets and distractors), no significant effect was found (pictures were matched with high frequency names only 6 milliseconds faster than with low frequency names). Jescheniak and Levelt attributed the difference in performance to differences in the processing stages required to perform each task. Picture naming requires access to L-level and phonological representations (to support oral production). In contrast, basic level word-picture matching is accomplished by comparing the semantic representations evoked by the pictorial and written word stimuli (DeCaro & Reeves, 2002). Thus, they argue, lexical frequency effects are observed only when post-semantic processing is required – consistent with the absence of feedback between these L-level and lexical semantic representations.

Mixed semantic-phonological error effects are absent at the lexical semantic level

Rapp and Goldrick (2000) examined the performance of KE, an individual with a deficit to lexical semantic processes. Like the individuals with L-level deficits described above, KE produced only semantic errors in speech production. As argued above, this suggests that his impairment was not at the phonological level. Unlike individuals with L-level deficits, KE exhibited remarkably similar performance across a range of perception and production tasks in a variety of modalities. For example, he produced similar rates of semantic errors in both writing and speaking, and made similar rates of semantic confusions in auditory, reading, and tactile

---

[13] Note that Bonin and Fayol (2002) found a reverse frequency effect in a picture categorisation task (e.g., pictures with low frequency names were more quickly categorised than those with high frequency names).

comprehension tasks. This is consistent with damage to an amodal lexical semantic system shared across perception and production (see Hillis, Rapp, Romani, & Caramazza, 1990, for further analyses arguing against multiple coincident deficits).

Using the same techniques applied to the analysis of individuals with L-level deficits (see above), Rapp and Goldrick (2000) found that KE's semantic errors exhibited no more phonological overlap than predicted by chance. This suggests that at the lexical semantic level, mixed semantic-phonological neighbours are no more active than those that are purely semantically related. This is consistent with the absence of feedback to lexical semantic representations. If such feedback were present, the activation advantage that mixed semantic-phonological neighbours have at the L-level (as evidenced by mixed semantic-phonological error effects at L-level selection) should be transferred to the lexical semantic level.

Selective deficits to speech production

As discussed above, if cascading activation from L-level to phonological representations is too strong, L-level deficits can indirectly disrupt phonological processing. Similar effects can arise due to feedback from L-level to semantic representations. If feedback is too strong, disruptions to L-level processing can feed back and indirectly disrupt lexical semantic processing (Rapp & Goldrick, 2000). For example, suppose L-level noise randomly boosts the activation of a semantic competitor at the L-level prior to lexical semantic selection (e.g., <DOG> is boosted prior to the selection of {CAT}). If feedback is strong, this increased activity can be fed back to its lexical semantic representation (e.g., {DOG}). Positive feedback loops between these two representations can drive the activity of the lexical semantic representation over that of the target, resulting in errors during lexical semantic selection. This would lead to the prediction that individuals with deficits to the L-level should show semantic deficits; as discussed above, they do not. They produce semantic errors in speech production, but do not have deficits to comprehension processes.

Figure 4 presents new simulation results further documenting the indirect disruption of lexical semantic processing under conditions of strong feedback from the L-level. The simulation implements a system with cascading activation and feedback throughout the production system (see Rapp & Goldrick, 2000, for implementation details).[14] Damage to the

---

[14] The 'High Interaction Account' simulation of Rapp & Goldrick (2000) was used. Parameter settings that deviated from default settings were: feedforward and feedback connections were set to 0.05 (except when varied as specified above); and the L-level jolt was set to 5.0.

L-level was simulated by setting L-level noise to a high level (0.7). Feedback strength from the L-level to lexical semantic representation was set to two very low levels (.01 and .025) and then varied from 0.05 to 0.50 in 0.05 increments. As shown in Figure 4, when feedback strength was very limited, lexical semantic processing was not disrupted. However, when feedback strength was increased beyond this point, many errors occurred at lexical semantic selection. Feedback from the L-level must be limited; if it is not, the occurrence of selective deficits to speech production following L-level damage cannot be explained.

Implications for the strength of feedback to lexical semantic representations

Existing evidence places an upper bound on the amount of feedback from L-level to lexical semantic representations. However, it is possible for theories with weak feedback between these two levels of processing to account for these data. First, the simulation studies of Rapp and Goldrick (2000) as well as those reported here showed that feedback strength can be attenuated to such a degree that it is functionally insignificant. For example, as shown in Figure 4, at very low levels of feedback there is no indirect disruption of lexical semantic processing by L-level damage. Feedback may therefore be technically present, but it may have no consequence on processing. (For further discussion of functionally

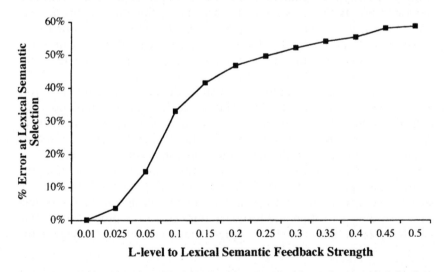

Figure 4. Indirect disruption to lexical semantic processing due to increases in L-level to lexical semantic feedback strength. Results show percentage of errors at lexical semantic selection over 10,000 simulated naming attempts in a system with both cascading activation and feedback between all levels in the production system. L-level noise was fixed at 0.7.

irrelevant feedback, see Rapp & Goldrick, 2000; Roelofs, 2003.) A second possibility is that feedback does exert an influence, but that this can only be found after lexical concepts have been selected. This would be analogous to the situation observed at the L-level for phonologically related neighbours. One area for future research is therefore the question of what lower bounds can be placed on the strength of feedback from L-level to semantic representations.

A related point is that theories assuming multiple levels of lexical representation (e.g., Levelt et al., 1999) can account for these findings while still allowing for strong feedback from some level of lexical representation to lexical semantics. This is possible so long as feedback is blocked from lexical representations that encode lexical frequency (e.g., feedback from frequency-insensitive lemmas is acceptable, so long as feedback from frequency-sensitive lexemes is blocked).

GENERAL DISCUSSION

Consideration of data from both major traditions of speech production research reveals support for limited interactivity in the speech production system. These studies provide strong constraints on both the upper and lower bounds of interaction in production theories. First, both chronometric and speech error studies set a lower limit on the degree of cascading activation from L-level to phonological representations. Unselected, semantically activated L-level representations must be able to enhance the activation of their phonological representations. However, there is an upper bound on this influence, as revealed by restrictions on the situations in which chronometric data show cascading activation effects and the lack of indirect disruptions to phonological processing following L-level damage. The second section reviewed evidence concerning feedback from phonological to L-level representations. Such feedback must be strong enough to facilitate the activation of mixed neighbours prior to L-level selection. It must also be able to combine with weak cascading activation to produce lexical effects within phonological processing. As with cascading activation, evidence was reviewed providing upper bounds on this type of interaction; prior to L-level selection, formal neighbours must not be significantly activated. Finally, existing evidence suggests that prior to selection lexical semantic representations are not influenced by feedback from lower levels in the speech production system. Such feedback is either absent or extremely weak.

Implications for theories of speech production

The results are most consistent with the Restricted Interaction Account (RIA) proposed by Rapp and Goldrick (2000, 2004; Goldrick & Rapp,

2002). This theory claims that: limited cascading activation is present throughout the production system; limited feedback exists between the phonological and L-levels; and feedback is absent between L-level and semantic representations. These previous papers have motivated this theory primarily through discussion of speech error data; as shown here, it is consistent with the existing chronometric data as well.

Although RIA provides the most explicit claims about restrictions on interaction, these claims resonate with properties of many other proposals in the literature. Theories with cascade and feedback often assume that the influence of these interactive mechanisms is restricted. Harley (1993, 1995) presented results from a simulation with cascading activation throughout the production system and feedback from phonological representations to the L-level. His results show that the influence of cascade and feedback can be minimised (or even eliminated) by the presence of inhibition and activation decay. Dell and O'Seaghdha (1991, 1992) pointed out that many spreading activation accounts are only *locally* interactive; these theories restrict interaction to adjacent representational levels and enforce rather strict selection points to increase the discreteness of spoken production processing.[15] Coming from the chronometric tradition, discrete theories often assume that cascade and feedback effects can appear in limited situations (see above for discussion of issues associated with these particular proposals). As noted above, Levelt et al. (1999) assume that cascading activation from L-level to phonological representations can occur in cases of near synonymy. Roelofs (2004a, 2004b) argues that feedback from phonological to L-levels can (optionally) occur, mediated by perceptual monitoring.

Directions for future research

In short, empirical data support the presence of limited interaction. Not surprisingly, then, all current theoretical proposals incorporate various forms of limited interaction. This suggests that the presence versus complete absence of interaction in the production system is no longer an issue under debate. If this is indeed the case, the empirical focus of research on interaction should focus on finer-grained questions on the

---

[15] Note that these restrictions on interaction are not a priori features of production theories. Plaut and Shallice (1993) proposed a theory of (semantically based) reading without strict selection points. In a similar context, Van Orden and colleagues (Farrar & Van Orden, 2001; Van Orden, op de Haar, & Bosman, 1997) have proposed that interactions can occur between non-adjacent representational levels.

manner and degree of interaction between speech production processes. Four such avenues for further investigation are sketched below.

Differences in the strength of interactive effects in chronometric and speech error data

One question that comes naturally out of the review above is why errors are more likely to show an influence of interaction than reaction times. As noted above, chronometric and speech error data disagree on the extent to which activation cascades from the L-level; specifically, chronometric data fail to reveal the activation of nonsynonymic semantically related words. Two possible accounts of this difference have been proposed.

The first of these focuses on methodological differences between the two types of studies. As noted above, chronometric studies reporting null effects often attempt to observe mediated effects, while speech error studies often focus on cases where activation largely converges with that of the target (Dell & O'Seaghdha, 1991). The presence versus absence of convergent activation may be sufficient to account for these differences.

A second possibility is that when errors occur, the dynamics and organisation of processing are shifted into a 'deviant' processing state that allows for greater interaction (for discussion of errors in reading aloud as the consequence of shifts in processing dynamics, see Farrar & Van Orden, 2001). A version of this hypothesis is Levelt et al.'s (1999: 35; see also Roelofs, 2004a) claim that cascading activation effects with near-synonyms are due to the erroneous selection of two L-level representations. In this proposal, interactive effects are due to extraordinary processing circumstances and do not reflect the normal state of processing. Note that this hypothesis is not identical to the thoroughly debunked claim that errors bear *no* relation to normal language processing (see, e.g., Fromkin, 1971, for a critique of this proposal). Rather, this hypothesis claims that certain *aspects* of errors are not indicative of normal processing.

The former hypothesis is more parsimonious in the sense that errors are assumed to be a natural consequence of spoken production processing; special mechanisms are not invoked purely to account for errors. However, it has not gone unchallenged. Levelt et al. (1991b) argued that the empirically observed strength of semantic priming is so great that interactive theories (specifically, Dell & O'Seaghdha, 1991) predict that some amount of priming should be observed in mediated situations. Resolution of this issue requires the development of accounts that simultaneously make fine-grained predictions regarding reaction times and errors. Analysis of such systems will allow a better test of these two proposals.

Interaction: Dynamic or static feature of production processes?

The question of whether the processing dynamics shift during error production relates to the broader question of whether interactivity is itself dynamic. Is the degree of interaction a hard-wired architectural feature of the production system, or does the extent of interaction across representations and processes shift across different processing situations?

For example, Kello, Plaut, & MacWhinney (2000) claimed that the strength of cascading activation to articulation could be modulated by task demands. A similar task-demand account might explain some of the results reviewed above. For example, the absence of lexical frequency effects in 'semantic' tasks (e.g., picture-word matching) might be due to the amount of resources they require. These tasks may simply be easier to perform than picture naming. The lower demand on processing resources, not a lack of feedback connections, may account for the absence of interactive effects. Note that it is unlikely that such an account can be offered for all the results reviewed here. For example, patients with lexical semantic vs. L-level deficits were all asked to perform the same task – untimed picture naming – yet their performance yielded contrasting patterns. Future research should more carefully explore how interactive effects can or cannot be modulated by the demands of different tasks.

Architectural accounts of the absence of feedback from L-level to semantic representations

Instead of contrasting task demands, is there instead some functional or architectural feature of the production system that could motivate this difference in interaction? One such account is connectivity distance. As pointed out above, feedback mechanisms may be present, but they may be too weak to exert an influence on lexical semantic selection processes. This is highly plausible for the case of phonological information. It must traverse many links in the production system before it can influence semantic processing; it may come too late or be too weak to influence selection of a lexical concept. It is less clear if this account could explain the lack of lexical frequency effects at the semantic level; in the three-level system discussed here these effects arise at a representational level adjacent to semantics. However, if there are instead two levels of lexical representation, and frequency effects are associated with the level more distant from semantics (e.g., a lexeme; Levelt et al., 1999), connectivity distance may provide a ready account of the lack of frequency effects.

A second proposal is that the lack of interaction stems from a representational distinction between semantic representations, on one hand, and L-level and phonological representations, on the other. If we assume (following Caramazza, 1997) that L-level representations are modality specific, the latter two levels of representation can be easily distinguished from amodal semantic representations. The lack of feedback can then be attributed to a more independent design principle – stronger interaction is restricted to similar representational types (Rapp & Goldrick, 2000).

Again, resolving these two proposals will most probably rely on the development of more detailed theories and simulations of speech production processing. Following the first proposal, is it even possible to set up such an interactive system? That is, can a system with a constant strength of cascade and feedback rely solely on connectivity distance to explain the absence of effects at the lexical semantic level? Future simulation studies of interactive theories are clearly required.

Mechanisms mediating feedback

This review explicitly avoided the issue of whether feedback was mediated by mechanisms and processes internal to speech production, or if speech perception processes may also play a role in mediating such effects. Roelofs (2004a, 2004b) claimed that feedback mediated by speech perception and monitoring systems provided the best account of the data supporting feedback. Rapp and Goldrick (2004) discussed some of the difficulties associated with this particular proposal. Since these papers, new data from Hartsuiker et al. (2005) provides further support for the claim that theories attributing all feedback effects to monitoring processes are clearly insufficient. Future theoretical and empirical work should continue to address the relative contributions of production-internal, perceptual and monitoring mechanisms in supporting feedback (see also Hartsuiker, 2006, for further discussion).

CONCLUSIONS

Speech production theories have tended to focus on a single type of evidence – based around reaction times or speech errors – to inform theory development. It has therefore been difficult to determine if disagreements between theories developed within each empirical tradition were merely due to differences in the type of evidence driving each theory. Consideration of both types of data shows that this is partially true – interactive effects appear to be more easily observed in speech errors than chronometric data. Recent work, however, reveals that interactive effects are not peculiar to speech error data; furthermore, discrete effects are not peculiar to chronometric data. Both types of evidence argue for the presence of interactivity; both types of evidence point to significant constraints on interactivity. These findings reveal the limitations of the 'highly discrete/highly interactive' dichotomy, and challenge us to explore the continuum of possibilities offered by limited interaction.

REFERENCES

Baars, B. J., Motley, J. T., & MacKay, D. (1975). Output editing for lexical status from artificially elicited slips of the tongue. *Journal of Verbal Learning and Verbal Behavior, 14*, 382–391.

Basso, A., Taborelli, A., & Vignolo, L. A. (1978). Dissociated disorders of speaking and writing in aphasia. *Journal of Neurology, Neurosurgery and Psychiatry, 41*, 556–563.

Berg, T., & Schade, U. (1992). The role of inhibition in a spreading-activation model of language production I: The psycholinguistic perspective. *Journal of Psycholinguistic Research, 21*, 405–434.

Best, W. (1996). When racquets are baskets but baskets are biscuits, where do the words come from? A single case study of formal paraphasic errors in aphasia. *Cognitive Neuropsychology, 13*, 443–480.

Blanken, G. (1990). Formal paraphasias: A single case study. *Brain and Language, 38*, 534–554.

Blanken, G. (1998). Lexicalisation in speech production: Evidence from form-related word substitutions in aphasia. *Cognitive Neuropsychology, 15*, 321–360.

Bloem, I., & La Heij, W. (2003). Semantic facilitation and semantic interference in word translation: Implications for models of lexical access in language production. *Journal of Memory and Language, 48*, 468–488.

Bloem, I., van den Boogaard, S., & La Heij, W. (2004). Semantic facilitation and semantic interference in language production: Further evidence for the conceptual selection model of lexical access. *Journal of Memory and Language, 51*, 307–323.

Bonin, P., Barry, C., Méot, A., & Chalard, M. (2004). The influence of age of acquisition in word reading and other tasks: A never ending story? *Journal of Memory and Language, 50*, 456–476.

Bonin, P., & Fayol, M. (2002). Frequency effects in the written and spoken production of homophonic picture names. *European Journal of Cognitive Psychology, 14*, 289–313.

Brédart, S., & Valentine, T. (1992). From Monroe to Moreau: An analysis of face naming errors. *Cognition, 45*, 187–223.

Burke, D. M., Locantore, J. K., Austin, A. A., & Chae, B. (2004). Cherry pit primes Brad Pitt: Homophone priming effects on young and older adults' production of proper names. *Psychological Science, 15*, 164–170.

Caramazza, A. (1997). How many levels of processing are there in lexical access? *Cognitive Neuropsychology, 14*, 177–208.

Caramazza, A., Bi, Y., Costa, A., Miozzo, M. (2004). What determines the speed of lexical access: Homophone or specific-word frequency? A reply to Jescheniak et al. (2003). *Journal of Experimental Psychology: Learning, Memory, and Cognition, 30*, 278–282.

Caramazza, A., Costa, A., Miozzo, M., & Bi, Y. (2001). The specific-word frequency effect: Implications for the representation of homophones in speech production. *Journal of Experimental Psychology: Learning, Memory, and Cognition, 27*, 1430–1450.

Caramazza, A., & Hillis, A. E. (1990). Where do semantic errors come from? *Cortex, 26*, 95–122.

Costa, A., Caramazza, A., & Sebastian-Galles, N. (2000). The cognate facilitation effect: Implications for models of lexical access. *Journal of Experimental Psychology: Learning, Memory, and Cognition, 26*, 1283–1296

Costa, A., Colomé, A., Gómez, O., & Sebastián-Gallés, N. (2003). Another look at cross-language competition in bilingual speech production: Lexical and phonological factors. *Bilingualism: Language and Cognition, 6*, 167–179.

Costa, A., Mahon, B., Savova, V., & Caramazza, A. (2003). Levels of categorization effect: A novel effect in the picture-word interference paradigm. *Language and Cognitive Processes, 18*, 205–233.

Cutting, J. C., & Ferreira, V. S. (1999). Semantic and phonological information flow in the production lexicon. *Journal of Experimental Psychology: Learning, Memory, and Cognition, 25*, 318–344.

Damian, M. F., & Bowers, J. S. (2003). Locus of semantic interference in picture-word interference tasks. *Psychonomic Bulletin and Review, 10*, 111–117.

Damian, M. F., & Martin, R. M. (1999). Semantic and phonological codes interact in single word production. *Journal of Experimental Psychology: Learning, Memory, and Cognition, 25*, 345–361.

DeCaro, S., & Reeves, A. (2002). The use of wordpicture verification to study entry-level object recognition: Further support for view-invariant mechanisms. *Memory and Cognition, 30*, 811–821.

del Viso, S., Igoa, J. M., & García-Albea, J. E. (1991). On the autonomy of phonological encoding: Evidence from slips of the tongue in Spanish. *Journal of Psycholinguistic Research, 20*, 161–185.

Dell, G. S. (1986). A spreading activation theory of retrieval in sentence production. *Psychological Review, 93*, 283–321.

Dell, G. S. (1990). Effects of frequency and vocabulary type on phonological speech errors. *Language and Cognitive Processes, 4*, 313–349.

Dell, G. S., & Gordon, J. K. (2003). Neighbors in the lexicon: Friends or foes? In N. O. Schiller & A. S. Meyer (Eds.), *Phonetics and phonology in language comprehension and production: Differences and similarities.* New York: Mouton de Gruyter.

Dell, G. S., & O'Seaghdha, P. G. (1991). Mediated and convergent lexical priming in language production: A comment on Levelt et al. (1991). *Psychological Review, 98*, 604–614.

Dell, G. S., & O'Seaghdha, P. G. (1992). Stages of lexical access in language production. *Cognition, 42*, 287–314.

Dell, G. S., & O'Seaghdha, P. G. (1994). Inhibition in interactive activation models of linguistic selection and sequencing. In D. Dagenbach & T. H. Carr (Eds.), *Inhibitory processes in attention, memory, and language* (pp. 409–453). San Diego: Academic Press.

Dell, G. S., & Reich, P. A. (1981). Stages in sentence production: An analysis of speech error data. *Journal of Verbal Learning and Verbal Behavior, 20*, 611–629.

Dell, G. S., Schwartz, M., Martin, M., Saffran, E. M., & Gagnon, D. A. (1997). Lexical access in aphasic and nonaphasic speakers. *Psychological Review, 104*, 801–838.

de Zubicaray, G. I., Wilson, S. J., McMahon, K. L., & Muthiah, S. (2001). The semantic interference effect in the picture-word paradigm: An event-related fMRI study employing overt responses. *Human Brain Mapping, 14*, 218–227.

Farrar IV, W. T., & Van Orden, G. C. (2001). Errors as multistable response options. *Nonlinear Dynamics, Psychology, and Life Sciences, 5*, 223–265.

Ferreira, V. S., & Griffin, Z. M. (2003). Phonological influences on lexical (mis-)selection. *Psychological Science, 14*, 86–90.

Fromkin, V. A. (1971). The non-anomalous nature of anomalous utterances. *Language, 47*, 27–52.

Gagnon, D. A., Schwartz, M. F., Martin, N., Dell, G. S. & Saffran, E. M. (1997). The origins of formal paraphasias in aphasics' picture naming. *Brain and Language, 59*, 450–472.

Garrett, M. F. (1976). Syntactic processes in sentence production. In R. J. Wales & E. Walker (Eds.), *New approaches to language mechanisms* (pp. 231–255). Amsterdam: North Holland.

Garrett, M. F. (1980). Levels of processing in sentence production. In B. Butterworth (Ed.), *Language production (Vol. 1): Speech and talk* (pp. 177–220). New York: Academic Press.

Goldrick, M., & Rapp, B. (2002). A restricted interaction account (RIA) of spoken word production: The best of both worlds. *Aphasiology, 16*, 20–55.

Goldrick, M., & Rapp, B. (in press). Lexical and post-lexical phonological representations in spoken production. *Cognition*.

Gollan, T. H., & Acenas, L.-A. R. (2004). What is a TOT? Cognate and translation effects on tip-of-the-tongue states in Spanish-English and Tagalog-English bilinguals. *Journal of Experimental Psychology: Learning, Memory, and Cognition, 30*, 246–269.

Gordon, J. K. (2002). Phonological neighborhood effects in aphasic speech: Spontaneous and structured contexts. *Brain and Language, 82*, 113–145.

Harley, T. A. (1984). A critique of top-down independent levels models of speech production: Evidence from non-plan-internal speech errors. *Cognitive Science, 8*, 191–219.

Harley, T. A. (1993). Phonological activation of semantic competitors during lexical access in speech production. *Language and Cognitive Processes, 8*, 291–309.

Harley, T. A. (1995). Connectionist models of anomia: A comment on Nickels. *Language and Cognitive Processes, 10*, 47–58.

Harley, T. A., & Bown, H. E. (1998). What causes a tip-of-the-tongue state? Evidence for lexical neighbourhood effects in speech production. *British Journal of Psychology, 89*, 151–174.

Harley, T. A., & MacAndrew, S. B. G. (1995). Interactive models of lexicalization: Some constraints from speech error, picture naming, and neuropsychological data. In J. P. Levy, D. Bairaktaris, & J. A. Bullinaria (Eds.), *Connectionist models of memory and language* (pp. 311–331). London: UCL Press.

Harley, T. A., & MacAndrew, S. B. G. (2001). Constraints upon word substitution speech errors. *Journal of Psycholinguistic Research, 30*, 395–417.

Hartsuiker, R. J. (2006). Are speech error patterns affected by a monitoring bias? *Language and Cognitive Processes, 21*, 856–891.

Hartsuiker, R. J., Corley, M., & Martensen, H. (2005). The lexical bias effect is modulated by context, but the standard monitoring account doesn't fly: Related beply to Baars et al. (1975). *Journal of Memory and Language, 52*, 58–70.

Hermans, D., Bongaerts, T., De Bot, K., & Schreuder, R. (1998). Producing words in a foreign language: Can speakers prevent interference from their first language? *Bilingualism: Language and Cognition, 1*, 213–229.

Hillis, A. E. (2001). The organization of the lexical system. In B. Rapp (Ed.), *The handbook of cognitive neuropsychology: What deficits reveal about the human mind* (pp. 185–210). Philadelphia: Psychology Press.

Hillis, A. E., Rapp, B., Romani, C., & Caramazza, A. (1990). Selective impairment of semantics in lexical processing. *Cognitive Neuropsychology, 7*, 191–243.

Humphreys, G. W., Lloyd-Jones, T. J., & Fias, W. (1995). Semantic interference effects on naming using a postcue procedure: Tapping the links between semantics and phonology with pictures and words. *Journal of Experimental Psychology: Learning, Memory, and Cognition, 21*, 961–980.

Humphreys, K. R. (2002). *Lexical bias in speech errors*. Doctoral dissertation, University of Illinois at Urbana-Champaign, USA.

Igoa, J. M. (1996). The relationship between conceptualization and formulation processes in sentence production: Some evidence from Spanish. In M. Carreiras, J. García-Albea, & N.

Sebastián-Galles (Eds.), *Language processing in Spanish* (pp. 305–351). Hillsdale, NJ: Lawrence Erlbaum Associates, Inc.

Indefrey, P., & Levelt, W. J. M. (2004). The spatial and temporal signatures of word production components. *Cognition, 92,* 101–144.

Jescheniak, J. D., Hantsch, A., & Schriefers, H. (2005). Context effects on lexical choice and lexical activation. *Journal of Experimental Psychology: Learning, Memory, and Cognition, 31,* 905–920.

Jescheniak, J. D., & Levelt, W. J. M. (1994). Word frequency effects in speech production: Retrieval of syntactic information and of phonological form. *Journal of Experimental Psychology: Learning, Memory, and Cognition, 20,* 824–843.

Jescheniak, J. D., Meyer, A. S., & Levelt, W. J. M. (2003). Specific-word frequency is not all that counts in speech production: Comments on Caramazza, Costa, et al. (2001) and new experimental data. *Journal of Experimental Psychology: Learning, Memory, and Cognition, 29,* 432–438.

Jescheniak, J. D., & Schriefers, H. (1998). Discrete serial versus cascaded processing in lexical access in speech production: Further evidence from the coactivation of near-synonyms. *Journal of Experimental Psychology: Learning, Memory, and Cognition, 24,* 1256–1274.

Jescheniak, J. D., & Schriefers, H. (2001). Priming effects from phonological related distractors in picture-word interference. *Quarterly Journal of Experimental Psychology, 54A,* 371–382.

Kello, C. T., Plaut, D. C., & MacWhinney, B. (2000). The task dependence of staged versus cascaded processing: An empirical and computational study of Stroop interference in speech production. *Journal of Experimental Psychology: General, 129,* 340–360.

Kulke, F., & Blanken, G. (2001). Phonological and syntactic influences on semantic misnamings in aphasia. *Aphasiology, 15,* 3–15.

Laine, M., Tikkala, A., & Juhola, M. (1998). Modelling anomia by the discrete two-stage word production architecture. *Journal of Neurolinguistics, 11,* 275–294.

Levelt, W. J. M. (1983). Monitoring and self-repair in speech. *Cognition, 14,* 41–104.

Levelt, W. J. M. (1989). *Speaking: From intention to articulation.* Cambridge, MA: MIT Press.

Levelt, W. J. M. (1999). Models of word production. *Trends in Cognitive Sciences, 3,* 223–232.

Levelt, W. J. M., Roelofs, A., & Meyer, A. S. (1999). A theory of lexical access in speech production. *Behavioral and Brain Sciences, 22,* 1–75.

Levelt, W. J. M., Schriefers, H., Vorberg, D., Meyer, A. S., Pechmann, T., & Havinga, J. (1991a). The time course of lexical access in speech production: A study of picture naming. *Psychological Review, 98,* 122–142.

Levelt, W. J. M., Schriefers, H., Vorberg, D., Meyer, A. S., Pechmann, T., & Havinga, J. (1991b). Normal and deviant lexical processing: Reply to Dell and O'Seaghdha (1991). *Psychological Review, 98,* 615–618.

Martin, N., Gagnon, D. A., Schwartz, M. F., Dell, G. S., & Saffran, E. M. (1996). Phonological facilitation of semantic errors in normal and aphasic speakers. *Language and Cognitive Processes, 11,* 257–282.

Martin, N., Dell, G. S., Saffran, E. M., & Schwartz, M. F. (1994). Origins of paraphasias in deep dysphasia: Testing the consequences of a decay impairment to an interactive spreading activation model of lexical retrieval. *Brain and Language, 47,* 609–660.

Martin, N., & Saffran, E. M. (2002). The relationship of input and output phonological processing: An evaluation of models and evidence to support them. *Aphasiology, 16,* 107–150.

Martin, N., Weisberg, R. W., & Saffran, E. M. (1989). Variables influencing the occurrence of naming errors: Implications for models of lexical retrieval. *Journal of Memory and Language, 28,* 462–485.

Melinger, A., & Abdel Rahman, R. (2004). Investigating the interplay between semantic and phonological distractor effects in picture naming. *Brain and Language, 90,* 213–220.

Meyer, D. E., & Gordon, P. C. (1985). Speech production: Motor programming of phonetic features. *Journal of Memory and Language, 24,* 3–26.

Miceli, G., Benvegnú, B., Capasso, R., & Caramazza, A. (1997). The independence of phonological and orthographic lexical forms: Evidence from aphasia. *Cognitive Neuropsychology, 14,* 35–70.

Miozzo, M., & Caramazza, A. (2003). When more is less: A counterintuitive effect of distractor frequency in the picture-word interference paradigm. *Journal of Experimental Psychology: General, 132,* 228–252.

Morsella, E., & Miozzo, M. (2002). Evidence for a cascade model of lexical access in speech production. *Journal of Experimental Psychology: Learning, Memory, and Cognition, 28,* 555–563.

Navarette, E., & Costa, A. (2005). Phonological activation of ignored pictures: Further evidence for a cascade model of lexical access. *Journal of Memory and Language, 53,* 359–377.

Nickels, L. (1992). The autocue? Self-generated phonemic cues in the treatment of a disorder of reading and naming. *Cognitive Neuropsychology, 9,* 307–317.

Nickels, L. (1995). Getting it right? Using aphasic naming errors to evaluate theoretical models of spoken word production. *Language and Cognitive Processes, 10,* 13–45.

Nickels, L. & Howard, D. (1995). Phonological errors in aphasic naming: Comprehension, monitoring, and lexicality. *Cortex, 31,* 209–237.

Nooteboom, S. G. (2005a). Lexical bias revisited: Detecting, rejecting, and repairing speech errors in inner speech. *Speech Communication, 47,* 43–58.

Nooteboom, S. G. (2005b). Listening to oneself: Monitoring speech production. In R. Hartsuiker, Y. Bastiaanse, A. Postma, & F. Wijnen (Eds.), *Phonological encoding and monitoring in normal and pathological speech* (pp. 167–186). Hove, UK: Psychology Press.

O'Seaghdha, P. G., & Marin, J. W. (1997). Mediated semantic-phonological priming: Calling distant relatives. *Journal of Memory and Language, 36,* 226–252.

Page, M. (2000). Connectionist modelling in psychology: A localist manifesto. *Behavioral and Brain Sciences, 23,* 443–467.

Peterson, R. R., & Savoy, P. (1998). Lexical selection and phonological encoding during language production: Evidence for cascaded processing. *Journal of Experimental Psychology: Learning, Memory, and Cognition, 24,* 539–557.

Plaut, D. C., & Shallice, T. (1993). Deep dyslexia: A case study of connectionist neuropsychology. *Cognitive Neuropsychology, 10,* 377–500.

Rapp, B., Benzing, L., & Caramazza, A. (1997). The autonomy of lexical orthography. *Cognitive Neuropsychology, 14,* 71–104.

Rapp, B., & Goldrick, M. (2000). Discreteness and interactivity in spoken word production. *Psychological Review, 107,* 460–499.

Rapp, B., & Goldrick, M. (2004). Feedback by any other name is still interactivity: A reply to Roelofs' comment on Rapp & Goldrick (2000). *Psychological Review, 111,* 573–578.

Roelofs, A. (1992). A spreading-activation theory of lemma retrieval in speaking. *Cognition, 42,* 107–142.

Roelofs, A. (1997). The WEAVER model of word-form encoding in speech production. *Cognition, 64,* 249–284.

Roelofs, A. (2003). Goal-referenced selection of verbal action: Modeling attentional control in the Stroop task. *Psychological Review, 110,* 88–125.

Roelofs, A. (2004a). Error biases in spoken word planning and monitoring by aphasic and nonaphasic speakers: Comment on Rapp and Goldrick (2000). *Psychological Review, 111,* 561–572.

Roelofs, A. (2004b). Comprehension-based versus production-internal feedback in planning spoken words: A rejoinder to Rapp and Goldrick (2004). *Psychological Review, 111*, 579–580.

Schade, U., & Berg, T. (1992). The role of inhibition in a spreading-activation model of language production II: The simulation perspective. *Journal of Psycholinguistic Research, 21*, 435–462.

Schatzman, K. B., & Schiller, N. O. (2004). The word frequency effect in picture naming: Contrasting two hypotheses using homonym pictures. *Brain and Language, 90*, 160–169.

Shelton, J. R., & Weinrich, M. (1997). Further evidence of a dissociation between output phonological and orthographic lexicons: A case study. *Cognitive Neuropsychology, 14*, 105–129.

Starreveld, P. (2000). On the interpretation of phonological context effects in word production. *Journal of Memory and Language, 42*, 497–525.

Starreveld, P. A., & La Heij, W. (1995). Semantic interference, orthographic facilitation, and their interaction in naming tasks. *Journal of Experimental Psychology: Learning, Memory, and Cognition, 21*, 686–698.

Starreveld, P. A., & La Heij, W. (1999). Word substitution errors in the picture-word task. *American Journal of Psychology, 112*, 521–553.

Stemberger, J. P. (1985). An interactive activation model of language production. In A. W. Ellis (Ed.), *Progress in the psychology of language* (Vol. 1, pp. 143–186). Hillsdale, NJ: Lawrence Erlbaum Associates Inc.

Stemberger, J. P. (2004). Neighbourhood effects on error rates in speech production. *Brain and Language, 90*, 413–422.

Taylor, J. K., & Burke, D. M. (2002). Asymmetric aging effects on semantic and phonological processes: Naming in the picture-word interference task. *Psychology and Aging, 17*, 662–676.

Van Orden, G. C., op de Haar, M. A. J., & Bosman, A. M. T. (1997). Complex dynamic systems also predict dissociations, but they do not reduce to autonomous components. *Cognitive Neuropsychology, 14*, 131–165.

Vigliocco, G., & Hartsuiker, R. J. (2002). The interplay of meaning, sound, and syntax in sentence production. *Psychological Bulletin, 128*, 442–472.

Vitevitch, M. S. (1997). The neighborhood characteristics of malapropisms. *Language and Speech, 40*, 211–228.

Vitevitch , M. S. (2002). The influence of phonological similarity neighborhoods on speech production. *Journal of Experimental Psychology: Learning, Memory and Cognition, 28*, 735–747.

Vitevitch, M. S., Armbrüster, J., & Chu, S. (2004). Sublexical and lexical representations in speech production: Effects of phonotactic probability and onset density. *Journal of Experimental Psychology: Learning, Memory, and Cognition, 30*, 514–529.

Vitevitch, M. S., & Sommers, M. S. (2003). The facilitative influence of phonological similarity and neighborhood frequency in speech production in younger and older adults. *Memory and Cognition, 31*, 491–504.

Zevin, J. D., & Seidenberg, M. S. (2002). Age of acquisition effects in word reading and other tasks. *Journal of Memory and Language, 47*, 1–29.

LANGUAGE AND COGNITIVE PROCESSES
2006, 21 (7–8), 856–891

 Psychology Press
Taylor & Francis Group

Are speech error patterns affected by a monitoring bias?

Robert J. Hartsuiker

Department of Experimental Psychology, Ghent University,
Ghent, Belgium

This paper reviews the proposal that observed patterns of speech errors are partly a function of language production mechanisms (that create an underlying pattern of errors), and partly a function of self-monitoring mechanisms (that intercept some errors more often than others and thus alter the underlying pattern). It is essential to find out whether such a 'monitoring bias' is real, because of the important role it plays in debates about the interactivity or modularity of the language production system. Data are reviewed that support an important precondition of monitoring bias accounts: The monitor is fast enough to intercept errors in the speech plan. Subsequently, a number of criteria are proposed for allowing a monitoring bias explanation, and five speech error patterns are compared with those criteria. I conclude that in no case is there unequivocal evidence for a monitoring bias, but that such an account is very plausible in the case of some speech error patterns (e.g., the lexical bias effect), but very implausible in the case of other patterns (e.g., morphophonological effects on errors of subject-verb number agreement).

There is a long tradition in which patterns of speech errors have informed theories of language production. This holds for patterns from corpora of spontaneous speech errors (Dell, 1986; Fromkin, 1971; Garrett, 1975; Harley, 1984; Stemberger, 1985) and for experimentally elicited speech error patterns (Baars, Motley, & MacKay, 1975; Bock & Miller, 1991; Dell,

Correspondence should be addressed to Robert J. Hartsuiker, Department of Experimental Psychology, Ghent University, Henri Dunantlaan 2, 9000 Ghent, Belgium. E-mail: Robert.Hartsuiker@ugent.be

Els Severens and Timothy Desmet are thanked for their comments on an earlier draft of this manuscript, and the participants of the International Workshop on Language Production in Marseille (September 2004) are thanked for stimulating discussion on many of the issues reviewed here.

http://www.psypress.com/lcp   DOI: 10.1080/016909600824609

1990; Vigliocco, Butterworth, & Semenza, 1995; see Stemberger, 1992 for a discussion of differences and similarities between conclusions derived from these two approaches). Speech error data have been used to make claims about the levels of processing in sentence production and lexical access, about the size of the planning units at each level, and about the nature of processing (i.e., are the levels modular or interactive?).

Notwithstanding the considerable influence of speech-error research, this approach has met with several criticisms (e.g., Cutler, 1982; Meyer, 1992). For example, Meyer (1992) noted that observed speech error patterns may inaccurately reflect real speech error patterns, because of a *listener's bias*. Some speech errors (e.g., those affecting phonemes in the word onset) might be detected more easily by speech error collectors than other errors (e.g., ones affecting phonemes in the middle of the word). As a result, the errors that are easier to detect will be over-represented in the corpora (one would overestimate any tendency for phonological errors to occur in the onset).

This article discusses another potential bias, which I will coin the *monitoring bias*. Speakers can monitor their own speech and, according to many proposals, also their speech *plans* before articulation (e.g., Baars et al., 1975; Hartsuiker & Kolk, 2001; Levelt, 1983, 1989). Monitoring the speech plan (i.e., a phonological code, Wheeldon & Levelt, 1995) is usually called internal-channel monitoring, whereas external-channel monitoring involves listening to one's own overt speech. This article will focus on internal- and external-channel monitoring, but it is important to note that the theories of Levelt (1989) and Postma (2000) distinguish additional channels. For example, there would be an 'innermost' channel, located in the production stage of conceptualising, which would check the appropriateness of the message that is constructed (e.g., is the message specific enough to achieve the communicative goals?). There would also be an 'outermost' channel, which would monitor listener feedback to check whether the message is coming across (this includes non-verbal feedback such as nods and frowns, and verbal responses expressing understanding or misunderstanding).

Most monitoring theories further suggest that errors in the speech plan can be *intercepted*, so that they never become overt. It is thus conceivable that, analogous to the listener's bias, some errors in the speech plan, presumably the ones that are easiest to detect, are intercepted more often than other errors. As a result, the final pattern of overt speech errors differs from the underlying error pattern in the speech plan (Figure 1).

As illustrated in Figure 1, a monitoring bias might interact with an underlying pattern of speech errors in several ways. Figure 1a displays the situation discussed most often in the literature (e.g., Levelt, Roelofs, & Meyer, 1999), namely the situation in which there is no difference in the

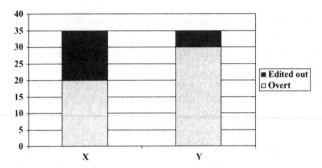

(a) Instantiation

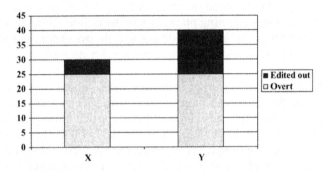

(b) Wipe-out

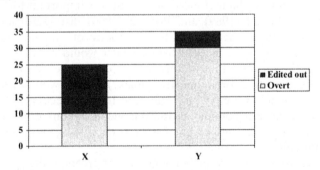

(c) Magnification

Figure 1. Illustration of how an observed pattern of speech errors can be altered as a result of a monitoring bias. The light bars represent the frequency of errors of two particular types X and Y, and the dark bars represent the frequency with which the monitor intercepts ('Edits out') errors of each type. Differences in the underlying pattern (the sum of light and dark bars) and interception rates (the dark bars) can have the effects that (a) a difference between conditions is observed, which does not exist in the underlying pattern; (b) no difference between conditions is observed, although there is one in the underlying pattern; (c) an underlying difference is magnified.

underlying rates of two types of error (e.g., lexical and non-lexical errors), but in which a monitoring bias *instantiates* a difference in overt error rates (e.g., more lexical than non-lexical errors). But other scenarios are also possible. In particular, there might already be a difference in the underlying error rates. If there is a monitoring bias, so that the most frequent underlying error is detected most often, this might *wipe-out* the underlying pattern (Figure 1b). In contrast, if the monitor detects the least frequent error most often, the result would be *magnification* of the underlying pattern (Figure 1c). This list is not exhaustive. A theoretical possibility might also be *reduction* of the speech error pattern (in which the underlying pattern survives the monitoring bias, but becomes smaller in the overt error pattern) and even *reversal* (in which the monitoring bias is so strong that the underlying pattern is reversed).

There is an important theoretical reason for testing the monitoring bias. If this bias exists, there are serious repercussions for the conclusions one can draw from speech error patterns. Such patterns would not only be a function of the speech production mechanisms themselves, but also be a function of monitoring mechanisms. And because there are two sets of candidate mechanisms, this limits the conclusions one can draw from such patterns. This problem is clearly illustrated in the current debate on whether language production should be conceived of as a series of modular processing levels, or whether there is interactivity between the levels (see Levelt et al., 1999; Rapp & Goldrick, 2000; Vigliocco & Hartsuiker, 2002). Advocates of modular theories (e.g., Levelt et al., 1999) often invoke the monitoring bias to attempt to explain speech error patterns that apparently support interactive theories. This includes the *lexical bias* (the tendency for phonological errors to result in existing words more often than is to be expected on the basis of chance; see Dell & Reich, 1981). The lexical bias can be taken to support an interactive account, whereby sublexical representations send feedback to lexical representations, thus increasing the probability that existing lexical representations (phonological neighbours of the target word) are produced (Dell, 1986). But it can also be explained by a monitoring bias account, whereby the monitor removes non-word errors more often than word errors (Baars et al., 1975; Levelt et al., 1999; Roelofs, 2004). Similar interactive and monitoring bias accounts have been proposed for the *mixed error bias* (the tendency for word substitution errors to be related more often in both form and meaning than is to be expected on the basis of chance; Dell & Reich, 1981).

Although one could argue that modular theories should be preferred to interactive ones on the basis of parsimony (Levelt et al., 1999), modular theories sacrifice parsimony when invoking the monitoring bias account. This is because such accounts are based on many (tacit) assumptions. These include assumptions about the time-course of monitoring (is the monitoring system fast enough to covertly detect and correct errors?) and about the detection criteria of monitoring (is it really true that the monitor detects one type of error more often than another?). The purpose of this article is to assess whether monitoring bias accounts are feasible in principle, to propose a number of preconditions such accounts must meet, and to illustrate this by considering a number of 'suspected' speech error patterns.

CAN THE MONITOR INTERCEPT PLANNING ERRORS?

A condition for monitoring bias accounts is that the verbal self-monitoring system (from now on *the monitor*) can intercept errors in the speech plan. This implies that (1) the monitor can inspect internal speech; (2) the monitor habitually *attends* to internal speech; (3) errors in the speech plan can be intercepted early enough to prevent them from becoming overt. This section discusses these implications.

There are several strands of evidence for internal-channel monitoring. For example, studies on error detection have manipulated whether speakers can or cannot hear their own overt speech. In one condition the participants receive normal auditory feedback, but in another (*noise-masking*) condition they are exposed to loud noise over headphones which prevents them from hearing their own overt speech. If speakers can still monitor speech in the noise-masking condition, they must do so internally. Such studies have revealed that speech errors can indeed be detected and corrected under noise-masking (Lackner & Tuller, 1979; Oomen, Postma, & Kolk, 2001; Postma & Noordanus, 1996). Additionally, speech errors are detected more quickly in the noise-masking condition than in the control condition. This follows from the architecture of the self-monitoring system (Hartsuiker & Kolk, 2001; Levelt, 1989): Internal-channel monitoring bypasses the processes of articulation and of auditory processing and is thus faster than external-channel monitoring.

Another argument for internal-channel monitoring is the finding that speakers can detect errors in silent speech, for example when silently reciting tongue twisters (Dell & Repka, 1992; Postma & Noordanus, 1996). Finally, incidents have been reported in which errors are aborted so early on that it is extremely unlikely that error-detection proceeded through external speech. An example is (1) in the context of a network description task (Levelt, 1983, 1989).

(1) To the left side of the purple disk is a v-, a horizontal line (Levelt, 1989, p. 13).

Given the context, it is very likely that the speaker first committed the error *vertical*, but aborted the error after the first phoneme /v/. Because phonemes such as /v/ only extend over roughly 70 ms of speech, and because it takes more time to perceive a phoneme, match it to the intended initial phoneme, and to abort speaking (the latter process is already estimated to take 200 ms), such incidents require an explanation in terms of internal monitoring. These findings strongly suggest that there is an internal monitoring mechanism (see Hartsuiker & Kolk, 2001 for a more elaborate discussion).

The second condition for a monitoring bias is that people habitually use this internal mechanism (rather than relying primarily on the external channel). Evidence for this second condition was obtained by Oomen et al. (2001). These authors conducted a study in which speakers with Broca's aphasia and matched control speakers produced speech in a normal auditory feedback condition and a noise-masking condition. The experimenters recorded the number of speech errors that were corrected, the number of speech errors that were not corrected, and the number of disfluencies (which they attributed to covert repair of speech errors and therefore called *covert repairs*). For the control speakers, noise-masking resulted in a decrease of corrected speech errors. For the speakers with aphasia, the distribution of these incidents was not affected by noise-masking. This suggests that the speakers with aphasia relied exclusively on internal-speech monitoring.

Hartsuiker, Kolk, and Martensen (2005b) applied a statistical model to these data (a so-called multinomial model) which had parameters for the efficiency of the internal and external monitoring channels (i.e., for the proportion of errors that each channel detected). These parameters were estimated from the observed distribution of incidents. They compared a constrained model (in which the efficiency of the internal and external channel was equal) with an unconstrained model (in which the two parameters were allowed to vary freely). The unconstrained model yielded a significantly better fit with the data, while taking into account the extra degree of freedom. Importantly, maximum-likelihood estimates of the parameters suggested that the internal channel was considerably more efficient than the external channel in the control speakers, and that a model *without* an external channel fit the data for the speakers with aphasia as well as model with external monitoring. These results suggest that the monitor strongly (and in some populations exclusively) relies on the internal channel.

A third precondition for a monitoring bias is that the monitor is fast enough to *remove* errors from the speech plan before these errors become (partly) overt. There are two arguments in favour of this precondition. First, studies with the so-called SLIP-task (e.g., Motley, Camden, & Baars,

1982) have provided experimental evidence for the suppression of taboo words. In these studies, participants silently read word pairs (e.g., *ball dove*, *bin dear*, *bark dome*) and they were occasionally cued to say a pair aloud (e.g., *darn bore*). The phonological composition of the biasing pairs, which precede the target pairs, and the target pair itself, namely with an exchange of word-initial phonemes between the biasing items and target item, promotes exchange errors (e.g., *barn door*). Motley et al. observed fewer exchanges when the exchange errors contained taboo words (e.g., *cool tits*) as opposed to neutral words. This is consistent with a monitoring bias, under the assumption that speakers want to avoid saying embarrassing things and thus intercept taboo-word errors more readily than neutral errors. Additionally, Motley et al. measured the Galvanic Skin Response (GSR), a physiological index of emotional arousal. In the trials where speakers *correctly* said the potential taboo-utterance (*tool kits*), the GSR was still elevated. This latter finding strongly suggests that the taboo utterance was really present in internal speech and was subsequently intercepted.

Second, studies with the SLIP-task have shown that the lexical bias effect is context-sensitive (Baars et al., 1975; Hartsuiker, Corley, & Martensen, 2005a). As discussed before, the lexical bias effect per se is not evidence for a monitoring bias; there are other (interactive) accounts that do not invoke the monitor. However, monitoring accounts predict that the lexical bias is sensitive to context (i.e., monitoring is a controlled process and can therefore adapt to the requirements of the speaking task at hand), whereas interactive accounts (that assume automatic feedback between levels) do not predict context-sensitivity.[1] In line with the monitoring accounts, Baars et al. (1975) and Hartsuiker et al. (2005a) demonstrated that the lexical bias effect (with non-word-stimuli as the target) was restricted to a mixed context of words and non-words, but disappeared in a pure context of non-words. This suggests that the monitor sets its error-detection criteria as a function of context so that the pattern of intercepted errors also varies with context. We turn to the question of what these error-detection criteria are in the next section.

In conclusion, there is experimental support for the preconditions of a monitoring bias account: Speakers can monitor the internal channel; they primarily attend to that channel rather than to the external channel; and they can remove internal speech errors.

---

[1] That is, in interactive models like Dell (1986), the input from the sublexical to the lexical level is automatically determined solely by the activation of sublexical units and the weights of the connections.

DOES THE MONITOR INTERCEPT SOME ERRORS MORE OFTEN THAN OTHER ERRORS?

Another aspect of monitoring bias accounts is the proposal that the monitor would intercept some errors more often than other errors. A precondition for such accounts is of course that we normally monitor our speech and detect considerable numbers of errors, but that monitoring is not perfect (if *all* errors were detected and corrected there could not be a monitoring bias). There is evidence from corpora of errors in normal conversational speech that people frequently, but not always, correct themselves (e.g., the observed correction rates of perseverations such as *good beer* → *good gear* vary from 40–80%, Nooteboom, 2005; Stemberger, 1989; the overall correction rate in a reanalysis of Meringer's 1908 corpus is 64%, Nooteboom, 1980).

It is worth pointing out that a monitoring bias is usually considered a *detection* bias, so that some errors are detected (and therefore corrected) more often than others, but a monitoring bias might in principle also result from a *correction* bias, so that some of the detected errors are corrected more often than others (i.e., because the monitor would not bother to correct some errors; Berg, 1986, 1992). Note however that there are no empirical data in support of a correction bias (Berg, 1992) and that there are data that seem to be inconsistent with such a bias (Levelt, 1989). Levelt noted that the correction rates of lexical errors in a corpus of spontaneous speech (Meringer, 1908, reanalysed by Nooteboom, 1980) and in an experiment (Levelt, 1983) were very similar, although the task requirements in the experiment made it essential to correct detected errors. Although one can only draw cautious conclusions from this comparison (as the data were collected in different places, periods in history, and languages), it is at least suggestive that both Meringer's and Levelt's speakers sometimes did not detect errors, but corrected the errors they did detect.

Which errors would be intercepted most often? Above, I already discussed the lexical bias (the monitor would intercept errors that are non-words more often than errors that are words), the 'appropriateness' bias (the monitor would intercept socially inappropriate errors more often than neutral errors), and the mixed error bias (the monitor would intercept errors that are related to the target in meaning only more often than errors that are related both in form and meaning). These claims about the relative interception rates of the monitor, although intuitively plausible, are usually not backed up by independent evidence, let alone by a theory of error-detection (or a theory of when the monitor would or would not bother to correct errors). As a result, there is a danger that monitoring bias accounts become ad-hoc (i.e., they are not constrained by information about error detection and correction).

One such an ad-hoc account was proposed by Baars et al. (1975). As mentioned earlier, these authors showed that the lexical bias effect occurred with non-word targets in a mixed context (of words and non-words), but not in a pure non-word context. In particular, the data suggested that non-word errors were suppressed in the mixed context, but not in the non-word context (Figure 2a).

They interpreted this data pattern as follows. One of the criteria that the monitor usually applies is lexicality. If an upcoming utterance is a non-

(a) Baars et al. (1975; Experiment 2)

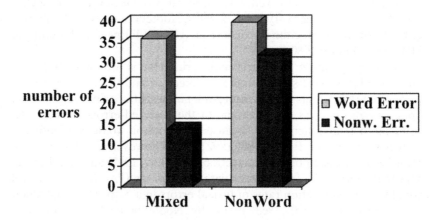

(b) Hartsuiker et al. (2005a; Experiment 2)

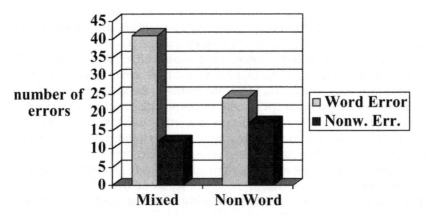

Figure 2. Number of word errors and nonword errors (Nonw. Err) in the mixed and nonword contexts of (a) Baars et al. (1975; Experiment 2), and (b) Hartsuiker et al. (2005a; Experiment 2).

word, this is evidence that something went wrong in the production process. Such a criterion is useful in contexts containing words, but not in contexts consisting of non-words only: In the latter case, the production of a non-word is no longer evidence that something went wrong. In other words, in a mixed context, when confronted with a non-word, the monitor would take this as evidence of an error, but in the non-word context it would ignore lexical status.

In a replication with an improved design Hartsuiker et al. (2005a) also showed contextual modulation: Again, the lexical bias was restricted to the mixed context. But importantly, our interaction had a different form (Figure 2b). Specifically, our data suggested that context affected the proportion of *word-errors* (suppressed in the non-word context), and not the proportion of *non-word* errors (as Baars et al. would have it). On our account, this error pattern supports a monitoring bias account, but one that resulted from *functional* monitoring criteria.

Consider the mixed context first. By definition, some items in this context are real words, whereas other items are non-words. In contrast to what Baars et al. assume, lexical status is therefore uninformative about the presence of an error: If it is a non-word, it could be right and it could be wrong, and the same is true for a word. Now consider the non-word context. If an upcoming item is a non-word, its lexical status provides no information about the correctness of that item. But if the upcoming item is a *word*, a consideration of lexicality is informative: If it is a word, it is surely wrong (because everything else is a non-word). In other words, the monitor *truly* adapts to context, so that in an exclusively deviant context, a non-deviant item becomes the odd-one-out.

Converging evidence for this account comes from the literature on sentence comprehension. It is often found that ungrammatical sentences (presented in blocks of grammatical sentences) elicit the P600 component in the ERP signal, a component which on many accounts is assumed to reflect reanalysis (*did I read this correctly?*). Recently, Coulson, King, and Kutas (1998) showed that if grammatical sentences were presented in blocks of ungrammatical sentences, the *grammatical* sentences elicited a P600. Again, this suggests that in a deviant context, something non-deviant is suspected to be the result of a processing error.

The Hartsuiker et al. (2005a) study is consistent with the existence of a monitoring-bias, resulting in the lexical bias effect. But that study also illustrates the importance of carefully considering the criteria an adaptive monitor would use: In our view, the monitoring criteria Baars et al. proposed were based on a (misleading) intuition, whereas the criteria we proposed followed from a consideration of what criteria would be functional (see below) given the goals of the speaker.

WHEN SHOULD WE ACCEPT A
MONITORING BIAS?

The previous sections have argued that existing data on self-monitoring are compatible with the hypothesis that errors in the speech plan can be intercepted, but that monitoring bias accounts are usually not supported by data on error detection (or by a theory on when the monitor bothers to correct detected errors). This raises the question of when we should accept a monitoring bias to account for particular speech error patterns. In this section, three demands are proposed before a particular monitoring bias account should be accepted, namely (1) the account poses functional monitoring criteria; (2) the bias can be altered by manipulations affecting monitoring performance; (3) the bias has an analogue in perception.

Demand 1. The monitoring criteria are functional

As discussed in the previous section, Hartsuiker et al. (2005a) proposed a different set of monitoring criteria from Baars et al. (1975). It is important to point out that this did not just lead to a different proposal about error interception (in which context does the monitor intercept which errors?), but also to a different proposal about the underlying error pattern. In particular, Hartsuiker et al. (2005a) proposed that the underlying pattern is one by which there is a lexical bias in both the mixed and non-word contexts. But because the monitor intercepts word-errors in the non-word context, a pattern results in which the lexical bias is wiped out in that context (Figures 1b and 3).

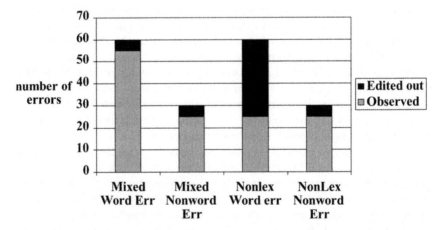

Figure 3. Hypothesized underlying and actual pattern in the Hartsuiker et al. (2005a) data. Mixed = mixed context; NonLex = nonlexical context; Word Err = word error; Nonword Err = nonword error.

One reason we rejected Baars et al.'s account (and embraced our own account) is that Baars et al. proposed a *dysfunctional* monitoring criterion, and we proposed a *functional* monitoring criterion. With functional, I mean here that the monitor sets criteria that are optimal for the task at hand. In conversation, it is functional to monitor for violations of lexical status, because non-words are likely to be errors. But in a context of exclusively deviant speech, it is functional to monitor for violations of deviancy, because such violations indicate that something went wrong in producing deviancy.

My proposal, then, is that *any* monitoring bias account should be rejected, if that account presupposes that the monitor hinders, rather than helps, the speaking task at hand. There is little doubt that speakers can flexibly invest attention to task-relevant characteristics of their speech (Levelt, 1989). This makes disfunctional monitoring criteria highly unlikely. I will allow only one exception to this demand. That is, it is conceivable that speakers with certain forms of language pathology have impaired monitoring systems, as a result of which they might set disfunctional monitoring criteria. For example, some authors have hypothesised that the monitor in people who stutter sets overly strict criteria; the many attempts at covert repair would then lead to disfluencies (Vasić & Wijnen, 2005; also see Lickley, Hartsuiker, Corley, Russell, & Nelson, 2005).

Demand 2. Monitoring manipulations affect the suspected bias (and these effects cannot be attributed to influences on the language production system)

If it is true that a given error pattern results from a monitoring bias, manipulations that affect monitoring performance should also affect that bias. However, an effect of monitoring manipulations is necessary but not sufficient to claim a monitoring bias, because it is possible that such manipulations affect *both* the language production system and the self-monitor. If that were the case, a difference in an error pattern might be the direct result of different language production, not of different monitoring. Thus, an important qualification of this demand is that the difference in bias should not be attributable to different performance of the language production system.

There are several manipulations that could alter monitoring performance. First, as monitoring can be considered a controlled process (e.g., Levelt, 1989) monitoring performance depends on the amount of effort invested in monitoring and on the focus of monitoring. Therefore, manipulations that decrease the amount of monitoring effort (e.g., by giving the speaker a secondary task) should reduce any monitoring bias. If the pattern is unaffected, it is likely not to be due to a monitoring bias. Similarly, even if the monitoring system invests the same amount of effort overall, but focuses more on speech characteristics that are irrelevant to the types of speech errors of interest, the monitoring bias should be reduced. For example, Vasić and Wijnen (2005) analysed disfluencies in the speech of participants who simultaneously played the computer game 'Pong', thereby decreasing the amount of attention that can be invested in monitoring. In another condition the secondary task was word-monitoring (push a button whenever a certain high-frequency function word was said), thus changing the monitor's focus. Both manipulations reduced the number of disfluencies produced by people who stutter, which the authors ascribed to reductions in covert repairing.

Manipulations of attention might of course also affect the language production system. For example, there is consensus in the literature that the process of conceptualising (constructing a message to be formulated) is (partly) constrained by attention (e.g., Levelt, 1989). Recently some evidence has also been reported that certain aspects of formulating (namely lexical access) are to some extent controlled (Ferreira & Pashler, 2002). Thus, secondary-task manipulations, like Vasić and Wijnen's computer game, conceivably exert an influence on language production. In the case of the Vasić and Wijnen experiments, however, any effect on the language production system works against the hypothesis of a monitoring bias. This is because most theorists assume that disfluencies occur more frequently when speaking becomes more difficult (e.g., Beattie & Butterworth, 1979; Maclay & Osgood, 1959). Thus, the effect of the secondary-task manipulation on language production itself should have been *more* disfluencies, whereas *fewer* were observed.

Another manipulation that can affect the monitor is available time. If there is less time for error interception, the monitoring bias should be reduced. Returning to the lexical bias effect, Humphreys (2002) also replicated Baars et al. (1975) but she used a procedure that left considerably less time to produce responses. In fact, in Humphreys' procedure, speakers had to produce each word pair before a 750 ms deadline (and 100 ms after this deadline, the next trial began). In Baars et al.'s and Hartsuiker et al.'s (2005a) procedure there was no response deadline, and naming latencies in that latter study were around 1000 ms. Hartsuiker et al. (2005a) argued that Humphreys' deadline procedure minimised the time for monitoring, and consistent with that argument, Humphreys observed a lexical bias effect in both the mixed and the non-lexical contexts. This is consistent with our argument, because on our account, the underlying pattern is one where lexical errors occur more frequently than non-word errors (see above). The monitoring bias wipes out the word-error advantage in the non-word condition, but if there is too little time for interception (as was the case in Humphreys, 2002), the underlying pattern remains.

Of course, manipulations of time might affect the language production system as well as the monitoring system. Particularly relevant in this context are the experiments and simulations of Dell (1986), which showed that with shorter response deadlines there is a reduction of the lexical bias. Manipulations of time thus affect the language production system in one way (i.e., increase of lexical bias with more time) but affect the monitor (in the non-word context) in the opposite way (reduction of lexical bias with more time). Thus, the monitoring bias Hartsuiker et al. (2005) propose is consistent with Demand 2.

Demand 3. The monitoring bias occurs in speech perception (with the qualification that listening to others and monitoring oneself differ)

According to Levelt's (1983, 1989) Perceptual Loop Theory of monitoring and Hartsuiker and Kolk's (2001) Perceptual Loop Model (PLM), internal speech is inspected using the speech-perception system. There is debate about this assumption (see Postma, 2000) and it certainly remains an empirical question. If one accepts a perception-based model, this has an important implication: A monitoring-bias account of a certain speech error pattern is not easily tenable if there are dissociations between the pattern of errors detected in internal speech, and the pattern of detected errors in external speech or the speech of others. This is because all three sources (internal speech, external speech, other-produced speech) are analysed by the same system (language compre-hension), and it would thus be odd to presume that a particular type of error is easily detected via one channel, but is detected with difficulty via another channel.

This Demand needs qualifying, because even though internal-channel monitoring, external-channel monitoring, and language comprehension would all use the same cognitive machinery, this machinery would not operate in the same way in all three cases (Rapp & Goldrick, 2004). Internal-channel monitoring only partly uses the same cognitive machinery as perception, because this type of monitoring bypasses the earliest stages of perception (up to phoneme identification). Additionally, monitoring one's own speech and listening to somebody else's speech differ in that the speaker, but not the listener, has knowledge of what the speech signal is supposed to mean. If prior knowledge can influence perception (i.e., on a theory of perception that allows for top-down influences), certain perceptual phenomena may *not* occur in monitoring. Finally, if monitoring uses the perception system, it is reasonable to assume that the success of monitoring depends on attention (Levelt, 1989). Attention in monitoring needs to be divided over at least two channels (the internal and external channel). Therefore, any observed differences between internal-channel and external-channel monitoring might result from differences in the amount of attention paid to each channel (see below). This implies that straightforward reaction-time error-detection experiments ('Press the button whenever you hear an error', e.g., Cole, 1973) inadequately reflect error-detection in monitoring, because in such experiments the focus of attention is specifically on errors, whereas in conversational speech the focus needs to be much broader. Based on these differences, I propose three qualifications to the Perceptual Demand. Each of these qualifications makes this Demand more conservative.

A. Low-level effects in perception do not support the Perceptual Demand. The assumed culprit of monitoring biases is the internal channel (the external channel is too slow for covert repair; Hartsuiker & Kolk, 2001). Since the internal channel does not have access to acoustic information, any error biases with respect to acoustic/phonetic differences cannot be attributed to a monitoring bias, even if an analogous bias occurs in perception. This is illustrated by a study conducted by Lackner and Tuller (1979). These authors showed that some errors (which were phonologically minimally different from the target, but were acoustically very distinct) can be easily detected under normal-feedback conditions, but were hardly ever detected when the speaker was exposed to loud noise (which masked the external channel). The ease with which these errors can be detected in external speech cannot be used to argue that these errors can also be detected easily in internal speech, causing a monitoring bias. Interestingly, Lackner and Tuller's paradigm might provide a way of testing whether internal monitoring is sensitive to a particular phonological difference, because it can 'knock out' the external channel, and thus isolate the internal channel.

B. Perceptual effects that disappear with prior knowledge do not support the Perceptual Demand. An important difference between internal- and external-channel monitoring and listening to the speech of others is that the listener, in contrast to the speaker, usually does not know what the speaker wants to say. There are many demonstrations in visual perception where prior knowledge about an ambiguous or degraded stimulus results in a clear and unambiguous percept of that stimulus. Similarly, prior knowledge about the meaning of an ambiguous or degraded stretch of speech might perceptually enhance it. It is thus important to consider whether any candidate perceptual effect still obtains if the listener has prior knowledge, before accepting that candidate as support for a monitoring bias.

For example, a well-established effect in language comprehension is that listeners and readers can mistakenly construct a certain interpretation of a lexically ambiguous word (e.g., *bat*) or of a (temporarily) ambiguous sentence (e.g., *Put the apple on the towel in the box*; Tanenhaus, Spivey-Knowlton, Eberhard, & Sedivy, 1995). When listeners/readers realise they have gone down the 'garden path', they need to revise their syntactic analysis and corresponding interpretation. Because the self-monitor would use the comprehension system, one might be tempted to conclude that speakers can sometimes lead *themselves* down the garden-path, detect the ambiguity, and perhaps repair with an unambiguous sentence (e.g., *Put the apple on the towel . . . um . . . Put the apple* that is *on the towel in the box*). However, there is empirical evidence that listeners use their knowledge of the situation to disambiguate sentences. For example, registration of eye-movements in a visual context containing two apples (one on a towel and one on a napkin), a box, and an empty towel suggested that listeners immediately chose the correct analysis (Tanenhaus et al., 1995). If knowledge of the situation can block the incorrect interpretation, it is very likely that knowing the intended meaning can do the same.

The issue of prior knowledge further mitigates against taking the results of error-detection experiments as evidence for the Perceptual Demand. But interestingly, there is an alternative paradigm (Oomen & Postma, 2002; Oomen et al., 2001) that allows a test of whether perceptual phenomena survive prior knowledge. Oomen and colleagues conducted experiments in which listeners heard a description of a route in a network of coloured line drawings, while seeing the same route at the same time. Listeners had prior knowledge about what the speaker was supposed to say at each moment. Whenever the listener detected an error, he or she was asked to push a button and to correct the error. Oomen et al. observed, for example, that syntactic errors were detected significantly less often than lexical or phonological errors. It seems that this paradigm can distinguish between detection accuracies of different error types, while ensuring that the listener (similar to the speaker monitoring their own speech) has prior knowledge.

C. Escape routes need to be motivated, before an exception to the Perceptual Demand should be made. As noted earlier, there may be differences in the amount of attention invested in internal-channel monitoring, external-channel monitoring, and listening to others. Some of the evidence suggests that speakers pay more attention to the internal channel than to the external channel (Oomen et al., 2001; Hartsuiker et al., 2005b). If it were the case that *quantitative* differences in amount of attention paid to a particular channel lead to *qualitative* differences in error detection, then any differences observed between channels might be attributed to attention, thereby providing an escape route from the Perceptual Demand.

One study that proposed such an escape route is Roelofs (2004), who commented on Nooteboom's (2005) corpus analysis of Dutch phonological speech errors and their corrections. Nooteboom tested whether the speech errors showed a lexical bias, but also whether the *corrections* of speech errors displayed such a bias. If it is true that the monitor detects non-word errors more often than word errors (yielding a lexical bias in the speech error pattern), the monitor should also correct overtly produced non-word errors more often than word errors. But whereas Nooteboom observed a lexical bias in the pattern of speech errors, the correction rates of non-word errors and word errors were identical. To account for this pattern, Roelofs (2004) argued that the monitor would mainly attend the internal channel (causing the lexical bias), but at the expense of attending the external channel (causing the absence of a repair bias). However, as Rapp and Goldrick (2004) noted, the most obvious prediction from a less efficient external-channel monitor is that there would be fewer corrections across the board, not that the corrections would be qualitatively different.

Of course, it is *conceivable* that qualitative differences arise as a result of decreased attention. As the results with the dichotic listening task (Cherry, 1953) demonstrated, we perceive some words (e.g., our own name) but not other words via an unattended channel. But the burden of proof that certain monitoring tests (i.e., the test for lexicality) are skipped when a particular channel is not sufficiently attended lies with the advocates of the escape route. Roelofs' escape route so far fails this qualification to the Perceptual Demand.

Roelofs (2004) also proposed a *second* escape route. On that account, there is no repair bias in Nooteboom's data because external-channel monitoring would detect all errors (lexical or non-lexical) but would not bother to correct all of them. This account runs into many difficulties. First, existing data strongly argue against the hypothesis that the external channel detects all errors. For example, the participants in Oomen and Postma (2002) listened to the speech of others, knew what the speech was about (they saw the network being described), and they were explicitly instructed to listen for errors. But even in such optimal conditions for error detection, the participants still missed 30–40% of errors. Second, as argued by Levelt (1989; see above), the correction rates are very similar in situations where the speaker *must* repair detected errors (in order to be understandable to an interlocutor) and in the situation of normal conversational speech, suggesting that speakers always bother to repair. Third, this account fails to specify when the monitor does or does not bother to correct errors. One might argue that the monitor bothers more about correcting non-lexical errors (which are both unintended utterances and linguistically ill-formed) than lexical errors. But one could just as easily argue that the monitor bothers more about correcting lexical errors (which introduce the wrong semantics) than non-lexical errors (which do not introduce semantics, so that the listener can guess that they are speech errors). Fourth, there is no empirical evidence that the monitor habitually evaluates whether an error needs to be corrected (Berg, 1992); the only evidence we have is introspection. Given these problems, a 'bothering to correct' escape route leads to a highly underspecified account.

In summary, the demand that a given monitoring bias also occurs as a perception bias is complicated by differences in perception between monitoring and listening to someone else. The internal channel does not have access to low-level perceptual information; monitoring differs from perception in that the monitor has prior knowledge; and monitoring and listening may very well differ in the demands on attention. This means that not all perceptual effects necessarily hold for monitoring. However, any escape routes based on differences between monitoring and normal perception need to be motivated.

THE SUSPECTS: FIVE SPEECH ERROR PATTERNS THAT MIGHT BE INFLUENCED BY MONITORING BIAS

This section briefly discusses five speech error patterns that can be considered 'suspects' of resulting from an interaction with a monitoring bias. Each suspect will be evaluated with respect to the three Demands proposed in the previous section. For all the selected patterns, both monitoring accounts and alternative accounts (mostly interactive accounts) have been developed. Rather than attempting to provide an exhaustive list, I have selected representative examples from many different stages of language production, including word retrieval, phonological encoding, and grammatical encoding.

The lexical bias effect

The lexical bias effect has already been discussed at length in this article. On a monitoring bias account, the monitor habitually applies the criterion of lexicality: If I am about to say a non-word, it is likely that I am about to make a mistake (in most circumstances). Because non-words are usually a sign of mistake, it is obvious that this criterion is functional (Demand 1). Furthermore, Hartsuiker et al.'s (2005a) experiments in which the context was manipulated supported the hypothesis that monitoring criteria can be adaptively changed in contexts where it is functional to consider words as errors.

Importantly, Hartsuiker et al. (2005a) inferred from their data that the underlying pattern of speech errors (i.e., the pattern before the monitor intercepts errors) already displays a lexical bias in both contexts and Humphreys (2002) showed that there was a lexical bias across the contexts, in a situation where the monitor had extremely little time for interception. Combined, these studies suggest that the lexical bias is modifiable by manipulations affecting the quality of monitoring: The monitoring bias disappears when there is not enough time for covert repair (Demand 2). Note that in the situation of normal conversational speech, it would of course be functional to treat upcoming non-words as errors. Given that the underlying pattern already displays lexical bias and that there is monitor involvement in lexical bias, I conclude that the lexical bias is a Magnification bias, so that monitoring increases the magnitude of the underlying bias (Figure 1C).

Finally, I am not aware of any studies that show a lexical bias effect in *perception* of others' speech (Demand 3), but Nooteboom's (2005) study, which showed lexical bias in speech errors but not in overt repairs is not compatible with this demand. As discussed above, Roelofs' (2004) escape routes via attention, or via evaluative processes (*Do I bother to correct this error?*) are insufficiently motivated (Demand 3, Qualification C) although it is possible of course that future studies can provide such a motivation. In conclusion, the lexical bias passes Demands 1 and 2, but fails on Demand 3.

The mixed error bias

The mixed error bias is the tendency for word substitution errors to be related in both meaning and form to the target (Dell & Reich, 1981). There are at least four explanations of this bias (see Levelt et al., 1999; Rapp & Goldrick, 2000, 2004; Roelofs, 2004, 2005; Vigliocco & Hartsuiker, 2002) for discussion. Some accounts explain this bias as the result of cascading of activation in a framework without feedback. Although Rapp and Goldrick

(2000) showed by simulation that such a model accounts for the mixed error bias in the general population, they rejected this account on the basis of data from a brain-damaged person (P.W.) who produced semantic errors and the mixed error bias but not other error types (such as non-word errors) that, on a cascading model, would necessarily co-occur with the mixed error bias (p. 481).

Another explanation allows cascading only in the special circumstance when two semantically related lemmas are both highly active. According to Levelt et al. (1999), in this situation two lemmas might be selected instead of one, and this would also account for so-called *blend* errors (e.g., *sleast* when both *least* and *slightest* are selected). When a double selection occurs there would be a 'horse-race' in phonological encoding. The lemma that is phonologically encoded first would be the one that is said, and the WEAVER++ model predicts that this race is more often won by the intruder when it is phonologically related to the target (Levelt et al., 1999, p. 35). However, as pointed out by Vigliocco and Hartsuiker (2002), a model that allows cascading in a growing number of special circumstances sacrifices parsimony.

The mixed error bias is also compatible with the notion of both cascading of activation and feedback between a level specified for meaning and one specified for form. If a speaker intends to say the word *cat*, semantic competitors such as the lemmas of *calf* and *dog* also become active. Assuming that there is cascading of activation, the word forms <Cat>, <Calf>, and <Dog> obtain some activation; but feedback deriving from the target's word form <Cat> will increase the activation of the lemmas of mixed competitors (*calf*) but not that of semantic-only competitors (*dog*). This makes it more likely that *calf* is said than *dog*.

A final explanation presumes a monitoring bias. According to Levelt et al. (1999) the error *rat* for *cat* is more likely than *dog* for *cat*, because *rat* and *cat* are perceptually closer than *dog* and *cat* and therefore the monitor will miss *rat* more readily than *dog*. In subsequent work this proposal has been elaborated (Roelofs, 2004). On that further monitoring account, the WEAVER++ model (Levelt et al., 1999) accomplishes self-monitoring by verifying whether a lemma recognised in comprehension corresponds to the target lexical concept in production. The mixed error bias would then result from a property of the comprehension system: On hearing a word like *cat* listeners activate a cohort of words beginning with the same initial sounds (*captain, capital, calf*; Zwitserlood, 1989). Since the internal error *calf* (when *cat* is intended) will activate the lemma for *cat*, the verification step is more likely to incorrectly decide that *cat* was just being perceived than *dog*, which is not in the comprehension cohort of *cat*.

There is debate on the tenability of this monitoring account.[2] However, since this debate appears to have stranded in a discussion about model details ('How plausible is it that certain connection weights have certain values?'), it is important to evaluate this monitoring bias with respect to other criteria, such as the three Demands proposed in this article. The first Demand is functionality. Roelofs (2004) assumes that lemmas, activated in comprehension, are compared with the target lexical concept for production. This process would be the same for each type of error, whereas the input (the pattern of lexical activation) would differ. Clearly, a system that verifies whether a lexical representation it has just heard itself produce matches with the intended concept is functional. This proposal thus conforms to Demand 1.

Second, the bias would automatically follow from the way speech is perceived. There is good evidence for the activation of begin-related cohorts in speech comprehension (e.g., Allopenna, Magnuson, & Tanenhaus, 1998; Zwitserlood, 1989). Importantly, Zwitserlood (1989) showed that cohort effects were not overridden by context effects. For example, in a discourse like 'With dampened spirit the men stood around the grave. They mourned the loss of their *captain*', there is still cross-modal priming for the word *money* (related to the cohort competitor *capital*) as the word *captain* unfolds acoustically. This finding is at least partial support for the assumption that cohort effects do not disappear as a result of top-down effects. It is important to note that there may also be production-internal reasons for the activation of begin-related cohorts in production.

---

[2] In particular, Rapp and Goldrick (2000) reported on two individuals with brain damage, whose impairments were consistent with a semantic locus (patient KE) and a post-semantic locus (patient PW). Whereas PW displayed a mixed error bias, KE did not, and this is difficult to reconcile with a monitoring bias account: There is no independent evidence to suggest that KE, but not PW, had a monitoring deficit. However, Roelofs (2004, 2005) argued that his version of the monitoring account is compatible with the patient findings, under the assumptions that (a) KE's semantic errors are errors of concept selection (because of the semantic locus of the impairment) whereas PW's semantic errors are errors of lemma selection (because of the post-semantic locus); (b) the cohort effect in speech perception results, in case of a mixed competitor (*calf*), in a relatively high activation of the target word (*cat*) at the *lemma* level; (c) but as a result of rather weak connections between lemma and concept levels, there is little propagation of this activation to the concept level. The *concept* CAT(X) would become about as active for a mixed and a semantic-only error. Therefore, KE, who can only detect the error by checking whether the selected concept is the right concept, is equally likely to detect the error *calf* and *dog* for *cat*, while PW, who can detect the error by checking whether the selected lemma is right, is more likely to detect the error *dog*. Rapp and Goldrick (2004, Footnote 8), criticized this proposal on the basis of plausibility. Because the connections between lemma and concept level are also used for language comprehension, it is unclear why these connections would be so weak that differences in activation levels at the lemma are 'washed out' at the concept level lemma.

On the assumption that phonological encoding proceeds from left to right (Dell, 1988), initial phonemes send feedback to the lexical representations at an earlier moment than final phonemes, thereby activating a begin-related lexical cohort. However, it is difficult to see how this mechanism could account for the cohort-effect in *perception*. Thus, Roelofs' proposal meets Demand 3.

That proposal also makes a testable prediction. Whereas there is compelling evidence for the activation of begin-related cohorts in comprehension, there is hardly any evidence for the activation of *end*-related cohorts (except for Allopenna et al., 1999). Thus, assuming that end-related cohorts are activated more weakly (or not at all), the mixed error bias should be reduced for cases in which target and intruder are end-related, such as *rat* and *cat*, or *lobster-oyster*. If a speaker incorrectly generates *rat* instead of *cat*, this should not lead to activation of the cohort competitor *cat*; therefore, the monitor should detect the error as easily as the error *dog*. Consistent with this prediction, Dell and Reich (1981; p. 624) showed a trend of more mixed errors with phonological similarity in the first position of the word than in later positions.

In sum, the monitoring bias account of Roelofs (2004) for the mixed error bias, is consistent with Demands 1 and 3; I do not know of any evidence pertaining to Demand 2.

The exchange rate

A speech error pattern that has been an important benchmark for models of phonological encoding is the relative frequency of anticipations (*good beer → bood beer*), perseverations (*good beer → good gear*), and exchanges (*good beer → bood gear*) involving single phonemes (Dell, 1986; Hartsuiker, 2002; Levelt et al., 1999). In short, anticipations are the most frequent type of phonological substitution errors, followed by perseverations, and exchange errors occur very rarely. For example, the corpus of Dutch reported by Nooteboom (1969) contained 76% anticipations, 17% perseverations, and only 7% exchanges (with ambiguous cases divided half-way between anticipations and perseverations). Hartsuiker (2002) simulated these data with Dutch versions of the Dell (1986) and the Dell (1988) models and obtained a reasonable fit, especially when a single model parameter was altered slightly (73% anticipations, 25% perseverations, and 2% exchanges). Levelt et al. (1999) also simulated these data in an adapted version of WEAVER++, and also appeared to obtain a fairly good fit (they reported the data only in their Figure 18, which suggested slight overestimations of the anticipations and perseverations, but a considerable underestimation of the exchanges).

Several authors have pointed out however that the basic data pattern may be subject to a monitoring bias (e.g., Dell & Reich, 1981; Nooteboom, 2005; Stemberger, 1989). The reason is that speech error corpora do not always distinguish between corrected and uncorrected speech errors, and that the correction *itself* can alter the classification a speech error gets. Suppose that the internal speech plan contains an exchange error, such as *mell wade* (intended: *well made*). If the speaker manages to correct half-way, the resulting utterance becomes *mell . . . well made*. A collector of speech errors might classify this as a corrected *anticipation*. But if the speaker is somewhat slower to correct the (internal) exchange, the resulting utterance will be a corrected exchange error (*mell wade ... well made*). If that is true, the number of scored corrected anticipations are an overestimation, and the number of scored corrected exchanges constitute an underestimation relative to the underlying pattern.

Of course, it is possible that errors like *mell . . . well made* (sometimes called incompletes in the literature) are in fact anticipations, and that the monitor stopped after having detected that the first word was wrong. An argument for that state of affairs comes from a study by Stemberger (1989), who analysed errors in a corpus of adult speech and in two children (longitudinally). He observed that as one child got older (i.e., after age 4), the rates of perseverations and complete exchanges began to resemble that of the adults, but that she produced far more complete anticipations and far fewer incompletes. The low rate of incompletes suggests that children are less efficient in monitoring (i.e., they do not detect the anticipation or exchange as easily as adults). Additionally, the high rate of complete anticipations in child speech strongly suggests that the majority of incompletes in adults should be regarded as anticipations.

In contrast, Nooteboom (2005) concluded that 64% of the incompletes are exchanges. He estimated the proportions of the incompletes that are really anticipations and really exchanges in a corpus of 1153 Dutch speech errors under the assumption that anticipations are detected as often as perseverations.[3] Given that assumption, the ratio of corrected vs. uncorrected anticipations should be equal to the ratio of corrected vs. uncorrected perseverations. Because the only unknown is the number of corrected anticipations, this equation is solvable, allowing estimates of the 'true' numbers of anticipations and exchanges. This estimate was further confirmed in the following way. Nooteboom observed that the chance for a perseveration to remain uncorrected is .60, and he assumed the same held for an anticipation. Because an exchange error is wrong in two places (it

---

[3] A speech-shadowing study in Dutch (Cohen, 1980) showed that participants indeed detected perseverations and anticipations at comparable rates (65% vs. 56%).

contains both an anticipation and a perseveration) the monitor should have two independent opportunities to detect such an error. This predicts that the probability for an exchange to remain uncorrected equals .60 × .60 = .36 and this prediction was confirmed in the reclassified data set (probability of .35 to remain uncorrected).

Consider how this monitoring bias fares on the three Demands. This monitoring bias is clearly functional: It is the job of the monitor to detect errors and correct them as soon as possible and it is functional for the monitoring system to have a higher detection rate when there are more opportunities for error detection (Demand 1).

It is more difficult to evaluate this bias on Demand 2 (the bias is modified by factors that affect monitoring). Language development clearly affects the efficiency of monitoring (and this is confirmed by the finding that adults corrected phonological perseverations much more often than children; Stemberger, 1989). However, language development of course also affects the language production system itself, and conceivably changes the underlying patterns of speech errors (i.e., Stemberger found a much larger percentage of perseverations in child speech than adult speech). Thus, developmental data cannot confirm or disconfirm that this bias passes Demand 2. Finally, there is no evidence I am aware of that speaks to Demand 3.

Morphophonological effects on attraction errors

Attraction errors are syntactic errors in which the rule of subject-verb (number) agreement is violated (2).

(2) *The position on the demonstrations were dumb

In this example the verb (*were*) does not agree in number with the subject head noun (position) but with the number of the 'local' noun (demonstrations). Bock and Miller (1991) introduced a sentence-fragment repetition and completion paradigm that elicits such agreement errors. Many studies with that paradigm have shown that agreement errors are more common when the two nouns mismatch in number (2) than when they match. Although Bock and colleagues initially argued that the rate of attraction errors is influenced only by syntactic factors and not by semantic or phonological factors (Bock & Cutting, 1992; Bock & Eberhard, 1993), subsequent studies have provided evidence that both of these latter factors play a role (e.g., Vigliocco et al., 1995; see Vigliocco & Hartsuiker, 2002, for a review).

An example of morphophonological effects on attraction was provided by Hartsuiker, Schriefers, Bock, and Kikstra (2003). In two of their experiments, these authors tested German-speaking participants, exploiting the fact that determiners in this language are sometimes ambiguous with respect to case or number (3).

(3) Die Stellungnahme gegen die Demonstrationen
       (The position against the demonstrations)
(4) Die Stellungnahme zu den Demonstrationen
       (The position on the demonstrations)

In (3), the preposition *gegen* (against) licenses accusative case. In the case of a feminine noun like *Demonstrationen*, this requires that the determiner *die* is chosen. This makes the entire noun phrase (*die Demonstrationen*) ambiguous in case, because the same forms of determiner and noun would be used in the nominative (subject) case. In contrast, in (4) the preposition *zu* (on) licenses dative case. As a result, the form *den Demonstrationen* needs to be chosen, which makes that phrase unambiguously dative. Case-ambiguity affected attraction error rates. Compared with control items in which the two nouns matched in number, there was an attraction effect for case-ambiguous items (3), but no attraction effect for case-unambiguous items (4).

To account for these data, Hartsuiker et al. (2003) offered several explanations, including a monitoring bias account. According to that explanation, the monitor would more easily detect (and intercept) an error in a case-unambiguous item (4) than in a case-ambiguous item (3), thus maintaining a model of language production in which later stages (concerned with sound) do not directly influence earlier stages (concerned with syntax).

If we apply our Demand of functionality to this account, however, that story appears unlikely. The task of the monitor is to *intercept* errors, including errors of agreement. The only likely reason for why errors after phrases like (4) would be detected more rapidly than phrases like (3) would be that the monitor applies a criterion of *local* well-formedness: . . . *die Demonstrationen* + V[plural] is locally well-formed, whereas . . . *den Demonstrationen* + V[plural] is locally ill-formed. But if such a bias causes the error pattern, one must assume that the monitor is checking the wrong thing. Instead of testing whether the verb agrees with the correct noun, it would test whether the combination of local noun and verb is coherent. That monitoring bias account therefore fails to meet the functionality demand (Demand 1). There are no data available that test this account against Demand 2. There are also no data from perception that test whether morphophonology affects any attraction effects in comprehension (Demand 3). It is worth pointing out, however, that attraction effects in comprehension do exist. In particular, studies on reading have shown a processing cost for correct verbs in sentences with a singular head noun and a plural local noun (Nicol, Forster, & Veres, 1997) as well as a reduced processing cost for incorrectly inflected verbs when the number of the local noun mismatched rather than matched the number of the head noun (Pearlmutter, Garnsey, & Bock, 1999). It might be tempting to conclude that this supports an account by which the comprehension system incorrectly considers the local noun as the controller of agreement. However, the results are equally compatible with an account by which the mechanisms of agreement computation are shared between production and comprehension, so that similar conditions lead to similar types of disruptions (Nicol et al., 1997; Pearlmutter et al., 1999).

Conceptual effects on attraction errors

Many studies have shown that agreement errors are more common when the head noun of a phrase can be construed as notionally plural (5) than when it is notionally singular (6); fragments like (5) are often called 'distributive' (e.g., Eberhard, 1999 for English; Vigliocco et al., 1995 for Italian; Vigliocco, Hartsuiker, Jarema, & Kolk, 1996 for Dutch and French).

(5) The label on the bottles
(6) The road to the islands

Would a monitoring bias account for the effect of distributivity, so that it is more difficult to detect and intercept an agreement error when the verb agrees with the notional number of the noun? One might argue that a functional monitor, when checking syntax, would be wise to ignore matters of meaning and simply compare the grammatical number of *label* with the number marking on the verb. On the other hand, there are many examples of semantic agreement. This is the case with collective nouns in English (7), or with collective noun phrases in Dutch (8) an 'error' so common, that prescriptive linguists have given up on considering it an error.

(7) The committee vote themselves a raise
(8) ?Een aantal mannen lopen (A number [of] men walk[pl.])

Bock, Nicol, and Cutting (1999) observed that when the controller of agreement was a collective noun (7), speakers of American English often used the notional number (plural) to mark agreement targets (although this was more common when the agreement target was a pronoun than a verb).

Additionally, semantic gender information safeguards speakers of French and Italian from gender-agreement errors (Vigliocco & Franck, 1999). These authors presented speakers with fragments like (9) and (10) and asked them to complete these fragments with an adjective (which is gender-marked in these languages).

(9) La ragazza nel parco
    [The(fem.) girl(fem.) in the(masc.) park(masc.)]
(10) La panchina nel parco
    [The(fem.) bench(fem.) in the(masc.) park(masc.)]

They observed far fewer gender-agreement errors when the subject carried conceptual gender (9) than when it only carried grammatical gender (10).

These considerations suggest that it may be functional for the monitor to consult semantic information when checking agreement; only in the rare case that semantics and syntax clash (as in distributive utterances) would this lead to a failure to detect errors.

Now consider the second demand: If distributivity were due to a monitoring bias, manipulations affecting the monitor should reduce the bias. Hartsuiker and Barkhuysen (2006) manipulated working memory, in two ways. First, they tested participants in conditions with or without an extrinsic memory load (a list of three words that had to be recalled). Second, they measured individual working memory spans using the Daneman and Green (1986) speaking span task, and divided participants in groups of high-span and low-span speakers. On the perceptual loop theory, monitoring is constrained by working memory (Levelt, 1989). Additionally, studies using dual-task paradigms have shown effects of secondary tasks on indices of monitoring, including the speed of error detection and repair (Oomen & Postma, 2002). Thus, if the distributivity effect were due to a monitoring bias, it should disappear when working memory is overloaded.

The data were clear-cut: There were main effects on the proportion of agreement errors of distributivity (as is to be expected), load, and span. In particular, there were more errors when span was low or when there was a memory load. Additionally, there was a Span × Load interaction, so that there were relatively many agreement errors in the condition with the greatest memory load (low-span speakers in the secondary-task condition). The larger number of errors when resources are scarce are of course compatible with worse monitoring performance under those conditions; but since a plausible effect of such manipulations on the language production system is that more errors are generated, that finding fails to pass Demand 2. Importantly, there were no second- or third-order interactions with distributivity. Thus, the increase in number of agreement errors as a result of resource limitations was the same for notionally singular and notionally plural fragments (5–6). In contrast, if the distributivity effect resulted from a monitoring bias, one would have expected it to disappear with resource limitations.

Are there distributivity effects in comprehension (Demand 3)? The only study that has considered this question is Nicol et al. (1997), who found that distributive sentences (*the ad on the billboards was very offensive*) and non-distributive sentences (*the bridge across the canyons is safe*) led to equivalent costs in reading time compared with their respective controls with singular local nouns. However, Nicol et al. did not test whether their stimuli elicited a distributivity effect in *production*. Given several earlier null-results in English production studies (Bock & Miller, 1991; Vigliocco, Butterworth, & Garrett, 1996; see Eberhard, 1999 for the suggestion that the effects are contingent on adequate control of item factors such as imageability), this evidence is not conclusive. In sum, the monitoring bias account of distributivity passes Demand 1, but it fails on Demand 2. Current evidence does not compellingly address Demand 3.

DISCUSSION

This article evaluated whether speech error patterns can be influenced by a monitoring bias. The first section made the case that this possibility should be taken seriously: Speakers can monitor speech before they say it (and do so habitually) and the data suggest that they are fast enough to intercept the errors in internal speech. The second section pointed out, however, that only very few studies have compellingly demonstrated what the monitor's criteria are exactly, allowing monitor bias accounts too many degrees of freedom. The third section proposed three main demands that one should impose on monitoring bias accounts: (1) Is the bias caused by functional monitoring criteria? (2) Can the bias be changed by manipulations affecting the monitor? (3) Is there a counterpart of the bias in speech comprehension? The fourth section assessed whether five candidate monitoring biases meet these demands (Table 1). These candidates are: (1) the lexical bias effect; (2) the mixed error effect; (3) the exchange rate; (4) morphophonological effects on agreement errors; (5) conceptual effects on agreement errors.

As Table 1 shows, the conclusions that can be drawn from this exercise will have to remain tentative, since none of the speech error patterns can be evaluated on all demands. Notwithstanding the tentativeness of the present exercise, it has several potential uses. First, by proposing explicit demands that monitoring bias accounts should meet, one can better evaluate the present status of such accounts. Thus, the case for a monitoring bias account of the lexical bias and of the mixed error bias is relatively strong, but by no means watertight. In contrast, the case for a monitoring account of morphophonological effects on number agreement errors is weak: Such an account fails on Demand 1 (functionality), and is not supported by any evidence pertaining to Demands 2 and 3.

Second, an evaluation of the monitoring bias has important repercussions for current theories of language production. One of these

TABLE 1
Evaluation of five suspected monitoring biases against the criteria of functionality (the monitor would set functional criteria), affectability (the bias is affected by manipulations that alter monitoring performance), and correspondence with perception (the bias would also occur in the perception of one's external speech and of others' speech)

	Functionality	Affectability	Perception analogue
Lexical bias	+	+	$0/-^a$
Mixed error bias	+	0	$0/+^b$
Exchange rate	+	0	0
Morphophonological effects on agreement errors	–	0	0
Conceptual effects on agreement errors	+	–	0

Explanation of symbols: ' + ' : the bias meets the demand; '–' : the bias does not meet the demand; '0' there is no compelling evidence that the bias does or does not meet the demand.

a. The '0' in the case of the perceptual demand refers to the general case (Do listeners detect non-word errors more readily than word errors?). The '–' refers to the specific proposal (Roelofs, 2004) that external-channel monitoring is qualitatively different, as a result of less attention being paid to it.

b. The '0' in the case of the perceptual demand refers to the general case (do listeners detect phonologically unrelated semantic errors more often than mixed errors?). The ' + ' refers to Roelofs' (2004) specific proposal that the internal channel will activate a cohort of phonologically similar (i.e., begin-related) competitors.

repercussions has already been discussed at some length: the issue of modularity. That is, proponents of modular theories often invoke a monitoring bias to attempt to explain error patterns that seemingly argue for interactivity. But it is important to note that monitoring bias accounts and modular accounts do not necessarily go together; they simply tend to go together in the literature (e.g., Levelt et al., 1999). As pointed out by Vigliocco and Hartsuiker (2002) there is no reason to exclude a theory that postulates both interactivity (i.e., cascading of activation and feedback) and a monitor. In fact, the data of Hartsuiker et al. (2005a) clearly make a case for such a theory. Likewise, the findings that suggest a monitoring account of the mixed bias effect are in no way incompatible with accounts of that effect in terms of feedback (Rapp & Goldrick, 2000).

In fact, one might argue that the discussion of whether there is feedback or not becomes obsolete when we consider monitoring accounts. As pointed out by Rapp and Goldrick (2004), if we assume (with Roelofs, 2004) that internal-channel monitoring activates representations in production (at the lemma level), this is effectively a form of feedback (albeit indirect feedback). Vigliocco and Hartsuiker (2002) even go a step further, and suggest the possibility that a main reason why (direct) feedback in the language production system has developed is in fact to be able to implement the monitoring function. This is based on Postma and Kolk's (1993) suggestion (also see MacKay, 1987) that unexpected patterns of feedback from a certain level in production can signal that something at that level went wrong.

The monitoring bias also has repercussions for other aspects of language production. In particular, the monitoring bias that alters the observed 'exchange rate' causes observed patterns of phonological speech errors to underestimate the number of exchange errors. This is important, because current models of phonological encoding are fit on observed (rather than on the internally planned) distributions of anticipations, perseverations, and exchanges (Dell, 1986; Hartsuiker, 2002; Levelt et al., 1999). An underestimation of the exchange rate is particularly problematic for Levelt et al.'s model, because that model considers the two component errors of an exchange as independent: An exchange occurs if there happens to be an anticipation and a perseveration involving the same two word positions. In contrast, in Dell's (1986, 1988) models, and in Hartsuiker's (2002) implementation of those models, there are mechanisms that promote the likelihood of exchanges. In particular, there are mechanisms in these models by which the probabilities of anticipating and perseverating are no longer independent, but rather positively correlated: A perseveration becomes more likely when an anticipation was made first. Levelt et al. note that WEAVER++ could be changed so that the independence assumption is given up, but such a change would be post-hoc. In contrast, the assumption of dependence in Dell's model follows from a general theoretical principle (namely the need to suppress representations that were just selected, and to prime representations that will be needed shortly).

Of course, the present paper has discussed only a subset of speech error patterns that are conceivably influenced by monitoring biases (i.e., mostly patterns that appear to argue for interactivity in language production, but that proponents of modular theories attempt to explain by invoking monitoring biases). At the same time, there are many speech error patterns reported in the literature (e.g., Stemberger, 1992) that could similarly be suspected of being at least partly the result of a monitoring bias. For example, the fact that phonological speech errors tend to be phonologically similar to the intended word can be explained as the result of feedback from phonological feature units (Dell, 1986), but also by a monitoring bias, on the assumption that the internal-channel finds it more difficult to discriminate more similar phonemes (i.e., Demand 3, Qualification A).

Another suspected monitoring bias was proposed by Shattuck-Hufnagel (1979). This bias relates to the phenomenon that if a certain phoneme (e.g.,

/b/) has been produced correctly, chances increase that an error is made on that phoneme in one of the next four words. This could be a result from a monitoring bias, by which the monitor would specifically look out for anticipations and perseverations, and incorrectly classify the next /b/ as an error. It is difficult to see, however, how such a monitoring bias might meet Demand 1 (functionality): It is clearly not functional for the monitor to raise many false alarms.[4]

Finally, the studies discussed in this article have a number of repercussions for research on the monitoring system. Rapp and Goldrick (2000) criticized monitoring accounts because the specific mechanisms of monitoring have remained unclear. Recently, improvements have been made in specifying these mechanisms. For example, Hartsuiker and Kolk (2001) proposed and implemented a computational model of monitoring (the Perceptual Loop Model, PLM; also see Hartsuiker, in press), with specific proposals about certain monitoring mechanisms. Simulations with this model could account for aspects of the time-course of self-monitoring (i.e., the time intervals between error onset and moment of speech suspension, and between suspension and resumption). However, a number of monitoring mechanisms that are important for monitoring bias accounts have remained unclear.

Most importantly, current accounts are underspecified with respect to the processes involved in error detection. As illustrated in Table 1, there are only few studies that allow an evaluation of monitoring biases with respect to Demand 3 (the bias also occurs in perception). For example, current accounts leave it unclear how exactly the monitor makes a comparison between the speech one intends to say and the speech that was actually said (or more precisely, the speech that the monitor *perceived* as having being said). On Levelt's (1989) account, which was largely followed in the PLM, comparison takes place at the conceptual level, so that the concept intended for production is compared to the concept recognized in perception. But this account runs into problems when one considers non-word errors. If such an error is fed back through comprehension, no word will be recognized (by definition) and therefore no concept will be recognized. How can the monitor then make a comparison?

In addition to a direct comparison of intended and realized speech, many monitoring bias accounts suggest that the monitor can make specific

---

[4] Additionally, the effect might follow from a mechanism of post-selection inhibition, which is incorporated in the model of Dell (1986). In order to prevent perseveration, the activation of a just-selected unit would be turned off, making it more difficult to select the unit again. Whether that explanation is sufficient to account for this effect remains to be seen however, because the activation level of the recently selected unit will quickly 'bounce back' (because of that unit's connections with highly active units at the lexical level).

tests (e.g., *Is this a word? Is this word appropriate?*), and as I have argued here, many of these tests pass the Demand of functionality. However, these accounts would be considerably strengthened if it could be established when and in which order such tests take place and whether they are optional or not.

Finally, it remains an empirical question whether internal-channel monitoring really uses language comprehension or rather uses certain mechanisms within language production (e.g., Postma, 2000). If the latter scenario is right, my Perceptual Demand (Demand 3) should of course be replaced by a new Demand, based on a new theory of how the monitor works. One possibility is that production-internal feedback serves as a monitoring cue (Postma & Kolk, 1993; Vigliocco & Hartsuiker, 2002). However, feedback is not necessary for production-monitoring, because the dynamics of activation at a given level of production (e.g., the lexical level) can also provide cues about the correctness of processing. Whenever we select a representation in error, the correct representation will also be very active (because it receives input from the correct representation at the previous level). But when we select a correct representation, representations of errors tend to be inactive. Because competition is a sign of error, a production-monitoring device might exploit the amount of competition at a given level. This can be done, for example, by a monitoring device that multiplies the activation levels of two response candidates; only if both are highly active will the end result have a high value (Botvinick, Braver, Barch, Carter, & Cohen, 2001). Of course, it remains to be seen whether such theoretical alternatives are viable.

In conclusion, monitoring bias accounts remain underspecified in terms of their precise mechanisms and the evidence for such biases, as tested against the three Demands I proposed, is mixed. However, given the continuing importance of speech error patterns for theories of language production and given the challenge to better understand the monitoring system, it is important to investigate such accounts more fully.

REFERENCES

Allopenna, P. D., Magnuson, J. S., & Tanenhaus, M. K. (1998). Tracking the time course of spoken word recognition using eye movements: Evidence for continuous mapping models. *Journal of Memory and Language, 38,* 419–439.

Baars, B. J., Motley, M. T., & MacKay, D. G. (1975). Output editing for lexical status in artificially elicited slips of the tongue. *Journal of Verbal Learning and Verbal Behavior, 14,* 382–391.

Beattie, G. W., & Butterworth, B. L. (1979). Contextual probability and word frequency as determinants of pauses and errors in spontaneous speech. *Language and Speech, 22,* 201–211.

Berg, T. (1986). The aftermath of error occurrence: Psycholinguistic evidence from cut-offs. *Language and Communication, 6,* 195–213.

Berg, T. (1992). Productive and perceptual constraints on speech-error correction. *Psychological Research, 54*, 114–126.

Bock, K., & Cutting, J. C. (1992). Regulating mental energy: Performance units in language production. *Journal of Memory and Language, 31*, 99–127.

Bock, K., & Eberhard, K. M. (1993). Meaning sound and syntax in English number agreement. *Language and Cognitive Processes, 8*, 57–99.

Bock, K., Nicol, J., & Cutting, J. C. (1999). The ties that bind: Creating number agreement in speech. *Journal of Memory and Language, 40*, 330–346.

Botvinick, M. M., Braver, T. S., Barch, D. M., Carter, C. S., & Cohen, J. D. (2001). Conflict monitoring and cognitive control. *Psychological Review, 108*, 624–652.

Bock, K., & Miller, C. A. (1991). Broken agreement. *Cognitive Psychology, 23*, 45–93.

Cherry, E. C. (1953). Some experiments on the recognition of speech with one and two ears. *Journal of the Acoustical Society of America, 25*, 975–979.

Cohen, A. (1980). Correcting speech errors in a shadowing task. In V. A. Fromkin (Ed.), *Errors in linguistic performance: Slips of the tongue, ear, pen, and hand* (pp. 157–163). New York: Academic Press.

Cole, R. A. (1973). Listening for mispronunciations. A measure of what we hear during speech. *Perception and Psychophysics, 11*, 153–156.

Coulson, S., King, J. W., & Kutas, M. (1998). Expect the unexpected: Event-related brain response to morphosyntactic violations. *Language and Cognitive Processes, 13*, 21–58.

Cutler, A. (1982). The reliability of speech error data. In A. Cutler (Ed.), *Slips of the tongue and language production* (pp. 728). Amsterdam: Mouton.

Daneman, M., & Green, I. (1986). Individual differences in comprehending and producing words in context. *Journal of Memory and Language, 25*, 118.

Dell, G. S. (1986). A spreading-activation theory of retrieval in sentence production. *Psychological Review, 93*, 283–321.

Dell, G. S. (1988). The retrieval of phonological forms in production: Tests of predictions from a connectionist model. *Journal of Memory and Language, 27*, 124–142.

Dell, G. S. (1990). Effects of frequency and vocabulary type on phonological speech errors. *Language and Cognitive Processes, 5*, 313–349.

Dell, G. S., & Reich, P. A. (1981). Stages in sentence production: An analysis of speech error data. *Journal of Verbal Learning and Verbal Behavior, 20*, 611–629.

Dell, G. S., & Repka, R. J. (1992). Errors in inner speech. In B. J. Baars (Ed.), *Experimental slips and human error: Exploring the architecture of volition* (pp. 237–262). New York: Plenum Press.

Eberhard, K. M. (1999). The accessibility of conceptual number to processes of subject-verb agreement in English. *Journal of Memory and Language, 41*, 560–578.

Ferreira, V. S., & Pashler, H. (2002). Central bottleneck influences on the processing stages of word production. *Journal of Experimental Psychology: Learning, Memory, and Cognition, 28*, 1187–1199.

Fromkin, V. A. (1971). The non-anomalous nature of anomalous utterances. *Language, 47*, 27–52.

Garrett, M. F. (1975). The analysis of sentence production. In G. H. Bower (Ed.), *The psychology of learning and motivation* (pp. 133–177). New York: Academic Press.

Harley, T. A. (1984). A critique of top-down independent levels models of speech production: Evidence from non-plan-internal speech errors. *Cognitive Science, 8*, 191–219.

Hartsuiker, R. J. (2002). The addition bias in Dutch and Spanish phonological speech errors: The role of structural context. *Language and Cognitive Processes, 17*, 61–96.

Hartsuiker, R. J. (in press). Studies on verbal self-monitoring: The Perceptual Loop Model and beyond. In A. S. Meyer, L. R. Wheeldon, & A. Krott (Eds.), *Automaticity and control in language processing.* Hove, UK: Psychology Press.

Hartsuiker, R. J., & Barkhuysen, P. N. (2006). Language production and working memory: The case of subject-verb agreement. *Language and Cognitive Processes, 21*, 181–204.

Hartsuiker, R. J., Corley, M., & Martensen, H. (2005a). The lexical bias effect is modulated by context, but the standard monitoring account doesn't fly: Related Beply to Baars, Motley, and MacKay (1975). *Journal of Memory and Language, 52*, 58–70.

Hartsuiker, R. J., & Kolk, H. H. J. (2001). Error monitoring in speech production: A computational test of the perceptual loop theory. *Cognitive Psychology, 42*, 113–157.

Hartsuiker, R. J., & Kolk, H. H. J., & Martensen, H. (2005b). The division of labor between internal and external speech monitoring. In R. J. Hartsuiker, R. Bastiaanse, A. Postma, & F. Wijnen (Eds.), *Phonological encoding and monitoring in normal and pathological speech* (pp. 187–205). Hove, UK: Psychology Press.

Hartsuiker, R. J., Schriefers, H. J., Bock, J. K., & Kikstra, G. M. (2003). Morphophonological influences on the construction of subject-verb agreement. *Memory and Cognition, 31*, 1316–1326.

Humphreys. K. R. (2002). *Lexical bias in speech errors*. Unpublished Doctoral dissertation, University of Illinois at Urbana-Champaign.

Lackner, J. R., & Tuller, B. H. (1979). Role of efference monitoring in the detection of self-produced speech errors. In: W. E. Cooper & E. C. T. Walker (Eds.), *Sentence processing: Psycholinguistic studies presented to Merrill Garrett* (pp. 281–294). Hillsdale, NJ: Lawrence Erlbaum Associates Inc.

Levelt, W. J. M. (1983). Monitoring and self-repair in speech. *Cognition, 14*, 41–104.

Levelt, W. J. M. (1989). *Speaking: From intention to articulation*. Cambridge, MA: MIT Press.

Levelt, W. J. M., Roelofs, A., & Meyer, A. S. (1999). A theory of lexical access in speech production. *Behavioral and Brain Sciences, 22*, 1–75.

Lickley, R. J., Hartsuiker, R. J., Corley, M., Russell, M., & Nelson, R. (2005). Judgment of disfluency in people who stutter and people who do not stutter: Results from magnitude estimation. *Language and Speech, 48*, 299–312.

MacKay, D. G. (1987). *The organization of perception and action: A theory of language and other cognitive skills*. New York: Springer.

Maclay, H., & Osgood, C. E. (1959). Hesitation phenomena in spontaneous English speech. *Word, 15*, 19–44.

Meyer, A. S. (1992). Investigation of phonological encoding through speech error analyses: Achievements, limitations, and alternatives. *Cognition, 42*, 181–211.

Motley, M. T., Camden, C. T., & Baars, B. J. (1982). Covert formulation and editing of anomalies in speech production: Evidence from experimentally elicited slips of the tongue. *Journal of Verbal Learning and Verbal Behavior, 21*, 578–594.

Nicol, J. L., Forster, K. I., & Veres, C. (1997). Subject-verb agreement processes in comprehension. *Journal of Memory and Language, 36*, 569–587.

Nooteboom, S. G. (1969). The tongue slips into patterns. In A. G. Sciarone, A. J. Van Essen, & A. A. Van Raad (Eds.), *Nomen. Leyden studies in linguistics and phonetics* (pp. 114–132). The Hague: Mouton.

Nooteboom, S. G. (1980). Speaking and unspeaking: Detection and correction of phonological and lexical errors in spontaneous speech. In V. A. Fromkin (Ed.), *Errors in linguistic performance: Slips of the tongue, ear, pen, and hand* (pp. 87–95). New York: Academic Press.

Nooteboom, S. G. (2005). Listening to oneself: Monitoring speech production. In R. J. Hartsuiker, R. Bastiaanse, A. Postma, & F. Wijnen (Eds.), *Phonological encoding and monitoring in normal and pathological speech* (pp. 167–186). Hove, UK: Psychology Press.

Oomen, C. C. E., & Postma, A. (2002). Limitations in processing resources and speech monitoring. *Language and Cognitive Processes, 17*, 163–184.

Oomen, C. C. E., Postma, A., & Kolk, H. H. J. (2001). Prearticulatory and postarticulatory self-monitoring in Broca's aphasia. *Cortex, 37,* 627–641.

Pearlmutter, N. J., Garnsey, S. M., & Bock, K. (1999). Agreement processes in sentence comprehension. *Journal of Memory and Language, 41,* 427–456.

Postma, A. (2000). Detection of errors during speech production: A review of speech monitoring models. *Cognition, 77,* 97–131.

Postma, A., & Kolk, H. H. J. (1993). The covert repair hypothesis: Prearticulatory repair processes in normal and stuttered disfluencies. *Journal of Speech and Hearing Research, 36,* 472–487.

Postma, A., & Noordanus, C. (1996). Production and detection of speech errors in silent, mouthed, noise-masked, and normal auditory feedback speech. *Language and Speech, 39,* 375–392.

Rapp, B., & Goldrick, M. (2000). Discreteness and interactivity in spoken word production. *Psychological Review, 107,* 460–499.

Rapp, B., & Goldrick, M. (2004). Feedback by any other name is still interactivity: A reply to Roelofs (2004). *Psychological Review, 111,* 573–578.

Roelofs, A. (2004). Error biases in spoken word planning and monitoring by aphasic and nonaphasic speakers: Comment on Rapp and Goldrick (2000). *Psychological Review, 111,* 561–572.

Roelofs, A. (2005). Spoken word planning, comprehending, and self-monitoring: Evaluation of WEAVER++. In R. J. Hartsuiker, R. Bastiaanse, A. Postma, & F. Wijnen (Eds.), *Phonological encoding and monitoring in normal and pathological speech* (pp. 42–63). Hove, UK: Psychology Press.

Shattuck-Hufnagel, S. (1979). Speech errors as evidence for a serial order mechanism in sentence production. In W. E. Cooper & E. C. T. Walker (Eds.), *Sentence processing: Psycholinguistic studies presented to Merrill Garrett* (pp. 295–342). Hillsdale, NJ: Lawrence Erlbaum Associates.

Stemberger, J. P. (1985). An interactive activation model of language production. In A. W. Ellis (Ed.), *Progress in the psychology of language, Vol. 1* (pp. 143–186). Hove, UK: Lawrence Erlbaum Associates Ltd.

Stemberger, J. P. (1989). Speech errors in early child language production. *Journal of Memory and Language, 28,* 164–188.

Stermberger, J. P. (1992). The reliability and replicability of naturalistic speech error data: A comparison with experimentally induced errors. In B. J. Baars (Ed.), *Experimental slips and human error: Exploring the architecture of volition* (pp. 195–215). New York: Plenum Press.

Tanenhaus, M. K., Spivey-Knowlton, M. J., Eberhard, K. M., & Sedivy, J. C. (1995). Integration of visual and linguistic information in spoken language comprehension. *Science, 268,* 1632–1634.

Vasić, N., & Wijnen, F. (2005). Stuttering as a monitoring deficit. In R. Hartsuiker, R. Bastiaanse, A. Postma, & F. Wijnen (Eds.), *Phonological encoding and monitoring in normal and pathological speech* (pp. 226–247). Hove, UK: Psychology Press.

Vigliocco, G., Butterworth, B., & Garrett, M. F. (1996). Subject-verb agreement in Spanish and English: Differences in the role of conceptual constraints. *Cognition, 61,* 261–298.

Vigliocco, G., Butterworth, B., & Semenza, C. (1995). Constructing subject-verb agreement in speech: The role of semantic and morphological factors. *Journal of Memory and Language, 34,* 186–215.

Vigliocco, G., & Hartsuiker, R. J. (2002). The interplay of meaning, sound, and syntax in language production. *Psychological Bulletin, 128,* 442–472.

Vigliocco, G., Hartsuiker, R. J., Jarema, G., & Kolk, H. H. J. (1996). One or more labels on the bottles? Notional concord in Dutch and French. *Language and Cognitive Processes, 11*, 407–442.

Vigliocco, G., & Franck, J. (1999). When sex and syntax go hand in hand: Gender agreement in language production. *Journal of Memory and Language, 40*, 455–478.

Wheeldon, L. R., & Levelt, W. J. M. (1995). Monitoring the time-course of phonological encoding. *Journal of Memory and Language, 34*, 311–334.

Zwitserlood, P. (1989). The locus of the effects of sentential-semantic context in spoken-word processing. *Cognition, 32*, 25–64.

LANGUAGE AND COGNITIVE PROCESSES
2006, 21 (7–8), 892–919

Ψ Psychology Press
Taylor & Francis Group

A further look at semantic context effects in language production: The role of response congruency

Jan-Rouke Kuipers

Leiden University, Cognitive Psychology Unit, P.O. Box 9555, 2300 RB Leiden, The Netherlands

Wido La Heij

Leiden University, Cognitive Psychology Unit, P.O. Box 9555, 2300 RB Leiden, The Netherlands

Albert Costa

University of Barcelona, Barcelona, Spain

Most current models of speech production predict interference from related context words in picture-naming tasks. However, Glaser and Düngelhoff (1984) reported semantic facilitation when the task was changed from basic-level naming to category-level naming. The authors explore two proposals to account for this change in polarity of the semantic context effect: the semantic selection account by Costa, Mahon, Savova, and Caramazza (2003) and a response-congruency account. Experiments 1a and 1b show that category names induce semantic interference in basic-level naming, a finding that disproves the semantic selection account and is in line with the response-congruency account. Experiment 2 reveals that response congruency is probably a major contributor to the overall facilitation effect in categorisation tasks. Finally, Experiment 3 tests and confirms a prediction of the response-congruency account in basic-level naming with subordinate-level distractors. The authors conclude that the available evidence support the response-congruency account and suggest that this congruency effect is localised at the stage of constructing a preverbal message.

Correspondence should be addressed to Jan-Rouke Kuipers, Leiden University, Cognitive Psychology Unit, P.O. Box 9555, 2300 RB Leiden, The Netherlands.
E-mail: kuipersj@fsw.leidenuniv.nl

This research was in part supported by a grant from the Spanish Government (SEJ 2005-00409/PSIC) and McDonnell grant 'Bridging Mind, Brain and Behaviour'. The authors wish to thank Ansgar Hantsch and two anonymous reviewers for their helpful comments on a previous version of this paper.

http://www.psypress.com/lcp   DOI: 10.1080/016909600824211

INTRODUCTION

In the last two decades, variants of the Stroop task have become increasingly popular in the study of speech production. In these tasks, researchers examine the effect of context stimuli on response latencies in picture naming (Schriefers, Meyer, & Levelt, 1990), definition naming (La Heij, Starreveld, & Steehouwer, 1993) and word translation (La Heij, Hooglander, Kerling, & Van der Velden, 1996). An often replicated finding in these studies is the semantic interference effect: when a target has to be named in the context of a distractor word, naming latencies are longer when the distractor word is semantically related to the picture than when it is unrelated.

This effect has played an important role in the development of models of speech production. In fact one of the basic tenets of several models of speech production, the existence of lexical competition, is largely based on the explanations given to the semantic interference effect (Glaser & Glaser, 1989; La Heij, 1988; Roelofs, 1992). A generally accepted explanation of the effect (Bloem & La Heij, 2003; Humphreys, Lloyd-Jones, & Fias, 1995; Levelt, Roelofs, & Meyer, 1999; Starreveld & La Heij, 1996) is as follows: When a target picture of, for instance, a dog is presented for naming, (a) this picture activates the representation DOG at the conceptual level, (b) activation spreads from this target concept to related concepts (e.g., CAT and HORSE), (c) activation spreads – dependent on the model – either directly from the target concept DOG or indirectly via the related concepts like CAT and HORSE, to semantically related words at the lexical level (e.g., 'cat', 'horse', etc.) and (d) these activated words compete in a process of lexical selection with the correct response word 'dog'. Thus, when participants are required to name the picture of a dog that is accompanied by the context word 'cat', the lexical representation of the word cat receives activation from two sources: from the word recognition system and from the target concept. In contrast, an unrelated context word only receives activation from the word recognition system and will, for that reason, induce less interference than a semantically related context word.

This account of semantic interference predicts an interference effect whenever target and distractor are semantically related. This prediction, however, is clearly at odds with experimental results obtained in variants of the picture-word interference task in which the target is not named at a basic level of categorisation. For instance, Glaser & Düngelhoff (1984) reported the results of a categorisation task in which the target picture (e.g., the picture of a cat) had to be named at the super-ordinate level (e.g., 'animal'). They used four context conditions: a 'concept-congruent condition', in which the context word was the basic-level name of the picture (e.g., 'cat'), a semantically related condition (e.g., 'dog'), an unrelated condition (e.g., 'glass') and a neutral condition. Although with simultaneous presentation of target and distractor a small semantic interference effect was obtained, at several stimulus-onset latencies (SOAs) close to zero the correct basic-level names and the related context words did not induce interference. In fact, at SOAs −400 ms, −300 ms, −200 ms and +100 ms facilitating effects were found. More recently, Costa, Mahon, Savova, and Caramazza (2003) found a significant semantic facilitation of 56 ms with simultaneous presentation of target picture and distractor word in a picture categorisation task.

This change in the polarity of the effects produced by semantically related distractors clearly asks for a reconsideration of simple models of semantic interference in terms of lexical competition. These models should be extended to accommodate semantic facilitation in categorisation tasks or – if that turns out to be impossible – be replaced by an alternative model that is able to account for the complete pattern of results. The main objective of the present study is to gather more information about the contribution of several factors to semantic context effects in this paradigm. Specifically, we explore the conditions for between-categorisation level interference and facilitation and consider the necessary adaptation for models of speech production.[1]

Previous explanations for semantic facilitation in categorisation tasks

In the literature, three proposals have been put forward to account for the change in the polarity of the semantic context effect in basic-level and category-level naming. First, Roelofs (1992) proposed that only words that belong to a predefined 'response set' compete for selection at the lexical level. In a categorisation task, these words are the category names in use in the experiment (e.g., 'animal', 'fruit', and 'vehicle'). Basic-level names do not belong to this set and hence do not induce interference. This approach, however, has been refuted by experimental results showing that context words that do not belong to the response set do induce lexical interference (Caramazza & Costa, 2000; 2001, Starreveld & La Heij, 1999; but see Roelofs, 2001). That is, although response set membership may exert some effects in this paradigm, it cannot account for both the presence of

---

[1] In this study we focus on categorising tasks, which have yielded rather consistent results across many studies. At this stage, no attempt will be made to account for subordinate level naming, a task that has yielded rather inconsistent findings (Hantsch et al., 2005; Vitkovitch & Tyrrell, 1999).

semantic facilitation in categorisation tasks and the presence of semantic interference in basic-level naming.

Secondly, in a proposal of Costa et al. (2003) it is assumed that the cognitive system can make use of several semantic dimensions to decide which semantic representation to prioritise for further processing (see also Costa, Alario, and Caramazza, 2005 for a further discussion of this issue). It is assumed that the level of categorisation of a given stimulus can be used by the semantic system to tease apart the semantic representation corresponding to the target and that corresponding to the distractor. Thus, when the two stimuli belong to different levels of categorisation (e.g., the target picture of a dog that is accompanied by the word 'animal'), the semantic system easily discards the semantic representation of the distractor for further processing, thereby reducing the chances for observing lexical interference. At the same time, however, the semantic representation of the distractor will enhance the activation of the semantic representation of the target, making it more available and leading to semantic facilitation. In this framework, when the level of categorisation of target and distractor is the same (the target picture of a dog accompanied by the word 'cat'), the semantic system cannot use such information to tease apart the two representations, and as a consequence a semantic relation between the two stimuli will increase the chance for observing semantic interference.

This account predicts that facilitation should not only be observed in categorisation tasks with basic-level distractors, but also in basic-level naming tasks with category-level distractors, a prediction that will be tested in Experiments 1a and 1b. This account of Costa et al. will be referred to as the 'semantic selection account'.

The third proposal explaining semantic facilitation in categorisation tasks is derived from observations by Lupker and Katz (1981). They argued that semantic interference is obtained when the two following conditions are met: (a) the context word is semantically related to the picture – similar but not the same as the picture, and (b) applying the task instruction to the target and distractor leads to an incompatible result. In other domains, this second principle is often referred to as 'response congruency'. In the flanker task, for instance, Eriksen and Eriksen (1974) observed facilitation when a target letter (e.g., K) was flanked by a distractor letter (e.g., H) that was associated with the same overt response (e.g., pressing a lever to the left).

Application of the response congruency principle to picture categorising with basic-level distractors leads to the prediction of facilitation when target and context stimuli are categorically related. For instance, in a categorisation task in which the target picture of a car is presented for naming, the context word 'bike' will result in facilitation compared to the context word 'apple', because 'bike' is response congruent and 'apple' is not. However, when the task is basic-level naming, the result of applying the task instruction to both stimuli will lead to different responses ('bike' and 'apple'). The proposal that the semantic facilitation effect in categorisation tasks is due to the convergence of target and context on the same response, will be referred to as the 'response congruency account'.

The response-congruency account predicts semantic facilitation in picture categorising, but for different reasons than the semantic selection account. Therefore, the picture-categorising paradigm is not appropriate to distinguish the two. To adjudicate between the two proposals, we need to examine a different experimental condition. Therefore, in Experiments 1a and 1b, we examine the effect of category-level distractors on basic-level naming. That is, participants are asked to name the picture of a dog (as 'dog'), while ignoring a semantically related category-level distractor ('animal') or an unrelated one ('vehicle'). In this condition, Costa et al.'s (2003) semantic selection account predicts semantic facilitation because target and distractor differ in their level of categorisation. In contrast, the response congruency account predicts semantic interference. The reason is that applying the task instruction ('name at basic level') to the target picture (e.g., of a dog) and a category distractor (e.g., 'animal') does not lead to the same response.

EXPERIMENT 1A

In this experiment participants were asked to name target pictures using basic-level names. The pictures were accompanied by distractor words that could be (a) semantically related or unrelated to the target and (b) basic-level names or category-level names.[2] For example, the target picture of a couch (response 'bank') was presented with the four distractor words: 'tafel' ('table'; basic-level, related), 'tomaat' ('tomato'; basic-level, unrelated), 'meubel' ('furniture'; category-level, related) and 'voertuig' ('vehicle'; category-level, unrelated).

The predictions of this study are clear. If a difference between the level of categorisation of target and distractor is enough to produce semantic facilitation, as proposed by Costa et al. (2003), then semantically related category-name distractors should lead to semantic facilitation, while semantically related basic-level distractors should lead to semantic

---

[2] A similar experiment was conducted by Roelofs (1992), who failed to find an effect of semantic similarity in a picture-naming task with category-level distractors. However, in that experiment the classical semantic interference effect from basic-level distractors in basic-level naming was also absent. Therefore, we refrain from interpreting these findings.

interference. Thus, an interaction between the variable 'semantic related-ness' and 'level of categorisation' should be present. In contrast, if the change in the polarity of related distractors is due to response congruency, then we should observe semantic interference from related distractors regardless of their level of categorisation. The reason is that applying the task instruction ('provide the basic-level name') to target (e.g., the picture of a couch) and distractor (e.g., the word 'furniture') does not lead to the same response.

Method

Participants.   Eighteen students from Leiden University took part in the experiment. They all had normal or corrected to normal vision and received 3.50 euro for their participation.

Materials.   Three line drawings of familiar objects or animals were selected from each of 10 categories, resulting in a total number of 30 target pictures. Most of the pictures used came from the Snodgrass and Vanderwart (1980) picture set. The targets were paired with four different distractors: related and unrelated words from the basic-level and category-level. For example: the picture of a car was accompanied with the Dutch words 'trein' (train), 'voertuig' (vehicle), 'banaan' (banana), and 'fruit' (fruit). The basic level and category level distractors were matched as far as possible with respect to length (in letters and in syllables) and familiarity (de Vries, 1986). Familiarity ratings were not available for one of the basic level words and four of the category level words. The mean familiarity ratings of the remaining basic- and category-level words were 8.1 and 7.9, respectively (values on a 9-point scale). The mean length of the words of the basic level words was 5.4 letters and 1.6 syllables. The corresponding values in the category level words were 6.2 and 1.9, respectively. Although no perfect match between category levels was achieved, it should be noted that the calculation of the semantic interference effect was conducted within each category level, which yields a comparison between identical word sets (related and unrelated). While constructing the picture-word pairs, care was taken to prevent a phonological relation between the names of the target pictures and the distractor words. The complete list of targets and distractors is presented in Appendix 1a.

Apparatus.   The experiment was programmed in MEL Professional software (version 2.0d; Schneider, 1988) on a TARGA Pentium PC. The stimuli were presented on a 17-inch Iiyama monitor, the correct answers and reaction times appeared on a 15-inch monochrome monitor. The reaction times were measured by means of a voice key.

Procedure. The participants had individual sessions in a dimly lit room. At the start of the session they were given a written instruction and a list containing the 30 pictures and their Dutch basic level name. They were instructed to inspect this list of stimulus materials. Next, all pictures were presented individually on the computer screen for naming. In the experimental series, which were preceded with 5 practice trials randomly drawn from the trial list, each trial involved the following sequence. First, a fixation point was presented in the centre of the display for 500 ms. The target picture and the distractor word appeared simultaneously in black centred at the point of fixation and remained on the screen until the voice key was triggered or an interval of 2000 ms had elapsed. The height and width of the target and context words were $1.4° \times 2°$ of visual angle for 3-letter words up to $1.4° \times 5°$ of visual angle for 8-letter words. The maximum size of the pictures was $7° \times 7°$ degree visual angle. A white edge around the distractor words ensured their legibility against the picture background. Viewing distance was approximately 80 cm. The experimenter judged the response for correctness and entered a code into the computer. Malfunctioning of the voice key could also be indicated. The order of presentation of the stimuli was random, with the restriction that a target picture was not repeated within a series of six trials. The total number of experimental trials was 120 (30 target pictures $\times$ 4 distractor conditions).

Results and discussion

The following reaction times (RTs) were excluded: RTs of incorrect responses (including failures to respond; a total of 2.1%), RTs of trials in which the voice key malfunctioned (0.83%) and RTs exceeding a cut-off criterion of 1500 ms (1.5%). The mean RTs and percentages of incorrect responses are shown in Table 1a.

Analyses of Variance (ANOVAs) were performed on both the participant means (F_1) and on the item means (F_2), with the category level of the distractor word (basic level versus category level) and the relation between target and distractor (semantically related or unrelated)

TABLE 1a

Reaction times in ms, percentage of error and semantic interference effects in the different conditions of Experiment 1a

	Related		*Unrelated*		*Semantic interference*	
Distractor type	*RT*	*%e*	*RT*	*%e*	*RT*	*%e*
Basic level	816	2.6	764	1.3	52	1.3
Category level	811	2.2	764	2.2	47	0.0

as within-participant variables. Variability is indicated by the 95% confidence intervals of the mean differences (Loftus & Masson, 1994). The main effect of semantic relatedness was significant, $F_1(1, 17) = 33.1$, $p < .001$, CI $= \pm 17.8$, $F_2(1, 29) = 36.7$, $p < .001$, CI $= \pm 16.7$. The main effect of level of categorisation was not significant, $F_1 < 1$, $F_2 < 1$. Importantly, the interaction between these two variables was not significant $F_1 < 1$, $F_2 < 1$. In an identical ANOVA on the error percentages there were no significant effects, semantic relatedness, $F_1(1, 17) = 1.06$, $p = 0.32$, CI $= \pm 0.5$, and all other Fs < 1.

The results of this experiment are clear: Semantically related distractors led to longer naming latencies than unrelated distractors regardless of their level of categorisation (52 ms and 47 ms for basic- and category-level distractors, respectively). The important new finding here is that semantically related category-name distractors induce semantic interference (rather than facilitation) in basic-level picture naming. Because of the importance of this finding for adjudicating between contrasting explanations of the contextual effects in this paradigm, it is appropriate that we replicate it in another paradigm in which context words can induce semantic interference and facilitation, the word translation task (cf. Bloem & La Heij, 2003; Bloem, van den Boogaard, & La Heij, 2004).

EXPERIMENT 1B

The goal of this experiment is to establish whether the main finding of Experiment 1a can be replicated using a different language-production task: translation of a second-language (L2) target word into the first language (L1). It is often assumed that this backward translation task, like picture naming, is conceptually mediated (Bloem & La Heij, 2003; see, however, Kroll & Stewart, 1994). The main argument in favour of this assumption is the presence of semantic context effects in backward translation. When, for example, Dutch–English bilinguals are asked to translate the L2 word 'dog' into the Dutch equivalent 'hond', the semantically related distractor word 'paard' (horse) delays responding in comparison to an unrelated distractor word (La Heij et al., 1990) and the semantically related distractor picture of a horse speeds up responding in comparison to an unrelated distractor picture (Bloem & La Heij, 2003; La Heij et al., 1996).

For very different reasons, Bloem and La Heij (2003) already examined the effect of category-level distractors on basic-level naming in a backward translation task. The results of their experiment seem to confirm the observation of our Experiment 1a in that basic-level distractors and category-level distractors induced similar amounts of semantic interference. However, for our present purposes, the interpretation of Bloem and

La Heij's finding is somewhat troublesome, given a difference in the number of repetitions of the two types of distractors in their experiment. Therefore, Experiment 1b reexamined the effect of basic-level and category-level distractors in a word-translation task. To induce maximum impact of the distractor on target processing, target and distractor were presented in the same display position, separated by an SOA interval of 150 ms (see Bloem et al., 2004, for a similar procedure).

Method

Participants. Twenty Leiden University students participated in the experiment. They all were Dutch native speakers and had sufficient command of English to participate in the experiment. They all had normal or corrected to normal vision and received 3.50 euro for their participation.

Materials. Three English basic-level words (non-cognates) were selected from each of 10 different semantic categories. Each of these 30 words was presented with a semantically related and an unrelated distractor word from both the basic-level (BL) and the category level (CL). For example the stimulus 'car', that had to be translated into the Dutch word 'auto', was accompanied by the Dutch distractor words 'fiets' (bike; related BL), 'tomaat' (tomato; unrelated BL), 'voertuig' (vehicle; related CL) and 'groente' (vegetable; unrelated CL). For two categories, the target words and the category distractors had a part-of relation (e.g., leg-body and window-house). The unrelated-word condition was created by re-pairing the target words and the semantically related context words. In re-pairing the words, care was taken to prevent a phonological relation between the distractor and the correct response word. The basic-level and category-level distractors were matched as far as possible with respect to length (in letters and in syllables) and familiarity (de Vries, 1986). Familiarity ratings were not available for four of the category level words. The mean familiarity ratings of the remaining basic level and category level distractor words were 8.4 and 8.3, respectively (values on a 9-point scale). The mean length of the basic-level words was 4.4 letters and 1.4 syllables. The corresponding values of the category-level words were 6.0 and 1.6, respectively. So, with respect to length in letters no perfect match was achieved.

In total, the participants were presented with 120 experimental trials. The complete set of stimuli is shown in Appendix 1b. The to-be-translated English target word was always presented in black lower-case letters against a white background. The height and width of the target and context words were 1.4° × 2° of visual angle for 3-letter words up to 1.4° × 5° of visual angle for 8-letter words. The target words were positioned such that the second letter appeared at the point of fixation. The context words were presented in red letters, 1.4° degree of visual angle (centre to centre) below the target word. Viewing distance was approximately 80 cm.

Apparatus. The apparatus was the same as the one used in Experiment 1a.

Procedure. The participants had individual sessions in a dimly illuminated room. At the start of the session they were given a written instruction and a list containing the 30 English target words and their Dutch translations. The correct responses to the stimulus words were practiced by presentation on the screen before the sessions started. The experimental series were preceded by 10 practice trials that were randomly selected from the experimental materials. Each trial involved the following sequence. First, a fixation point was presented in the centre of the display for 500 ms. The stimulus appeared in black at the point of fixation for 150 ms and was immediately replaced by the red context word. The context word remained on the screen until the voice-key was triggered. The presentation of the stimuli was randomised with the restriction that a target word was not repeated within a series of six consecutive trials. The experimenter judged the response for correctness and entered a code into the computer. Malfunctioning of the voice-key could also be indicated.

Results

Response times were treated in the same way as in Experiment 1a. The following were excluded: 3.8% incorrect responses, 0.08% voice key errors, and 2.6% exceeding the 1500 ms cutoff criterion. The mean RTs and percentages of incorrect responses are shown in Table 1b.

An ANOVA with category level (basic level versus category level) and relatedness (semantically related versus unrelated) as within-participant

TABLE 1b

Reaction times in ms, percentage of error and semantic interference effects in the different conditions of Experiment 1b

Distractor type	Related		Unrelated		Semantic interference	
	RT	%e	RT	%e	RT	%e
Basic level	882	3.7	850	3.0	32	0.7
Category level	872	5.2	840	3.3	32	1.9

variables showed a significant main effect of relatedness, $F_1(1, 19) = 32.6$, $p < .001$ CI $= \pm 11.7$, $F_2(1, 29) = 23.4$, $p < .001$, CI $= \pm 13.9$. The effect of Level failed to reach significance $F_1(1, 19) = 2.4$ $p > .1$, CI $= \pm 20.5$, $F_2(1, 29) = 2.7, p > .1$, CI $= \pm 12.5$. Most importantly, the interaction between both factors was far from significant, $F_1 < 1$, $F_2 < 1$. In fact, the semantic interference effects produced by category-level and basic-level distractors were numerically identical (32 ms).

In the error analysis, the effect of semantic relatedness was nearly significant, $F_1(1, 19) = 3.7$, $p = .07$, CI $= \pm 0.5$, $F_2(1, 29) = 3.3$, $p = .08$, CI $= \pm 0.4$. The effect of Level was not significant $F_1(1, 19) = 2.1$, $p = .16$, CI $= \pm 0.2$, $F_2 < 1$, and the interaction was far from significant, $F_1 < 1$, $F_2 < 1$.

Discussion

In this experiment we replicated the finding that in a word-translation task related basic-level names induce semantic interference compared to unrelated basic level names (cf. La Heij et al., 1990, 1996). More important for our purposes is the observation that in a word-translation task, just as in the picture-naming task of Experiment 1a, category-level distractors induce semantic interference. This finding indicates semantic interference across levels of categorisation. This result contrasts sharply with the presence of semantic facilitation when pictures need to be categorised and distractors are basic-level names (e.g., Glaser & Düngelhoff, 1984). That is, our study in combination with related observations allows for the following empirical generalisation: a difference between the level of categorisation of the distractor and that of the target leads to semantic facilitation when the response is given at the category level and to semantic interference when the response is given at the basic level.

This empirical generalisation is at odds with the predictions derived from the semantic selection account. In contrast, the response congruency account predicted the outcome of these experiments correctly. As discussed above, this account predicts semantic facilitation when (a) target and distractor are semantically related and (b) target and context are response congruent. In the basic-level naming task employed in Experiments 1a and 1b, however, the target (e.g., couch) and the semantically related context word (e.g., 'furniture') clearly do not converge on the same response. Hence, the account predicts semantic interference instead of facilitation. In conclusion, the results obtained in Experiments 1a and 1b suggest that response congruency is an important determinant of the polarity of the semantic context effect in picture naming and word translation. In Experiment 2 we set out to investigate whether response congruency is a major contributor to this effect in categorisation tasks.

EXPERIMENT 2

Glaser and Düngelhoff's (1984) observation of semantic facilitation in picture categorisation can be accounted for in terms of response congruency, but it cannot be excluded that part of the effect is due to facilitation at the level of target identification (concept activation). For example, in the situation in which the picture of a dog has to be categorised as 'animal', the context word 'cat' may (a) facilitate target processing due to response congruency (the word 'cat' also leads to the correct response 'animal' in a categorisation task) but may also (b) facilitate target processing due to a process of spreading activation from the concept CAT to the concept DOG.[3]

To assess the relative contribution of response congruency and facilitation of target-concept activation, in Experiment 2 participants were asked to produce the category name (e.g., 'meubel', furniture) of a target while ignoring three types of distractor: (a) the correct basic-level name of the target (e.g., 'bank', couch), (b) a semantically related basic-level name (e.g., 'tafel', table), and (c) an unrelated basic-level name (e.g., 'hond', dog). In the first of these conditions, the semantically related context word is both response congruent and 'concept congruent'. That is, the context word and target converge on the same response but also on the same conceptual representation. In the second of these conditions, the semantically related context word is response congruent and may add to the activation of the target concept via a process of spreading activation. In the unrelated condition, the context word is not response congruent and does not speed up target identification. If a difference between the first two conditions is observed, this indicates that facilitation of concept activation may play a role in the overall semantic facilitation effect in categorisation tasks. If, however, the first two conditions show similar results, it seems likely that response congruency is the major contributor to the overall facilitation effect.

To our knowledge, there are two studies in which the results of these three conditions are reported. In the study of Glaser and Düngelhoff (1984) in which a picture-categorisation task was used, the facilitation effects induced by 'concept-congruent distractors' (correct basic-level words) and 'category-congruent distractors' (basic-level words from the same semantic category) were, averaged across the SOA conditions close to zero (−200 ms, −100 ms, 0 ms and +100 ms), 13 ms and 18 ms respectively. Although this finding suggests that there is no substantial

---

[3] Because the target concept used in the process of lexicalisation is 'animal', it seems unlikely that the context words 'cat' and 'dog' differentially affect the process of lexical selection.

effect of concept congruency, the facilitation effects varied too strongly across the SOA range to draw a firm conclusion. For instance, at SOA = −100 ms, the facilitation effect induced by category-congruent distractors was larger than the facilitation effect induced by concept-congruent distractors (29 ms and 4 ms respectively).

Glaser and Glaser (1989; Experiment 6) reported the results of a word-categorisation task with word distractors. Because it is generally assumed that word-categorisation is conceptually mediated, the results of this task are relevant for our current issue. Averaged across the two SOA values close to zero (−50 ms and +50 ms), the facilitation effects induced by correct basic-level words and words from the same semantic category (in comparison to the unrelated-word condition) were 127 ms and 79 ms, respectively. These findings suggest a concept-congruency effect of approximately 50 ms. However, as discussed by Damian and Bowers (2003) and La Heij, Heikoop, Akerboom, and Bloem (2003), Glaser and Glaser's results are difficult to interpret, because of the use of the 'sequential discrimination task'. In this task, target and context are presented above or below the central fixation point and the participants are instructed to react to the first or second stimulus that appears on the display. As has been shown by La Heij et al. (2003), this task is difficult to perform and incorrect selections are easily made. Clearly, target selection will be much easier when target and distractor are identical words, as in Glaser and Glaser's concept-congruent condition. So, this 'selection effect' alone may account for the 50 ms difference observed between the concept-congruent and category-congruent conditions.

To increase the sensitivity of the task for facilitation effects at the level of target identification, in Experiment 2, like in Experiment 1b, L2 words were presented as targets (see Bloem, van den Boogaart & La Heij, 2004, for a further discussion of this issue). In the experiment these L2 words (e.g., the English word 'couch') had to be responded to by their category names in Dutch ('meubel', furniture).

Method

Participants.   Twenty students from Leiden University took part in the experiment. They all had sufficient command of English to participate, had normal or corrected to normal vision and received 3.50 euro for their participation.

Materials.   The same target words were used as in Experiment 1b. For most target words, the correct response was the category name (e.g., 'voertuig', vehicle), sometimes abbreviated for ease of responding (e.g., 'lichaam', body, was used instead of 'lichaamsdeel', body part). For two sets of three target words a part-of relation was used: the words 'room', 'wall', and 'window' had to be responded to with 'house' and the words 'leg', 'chest', and 'face' had to be responded to with 'body'. None of the participants reported problems with this type of categorisation and the results obtained with these categories were not different from the results obtained in the other categories. Four sets of distractor words were used (examples are given for the target word 'bike'): (1) the correct Dutch translation equivalents of the target words ('fiets', bike), (2) the same set of words as under (1) re-paired with the target words to obtain unrelated pairs ('kast', cupboard), (3) basic-level words denoting objects from the same semantic category as the target word ('trein', train), and (4) the same set of words as under (3) re-paired with the targets to obtain unrelated pairs ('rood', red). Thus, the total number of trials in the experiment was 120 (30 target words × 4 sets of context words).

For the two sets of distractor words used, the correct Dutch basic-level names and the semantically related Dutch basic-level names were matched as far as possible with respect to length (in letters and in syllables) and familiarity (de Vries, 1986). Familiarity ratings were not available for two of the words in the semantically related list. The mean familiarity ratings of the remaining distractor words in the correct and semantically related lists were 8.22 and 8.20, respectively (values on a 9-point scale). The mean length of the words in the correct basic-level names list was 5.0 letters and 1.4 syllables. The corresponding values in the semantically related word list were 5.3 and 1.4, respectively. The complete set of stimuli is presented in Appendix 2.

Apparatus.   The apparatus was the same as the one used in Experiments 1a and 1b.

Procedure.   The procedure was identical to the one in Experiment 1b, with the only difference that the participants were instructed to produce the Dutch category name of the English target word.

Results and discussion

The following RTs were excluded: 10.0% incorrect responses and 0.8% voice key errors. The upper limit was set to 2000 ms (eliminating 0.5% of the data), because the response latencies in this categorisation task proved to be larger than those in the basic-level naming tasks of Experiments 1a and 1b. The mean reaction times and percentages of incorrect responses are shown in Table 2. ANOVAs were performed on these data with type of relation (correct versus semantically related) and relatedness (related versus unrelated) as within-participants factors. The effect of relatedness

TABLE 2

Reaction times in ms, percentages of error and facilitation effects in the various conditions of Experiment 2

Concept and response congruent		Unrelated		Facilitation	
RT	%e	RT	%e	RT	%e
1098	10.0	1121	11.8	23	1.8

Response congruent		Unrelated		Facilitation	
RT	%e	RT	%e	RT	%e
1093	8.0	1126	10.2	33	2.1

was significant $F_1(1, 19) = 7.5, p < .05$, CI $= \pm 20.9$, $F_2(1, 29) = 8.8, p < .01$, CI $= \pm 23.7$. The type of relation and the interaction were not significant, all $Fs < 1$. The error analysis did not yield any significant effects: relatedness, $F_1(1, 19) = 2.4, p = .14$, CI $= \pm 0.8$, $F_2(1, 29) = 2.0, p = .17$, CI $= \pm 0.6$, type of relation, $F_1(1, 19) = 2.4, p = .14$, CI $= \pm 0.7$, $F_2(1, 29) = 2.0, p = .17$, CI $= \pm 0.5$ and the interaction was far from significant, $F_1 < 1$, $F_2 < 1$.

The results of this experiment are in line with the picture-naming results reported by Glaser and Düngelhoff (1984). At SOA +150 ms, correct basic-level names facilitate categorisation responses. For instance, categorising the word 'bike' as 'voertuig' (vehicle) was facilitated by the Dutch translation equivalent 'fiets' (bike) in comparison to an unrelated Dutch context word (e.g., 'kast', cupboard). Most importantly, a similar amount of facilitation was observed when instead of the correct translation equivalent a different word from the target's semantic category was presented as context. For instance, categorising the word 'bike' was facilitated to the same degree by the context words 'fiets' (bike) and 'trein' (train). Since the two sets of context words only differed in the aspect 'concept congruency' and this difference did not influence the size of the facilitation effect, concept congruency does not contribute substantially to the facilitation effect induced by correct basic-level names in categorisation tasks. We conclude that response congruency is most probably a major contributor to semantic facilitation effects in categorisation tasks.

Up to now we have explored the contribution of response congruency in category-level and basic-level naming. We argued that such a principle seems to capture nicely the various results observed with semantically related distractors in these two tasks. A further test of this principle can be gathered if we consider a third level of categorisation, namely the subordinate level. At present, however, the findings regarding the effects of semantically related distractors in subordinate naming and in basic-level naming with subordinate distractors are rather inconsistent.

Vitkovitch and Tyrrell (1999) observed semantic facilitation from basic-level distractors in subordinate naming. For instance, the naming of the picture of a cobra as 'cobra' was facilitated by the related basic-level word 'snake' in comparison with the basic-level word 'table'. However, in a similar experiment, Hantsch, Jescheniak, and Schriefers (2005) observed semantic interference, a finding that is in line with our response congruency account. Unfortunately, in this latter study subordinate distractors induced semantic interference in basic-level naming, a result that runs counter the prediction derived from a response congruency interpretation.

Both in the Vitkovitch and Tyrrell (1999) study and in the Hantsch et al. (2005) study, the conventional picture-word paradigm was used. A potential problem with this paradigm is that a picture may be rather ambiguous with respect to level of categorisation. For example, it is not completely clear what the response should be in a basic-level naming task to the pictures of a crow, a cobra, a shark, or a chicken. Most likely, participants spontaneously use the names 'bird', 'snake', 'shark', and 'chicken', respectively. The first two of these responses are often categorised as basic-level names, and the latter two as sub-ordinate level names. Clearly, in this situation one of the defining characteristics of the basic level of categorisation, the preferred name of an object (Rosch, Mervis, Gray, Johnson, & Boyes-Bream, 1976), does not result in the same label as a definition based on the object's position in a natural hierarchy.

These problems can be resolved by using word targets (cf. Glaser & Glaser, 1989) since there is less doubt on what the level of categorisation a word is. More specific, with words there is little doubt whether two words are on the same level or on different levels of categorisation. For instance, the words shark and sparrow are on the same, subordinate level of categorisation, with as corresponding basic-level names fish and bird, respectively. To prevent problems with the categorisation level of pictures, in Experiment 3 we used a word categorisation task with context words to investigate whether the response congruency effect can also be found in lower levels of categorisation.

EXPERIMENT 3

In this experiment we further test the 'response congruency' hypothesis, by inspecting the effects of semantically related subordinate distractors in basic-level naming. In this experiment participants were asked to name subordinate level words (e.g., 'tulip') using their most common basic-level name ('flower'), while ignoring a related subordinate level distractor (e.g., 'rose') or an unrelated subordinate level distractor (e.g., 'volvo'). Because there is no need for using L2 words in the present experiment, stimuli and responses were presented in Dutch (L1).

Unless additional assumptions are made (like Roelofs', 1992, response set mechanism), current models of language production predict semantic interference in the present task. The reason is that – because of its semantic similarity to the correct response – the distractor word 'rose' will induce more lexical interference in responding 'flower' to the word 'tulip' than the distractor word 'volvo'. The response-congruency account, however, predicts semantic facilitation, because target and distractor converge on the same response when the task instruction – provide the basic-level name – is applied to both of them.

Method

Participants.   Twenty Dutch University students participated in this experiment and received 4 euros. They all had normal or corrected to normal vision.

Materials.   Twenty-one Dutch target words were selected from different basic level categories. These words were paired with another member of the same basic level for the related condition. The unrelated condition was made by re-pairing the related distractor words. Care was taken to prevent phonological or associative relations between target and context words. The resulting 42 target-distractor pairs were presented twice, thus each participant received a total of 84 experimental trials.

Apparatus.   The experiment was programmed in E-Prime (Psychology software tools, 2002) using a Pentium 4 computer and two monitors with a refresh rate of 100MHz. Response latencies were measured by means of a voice key.

Procedure.   The experiment took place in a dimly lit room with seating for two. The participant received an instruction on the monitor and was then presented with a sheet that contained the 21 target words and the corresponding basic level names. The participant was required to study the list and indicate when their preferred basic-level name did not match the basic-level name provided. None of the participants reported such a problem. Next, the target words were presented one by one in the display in isolation and the participants were required to produce the corresponding basic-level name as fast as possible. In a second practice series the participants were familiarised with the target-context stimuli. To that end, five stimuli were randomly chosen from the experimental materials. The presentation sequence in each of these trials and in the experimental series was identical to the one in Experiments 1b and 2. So, SOA was again set at +150 ms. The complete list of 42 stimuli was presented twice in a different randomised order. Target words were not repeated within a series of three consecutive trials.

Results and discussion

The reaction times were treated the same way as in Experiment 2. The excluded data were 2.6% wrong or long responses and 4.3% voice key errors. The mean RTs and errors are presented in Table 3. The data were analysed with an ANOVA with semantic relatedness as a within-participants factor. The effect of relatedness (30 ms) was significant: $F_1(1, 19) = 8.4$, $p < .01$, CI $= \pm 21.4$, $F_2(1, 20) = 9.3$, $p < .01$, CI $= \pm 26.0$. In the error analysis, the effect of relatedness was far from significant, all $Fs < 1$.

The finding of a semantic facilitation effect is clearly in line with the response congruency account and shows that response congruency also plays an important role in categorisation tasks in which subordinate levels of categorisation are involved. The present result is at variance with the recently reported findings of Hantsch et al. (2005), who obtained semantic interference in basic-level picture naming when using a subordinate, response-congruent distractor word. For instance, the word 'shark' hampered the naming of the picture of a shark as 'fish'. One possible explanation for this discrepancy is the fact that the participants in the Hantsch et al. study did not receive the instruction to respond to the pictures at a certain level of categorisation. Instead, they were simply instructed to respond to the target pictures with the verbal labels provided by the experimenter. It is conceivable that in that situation, the word 'fish' in response to the picture of a shark was not perceived as a categorisation response. If that is true, our account of facilitation in categorisation tasks in terms of 'applying the task instruction to both target and distractor' does not hold for the Hantsch et al. experiment.

TABLE 3

Reaction times in ms, percentage of error and semantic interference effects in the different conditions of Experiment 3

Distractor type	Related		Unrelated		Semantic interference	
	RT	%e	RT	%e	RT	%e
Subordinate level	912	2.7	942	2.5	30	−0.1

A final point that we want to discuss here is the fact that, with picture stimuli, preferred names do not always coincide with their basic-level names (see also Hantsch et al., 2005). The preferred name may depend on the context (participants will prefer 'cobra' when pictures of different snakes are used in the experiment, but will prefer 'snake' when no other snakes are present) and amount of detail in combination with the participant's familiarity with the object (some participants will prefer 'Porsche' as the name for a Porsche, whereas others will use the word 'car'). If there is uncertainty about the entry level of categorisation of the various pictures, inconsistencies in results may appear.

GENERAL DISCUSSION

Glaser and Düngelhoff (1984) and Costa et al. (2003) reported that picture categorisation is facilitated by semantically related, basic-level words in comparison with unrelated words. In the introduction we argued that models of language production provide no, or unsatisfactory explanations for this semantic facilitation effect. To account for the effect, we distinguished three possible approaches. The 'response set' account (Roelofs, 1992) was discarded on the basis of rather compelling evidence that distractors that are not part of the response set do compete for lexical selection. In the semantic-selection account, proposed by Costa et al. (2003) it is assumed that category-level information is embedded in the conceptual representations and that speakers can make use of this information to tease apart target and context information. This account predicts semantic facilitation in a categorisation task with basic-level distractors, but also semantic facilitation in a basic-level naming task with category distractors. This latter prediction was tested and disproved in Experiments 1a and 1b. Instead of facilitation, category names induced semantic interference, both in a picture-naming and in a word-translation task. The third account was phrased in terms of 'response congruency' and stated that semantic facilitation will occur in naming tasks whenever target and distractor converge on the same response, given the current task instruction. This account correctly predicted the results of Experiments 1a and 1b.

Glaser and Düngelhoff (1984) have shown that categorisation is not only facilitated by semantically related basic-level words, but – not surprisingly – also by the correct basic-level name of the target. For example, categorising the picture of a dog as 'animal' is not only facilitated by the word 'cat' but also by the word 'dog'. Experiment 2 investigated the relative contribution of response congruency and concept congruency to this latter finding. The results show that semantically related basic-level words and the correct basic-level names induce a comparable amount of facilitation, a finding that suggests that response congruency is a major determinant of the facilitation effects observed in categorisation tasks.

In Experiment 3 we tested the response congruency account in a situation in which targets and distractors are on the subordinate level and responses on the basic level of categorisation. We argued that the rather inconsistent results obtained in studies using the subordinate level of categorisation may have been due to differences in instruction: the instruction to name pictures at a certain level of categorisation versus the instruction to use predefined verbal labels in response to these pictures. In addition, we mentioned a potential problem in using pictures in categorisation tasks, given the fact that the preferred level of categorisation of other pictures seems to depend on the amount of detail provided and the specific set of stimuli used. Whereas the picture of a codfish is spontaneously named as 'fish', the picture of a shark is most often named as 'shark'. To eliminate the ambiguity in the level of categorisation of the targets, in Experiment 3 a word-categorisation task was used. In this experiment we tested and confirmed the prediction of the response-congruency account that a semantically related subordinate-level distractor word (e.g., 'rose') should facilitate the naming of a subordinate-level target (e.g., 'tulip') at the basic level (response: 'flower').

The response congruency account predicts that semantic facilitation will occur in all situations in which the context and target converge on the same response. This prediction is in line with a number of other findings. First, naming the picture of an object in a second language (L2) is facilitated by the picture's name in the first language (L1) (Costa & Caramazza, 1999; Costa, Miozzo, & Caramazza, 1999). Here, the instruction 'provide the English name of . . .' leads to the same response when applied to the target picture (e.g., of a dog) and when applied to the context word (e.g., the Dutch translation equivalent of the word dog: 'hond'). A semantically related L1 context word (e.g., kat, 'cat') should not induce facilitation, because it does not lead to the same response as the target. Indeed, reported semantic interference effects of L1 basic-level words in L2 picture naming have been reported (Costa et al., 1999; Hermans, Bongaerts, de Bot, & Schreuder, 1998).

Second, the response-congruency account also predicts facilitation effects in a function-naming task with distractors that are associated with the same or a different function. For instance, the response 'to wear' to the target word 'trousers' should be facilitated by the context picture of a shirt in comparison to the unrelated picture of a tree. Recently, Kuipers and La Heij (2006) tested and confirmed this prediction.

Finally, effects of response congruency are also observed in Stroop-like colour categorisation tasks. Glaser and Glaser (1989; Footnote 5) briefly mentioned the results of a Stroop task in which the participants were required to categorise colour words and colours as 'warm' (red and yellow) or 'cold' (blue and green). In line with our response congruency principle, they observed a complete reversal of the usual asymmetry in Stroop interference: words hardly interfered with colour categorisation whereas the categorisation of words (e.g., the categorisation of the word 'green' as 'cold') was hampered by the response-incongruent colour yellow in comparison to the response-congruent colour blue.

To conclude, current models of lexical access are able to account for semantic interference effects in basic-level naming, but have difficulty in accounting for semantic facilitation effects in category naming. Our present results indicate that the response congruency of target and distractor is a major factor in accounting for the polarity of semantic context effects in naming tasks. If this conclusion is correct, it is interesting to speculate about the locus of the response congruency effect in language production. On the basis of our present findings and those of Bloem and La Heij (2003) and Bloem et al. (2004), we propose that the effect is localised at a processing level that Kempen (1977; see also Levelt, 1989) referred to as 'conceptualising'; the level at which a 'preverbal message' is constructed on the basis of (a) the stimuli presented and (b) the current task instruction. If this interpretation is correct, context stimuli may affect target processing in at least three processing stages. First, semantic facilitation may occur in a stage of target identification. Through, for instance, a process of spreading activation, a semantically related context may facilitate the activation of the target concept. Semantic facilitation induced by context pictures in a word-translation task (Bloem & La Heij, 2003; La Heij et al., 1996) may largely be localised at this processing level.

Second, context effects may be localised at a stage of conceptualisation. Context stimuli may facilitate this process when – given the task instruction – target and context converge on the same preverbal message. This process may underlie facilitation in categorisation tasks, including the 'warm-cold' colour-classification task briefly discussed by Glaser and Glaser (1989). If this interpretation is correct, the term 'response congruency' may better be replaced by 'message congruency', to avoid confusion with later processing stages.

Finally, interference effects may arise at the level of lexical selection. Most models (but see Costa et al., 2003) assume that this is the level at which context words induce semantic interference. We suggest that semantically related context words may always induce lexical interference, but that this effect can be outweighed by larger facilitation effects at the earlier two processing stages. Indeed, Kuipers and La Heij (2006) report results indicating that the effects of message congruency are larger than the semantic interference effects usually obtained in picture-word interference tasks.

It should be stressed that in our proposal one and the same context stimulus may – to some degree – affect each of these three processing stages. As discussed above, in a picture-categorisation task with word context (e.g., the target picture of a dog with the distractors 'cat' or 'pen'), a semantically related context word may facilitate target identification, facilitate the construction of a preverbal message and hamper lexical selection. In this task the former two effects may outweigh the latter (see Navarrete and Costa, 2005 for a similar argument). In a word-translation task with picture context (e.g., the L2 target word 'dog' with the distractor pictures of a cat or a pen), a semantically related context picture may strongly facilitate target identification, and have little effect on conceptualisation and lexical selection (see Bloem et al., 2004), resulting in an overall semantic facilitation effect.

To summarise, in this article we set out to provide an explanation for the semantic facilitation effect in categorisation tasks. We conclude that this effect is most probably not due to the elimination of lexical interference (Roelofs, 1992) nor to the facilitation of selection at a semantic level (Costa et al., 2003). Instead, the effect may result from facilitation at the level of conceptualisation: the preparation of a preverbal message. It should be noted that the reintroduction of this processing level not only provides an attractive explanation for semantic facilitation in category naming, but may also provide a useful starting point for future studies on executive control in naming tasks.

REFERENCES

Bloem, I., & La Heij, W. (2003). Semantic facilitation and semantic interference in word translation: Implications for models of lexical access in language production. *Journal of Memory and Language, 48*, 468–488.

Bloem, I., van den Boogaard, S., & La Heij, W. (2004). Semantic facilitation and semantic interference in language production: Further evidence for the Conceptual Selection Model of lexical access. *Journal of Memory and Language, 51*, 307–323.

Caramazza, A., & Costa, A. (2000). The semantic interference effect in the picture-word interference paradigm: Does the response set matter? *Cognition, 75*, 51–64.

Caramazza, A., & Costa, A. (2001). Set size and repetition in the picture-word interference paradigm: implications for models of naming. *Cognition, 80*, 291–298.

Costa, A., Alario, F. X., & Caramazza, A. (2005). On the categorical nature of the semantic interference effect in the picture-word interference paradigm. *Psychonomic Bulletin and Review, 12*, 125–131.

Costa, A., & Caramazza, A. (1999). Is lexical selection in bilingual speech production language-specific? Further evidence from Spanish–English and English–Spanish bilinguals. *Bilingualism: Language and Cognition, 2*, 231–244.

Costa, A., Mahon, B., Savova, V., & Caramazza, A. (2003). Level of Categorisation effect: A novel effect in the picture-word paradigm. *Language and Cognitive Processes, 18*, 205–233.

Costa, A., Miozzo, M., & Caramazza, A. (1999). Lexical selection in bilinguals: Do words in the bilingual's two lexicons compete for selection? *Journal of Memory and Language, 41*, 365–397.

Damian, M. F., & Bowers, J. S. (2003). Locus of semantic interference in picture-word interference tasks. *Psychonomic Bulletin and Review, 10*, 111–117.

De Vries, K. L. M. (1986). Vertrouwdheid van woorden en woordherkenning [Familiarity of words and word recognition]. *Nederlands Tijdschrift voor de Psychologie, 41*, 295–304.

Eriksen, B. A., & Eriksen, C. W. (1974). Effects of noise letters upon the identification of a target letter in a nonsearch task. *Perception and Psychophysics, 16* (1), 143–149.

Glaser, W. R., & Düngelhoff, F. J. (1984). The time course of picture-word interference. *Journal of Experimental Psychology: Human Perception and Performance, 10*, 640–654.

Glaser, W. R., & Glaser, M. O. (1989). Context effects in Stroop-like word and picture processing. *Journal of Experimental Psychology: General, 118*, 13–42.

Hantsch, A., Jescheniak, J. D., & Schriefers, H. J. (2005). Semantic competition between hierarchically related words during speech planning. *Memory and Cognition, 33*, 984–1000.

Hermans, D., Bongaerts, T., de Bot, K., & Schreuder, R. (1998). Producing words in a foreign language: Can speakers prevent interference from their first language? *Bilingualism, Language and Cognition, 1*, 213–229.

Humphreys, G. W., Lloyd-Jones, T. J., & Fias, W. (1995). Semantic interference effects on naming using a postcue procedure: Tapping the links between semantics and phonology with pictures and words. *Journal of Experimental Psychology: Learning, Memory, and Cognition, 21*, 961–980.

Kempen, G. (1977). Conceptualizing and formulating in sentence production. In S. Rosenberg (Ed.), *Sentence production: Developments in research and theory*. Hillsdale, NJ: Lawrence Erlbaum.

Kroll, J. F., & Stewart, E. (1994). Category interference in translation and picture naming: Evidence for asymmetric connections between bilingual memory representations. *Journal of Memory and Language, 13*, 149–174.

Kuipers J. R., & La Heij, W. (2006). *Semantic facilitation in category and action naming: Testing the message-congruency account*. Manuscript submitted for publication.

La Heij, W. (1988). Components of Stroop-like interference in picture naming. *Memory and Cognition, 16*, 400–410.

La Heij, W., de Bruyn, E., Elens, E., Hartsuiker, R., Helaha, D., & Van Schelven, L. (1990). Orthographic facilitation and categorical interference in a word-translation variant of the Stroop task. *Canadian Journal of Experimental Psychology, 44*, 76–83.

La Heij, W., Heikoop, K. W., Akerboom, S., & Bloem, I. (2003). Picture naming in picture context: Semantic interference or semantic facilitation? *Psychology Science, 45*, 49–62.

La Heij, W., Starreveld, P. A., & Steehouwer, L. C. (1993). Semantic interference and orthographic facilitation in definition naming. *Journal of Experimental Psychology: Learning, Memory, and Cognition, 19*, 352–368.

La Heij, W., Hooglander, A., Kerling, R., & Van der Velden, E. (1996). Nonverbal context effects in forward and backward word translation: Evidence for concept mediation. *Journal of Memory and Language, 35*, 648–665.

Levelt, W. J. M. (1989). *Speaking: From intention to articulation*. Cambridge, MA: MIT Press.

Levelt, W. J. M., Roelofs, A., & Meyer, A. S. (1999). A theory of lexical access in speech production. *Behavioral and Brain Sciences, 22*, 1–75.

Loftus, G. R., & Masson, M. E. J. (1994). Using confidence intervals in within-subject designs. *Psychonomic Bulletin and Review, 1*, 476–490.

Lupker, S. J., & Katz, A. N. (1981). Input, decision, and response factors in picture-word interference. *Journal of Experimental Psychology: Human Learning and Memory, 7*, 269–282.

Navarrete, E., & Costa, A. (2005). Phonological activation of ignored pictures: Further evidence for a cascaded model of lexical access. *Journal of Memory and Language, 53,* 359–377.

Psychology Software Tools (2002). E-Prime. http://www.pstnet.com.

Roelofs, A. (1992). A spreading-activation theory of lemma retrieval in speaking. *Cognition, 42,* 107–142.

Roelofs, A. (2001). Set size and repetition matter: comment on Caramazza and Costa (2000), *Cognition, 80,* 283–290.

Rosch, E., Mervis, C. B., Gray, W., Johnson, D., & Boyes-Bream, P. (1976). Basic objects in natural categories. *Cognitive Psychology, 8,* 382–439.

Schneider, W. (1988). Micro experimental laboratory: An integrated system for IBM-PC compatibles. *Behavior Research Methods, Instruments, and Computers, 20,* 206–217.

Schriefers, H., Meyer A. S., & Levelt, W. J. M. (1990). Exploring the time course of lexical access in language production: picture-word interference studies. *Journal of Memory and Language, 29,* 86–102.

Snodgrass, J. G., & Vanderwart, M. (1980). A standardized set of 260 pictures: Norms for name agreement, image agreement, familiarity, and visual complexity. *Journal of Experimental Psychology: Human Learning and Memory, 6,* 174–215.

Starreveld, P. A., & La Heij, W. (1996). Time-course analysis of semantic and orthographic context effects in picture naming. *Journal of Experimental Psychology: Learning, Memory, and Cognition, 22,* 896–918.

Starreveld, P. A., & La Heij, W. (1999). What about phonological facilitation, response-set membership, and phonological co-activation? *Behavioral and Brain Sciences, 22,* 56–58.

Vitkovitch, M., & Tyrrell, L. (1999). The effects of distractor words on naming pictures at the subordinate level. *Quarterly Journal of Experimental Psychology: Human Experimental Psychology, 52A,* 905–926.

APPENDIX 1a

Stimulus materials used in Experiment 1a

		Related Distractors		Unrelated Distractors	
Picture	Response	BL	CL	BL	CL
car	auto	trein (train)	voertuig (vehicle)	banaan	groente
bicycle	fiets	trein (train)	voertuig (vehicle)	tafel	meubel
motorbike	motor	trein (train)	voertuig (vehicle)	tomaat	insect
onion	ui	tomaat (tomato)	groente (vegetable)	fabriek	kleding
carrot	wortel	tomaat (tomato)	groente (vegetable)	geweer	gebouw
lettuce	sla	tomaat (tomato)	groente (vegetable)	tafel	vogel
couch	bank	tafel (table)	meubel (furniture)	tomaat	voertuig
closet	kast	tafel (table)	meubel (furniture)	banaan	wapen
chair	stoel	tafel (table)	meubel (furniture)	geweer	sieraad
lemon	citroen	banaan (banana)	vrucht (fruit)	trein	sieraad
pear	peer	banaan (banana)	vrucht (fruit)	vlieg	meubel
cherry	kers	banaan (banana)	vrucht (fruit)	fabriek	wapen
dress	jurk	sok (sock)	kleding (clothes)	kraai	vrucht
trousers	broek	sok (sock)	kleding (clothes)	trein	voertuig
coat	jas	sok (sock)	kleding (clothes)	fabriek	insect
owl	uil	kraai (crow)	vogel (bird)	sok	kleding
duck	eend	kraai (crow)	vogel (bird)	trein	groente
vulture	gier	kraai (crow)	vogel (bird)	oorbel	sieraad
ant	mier	vlieg (fly)	insect (insect)	sok	meubel
mosquito	mug	vlieg (fly)	insect (insect)	trein	kleding
spider	spin	vlieg (fly)	insect (insect)	oorbel	wapen
church	kerk	fabriek (factory)	gebouw (building)	tomaat	vogel
house	huis	fabriek (factory)	gebouw (building)	kraai	groente
castle	kasteel	fabriek (factory)	gebouw (building)	vlieg	vrucht
necklace	ketting	oorbel (earring)	sieraad (jewellery)	tafel	gebouw
watch	horloge	oorbel (earring)	sieraad (jewellery)	banaan	voertuig
ring	ring	oorbel (earring)	sieraad (jewellery)	vlieg	insect
canon	kanon	geweer (rifle)	wapen (weapon)	sok	vrucht
knife	mes	geweer (rifle)	wapen (weapon)	kraai	vogel
pistol	pistool	geweer (rifle)	wapen (weapon)	oorbel	gebouw

APPENDIX 1b

Stimulus materials used in Experiment 1b

Picture	Response	Related Distractors		Unrelated Distractors	
		BL	CL	BL	CL
car	auto	trein (train)	voertuig (vehicle)	tomaat	groente
bike	fiets	trein (train)	voertuig (vehicle)	tafel	meubel
plane	vliegtuig	trein (train)	voertuig (vehicle)	banaan	beroep
onion	ui	tomaat (tomato)	groente (vegetable)	bakker	kleding
carrot	wortel	tomaat (tomato)	groente (vegetable)	trein	kleur
lettuce	sla	tomaat (tomato)	groente (vegetable)	tafel	dier
couch	bank	tafel (table)	meubel (furniture)	tomaat	vrucht
closet	kast	tafel (table)	meubel (furniture)	banaan	lichaam
chair	stoel	tafel (table)	meubel (furniture)	bakker	huis
grape	druif	banaan (banana)	vrucht (fruit)	bakker	beroep
lemon	citroen	banaan (banana)	vrucht (fruit)	trein	meubel
cherry	kers	banaan (banana)	vrucht (fruit)	rood	dier
dress	jurk	sok (sock)	kleding (clothes)	arm	vrucht
trousers	broek	sok (sock)	kleding (clothes)	kat	voertuig
coat	jas	sok (sock)	kleding (clothes)	dak	huis
yellow	geel	rood (red)	kleur (color)	kat	voertuig
black	zwart	rood (red)	kleur (color)	arm	lichaam
purple	paars	rood (red)	kleur (color)	sok	meubel
horse	paard	kat (cat)	dier (animal)	arm	beroep
lion	leeuw	kat (cat)	dier (animal)	dak	vrucht
pig	varken	kat (cat)	dier (animal)	rood	kleding
lawyer	advocaat	bakker (baker)	beroep (occupation)	tomaat	groente
teacher	leraar	bakker (baker)	beroep (occupation)	banaan	huis
dentist	tandarts	bakker (baker)	beroep (occupation)	rood	meubel
leg	been	arm (arm)	lichaam (body)	sok	voertuig
chest	borst	arm (arm)	lichaam (body)	tafel	kleur
face	gezicht	arm (arm)	lichaam (body)	dak	huis
room	kamer	dak (roof)	huis (house)	trein	groente
wall	muur	dak (roof)	huis (house)	kat	dier
window	raam	dak	huis (house)	sok	kleding

APPENDIX 2
Stimulus materials used in Experiment 2

Stimulus	Response	Congruent distractors	Related distractors	Unrelated distractors	
car	voertuig	auto	bus (bus)	geel	rok
bike	voertuig	fiets	trein (train)	kast	rood
plane	voertuig	vliegtuig	brommer (moped)	wortel	tafel
onion	groente	ui	erwt (pea)	muur	enkel
carrot	groente	wortel	tomaat (tomato)	druif	douche
lettuce	groente	sla	spruitje (sprout)	borst	kapper
couch	meubel	bank	tafel (table)	jas	hond
closet	meubel	kast	bed (bed)	jurk	bakker
chair	meubel	stoel	kruk (stool)	auto	hemd
grape	vrucht	druif	peer (pear)	ui	trui
lemon	vrucht	citroen	aardbei (strawberry)	vliegtuig	vogel
cherry	vrucht	kers	pruim (plum)	leeuw	oranje
dress	kleding	jurk	hemd (shirt)	sla	trein
trousers	kleding	broek	trui (sweater)	raam	aardbei
coat	kleding	jas	rok (skirt)	fiets	groen
yellow	kleur	geel	rood (red)	broek	peer
black	kleur	zwart	groen (green)	leraar	deur
purple	kleur	paars	oranje (orange)	advocaat	spruitje
horse	dier	paard	vogel (bird)	stoel	knie
lion	dier	leeuw	hond (dog)	paars	kruk
pig	dier	varken	kip (chicken)	tandarts	bus
lawyer	beroep	advocaat	piloot (pilot)	kers	pruim
teacher	beroep	leraar	kapper (barber)	kamer	brommer
dentist	beroep	tandarts	bakker (baker)	citroen	tomaat
leg	lichaam	been	hand (hand)	paard	kip
chest	lichaam	borst	knie (knee)	bank	erwt
face	lichaam	gezicht	enkel (ankle)	varken	gang
room	huis	kamer	gang (hall)	gezicht	hand
wall	huis	muur	douche (shower)	zwart	bed
window	huis	raam	deur (door)	been	piloot

APPENDIX 3

Stimulus materials used in Experiment 3

Target	Response	Related distractor	Unrelated distractor
roos (rose)	bloem (flower)	tulp (tulip)	forel (trout)
volvo (idem)	auto (car)	skoda (idem)	adder (idem)
merrie (mare)	paard (horse)	hengst (stallion)	heineken (idem)
cobra (idem)	slang (snake)	adder (viper)	ijssel (idem)
poedel (poodle)	hond (dog)	tekkel (idem)	telegraaf (idem)
villa (idem)	huis (house)	flat (idem)	kraai (crow)
bordeaux (idem)	wijn (wine)	bourgonje (idem)	konmar (idem)
mus (sparrow)	vogel (bird)	kraai (crow)	sloep (cutter)
grolsch (idem)	bier (beer)	heineken (idem)	elstar (idem)
parool (idem)	krant (newspaper)	telegraaf (idem)	sinas (idem)
c1000 (idem)	supermarkt (supermarket)	konmar (idem)	tulp (tulip)
detective (idem)	boek (book)	roman (novel)	gorilla (idem)
goudreinet (idem)	appel (apple)	elstar (idem)	bourgonje (idem)
elle (idem)	tijdschrift (magazine)	story (idem)	berk (birch)
eik (oak)	boom (tree)	berk (birch)	fokker (idem)
maas (idem)	rivier (river)	ijssel (idem)	story (idem)
kano (canoe)	boot (boat)	sloep (cutter)	roman (novel)
boeing (idem)	vliegtuig (airplane)	fokker (idem)	hengst (stallion)
bonobo (idem)	aap (monkey)	gorilla (idem)	skoda (idem)
zalm (salmon)	vis (fish)	forel (trout)	flat (idem)
cola (idem)	frisdrank (soda)	sinas (idem)	tekkel (idem)

LANGUAGE AND COGNITIVE PROCESSES
2006, 21 (7–8), 920–944

A chatterbox is a box:
Morphology in German word production

Heidi Gumnior, Jens Bölte, and Pienie Zwitserlood

Westfälische Wilhelms-Universität Münster, Münster, Germany

Two experiments are reported in which university students translated visually presented English words into German, while German distractor words were simultaneously presented. Distractors were morphologically related, merely form-related or unrelated to the German translations (target words). The transparency of the semantic relation between target words and morphological distractors was also varied. Morphological distractors facilitated word-translation latencies irrespective of their semantic transparency, replicating results obtained with other tasks. Thus, in German word production, effects of morphological complexity seem to be largely independent of semantics. Morphological facilitation is also not due to mere form relatedness, since phonological distractors had no impact on translation latencies, relative to unrelated distractors. Our data corroborate the usefulness of word-translation for investigating spoken word production, in particular, for morphological processing.

INTRODUCTION

The generation of spoken words is normally a fast and effortless process which proceeds from meaning to sound. The non-linguistic information that speakers convey has to be transformed by several linguistic processes, before eventually the appropriate articulatory gestures are produced. In the research presented here, we concentrate on the role of morphology at the interface between speech production and comprehension. Our aims are

Correspondence should be addressed to Heidi Gumnior, Westfälische Wilhelms-Universität Münster, Psychologisches Institut II, Fliedner Str. 21, Münster 48149, Germany. E-mail: gumnior@psy.uni-muenster.de

We thank F.-Xavier Alario, Marc Brysbaert and two anonymous reviewers for helpful comments on an earlier version of this manuscript. We would also like to thank Ann-Kathrin Bröckelmann for her help with the selection of materials and running the experiments.

http://www.psypress.com/lcp   DOI: 10.1080/016909600824278

twofold. First, we investigate the nature and structure of lexical representations used in speaking, by assessing the impact of morphologically complex words on the production of simple words. Since most speech production experiments focus on semantic or phonological processing, data on morphology are still quite meagre. Second, we evaluate the suitability of a variant of the word translation task for these purposes. Most research on word production relies on the picture-word interference paradigm. The fact that this task requires concrete, depictable objects poses clear restrictions on the materials which can be used. This is particularly violent for the issue of morphology. If it is shown that picture-word interference and word translation generate similar results, these limitations can be overcome.

Morphology in speech production is a relatively new field of experimental research. This contrasts with the plethora of studies in word recognition, with the diverse theoretical implementations based on data from such studies, and with the clear role of morphology in theories of speech production (Dell, 1986; Levelt, Roelofs, & Meyer, 1999). Taking the model by Levelt and colleagues (Levelt et al., 1999) as an example, monomorphemic words, and words with a degenerate morphology (e.g., *replicate*), have single units at each processing level. This is different for morphologically complex words (e.g., *outsource, handbag, lively*) and idioms (e.g., *to bite the dust*). For most morphologically complex words, a single concept node activates a single lemma node (which codes syntactic properties of a word), which in turn activates multiple, morpheme-sized nodes at a word-form stratum. This holds equally for semantically transparent and opaque complex words (e.g., *blackbird* and *jailbird*). Complex words which are novel or of low frequency can have more than one lemma and obviously more than one morpheme at the form level. So, in the model by Levelt et al., a word's morphological complexity is always coded in a decomposed way at the form level, regardless of the degree of decomposition at the lemma or concept level. The model proposed by Dell (Dell, 1986), which has a different architecture, also has morphemes as the core units at the form level.

From a broader theoretical perspective, taking models of language comprehension into account, the obligatory decomposed representation of morphologically complex words represents one extreme position on a continuum. The other extreme denotes that complex words are stored as whole-word units (Butterworth, 1983; Manelis & Tharp, 1977). Between these poles are various graded positions, for instance that decomposition is restricted to infrequent words (Caramazza, Laudanna & Romani, 1988; Chialant & Caramazza, 1995; Schreuder & Baayen, 1995), to semantically transparent words (Marslen-Wilson, Tyler, Waksler, & Older, 1994; Schreuder & Baayen, 1995), or that there is a race between decomposed and whole-word access units (Baayen & Schreuder, 1999; Frauenfelder & Schreuder, 1992).

Clearly, such models are based on results from comprehension studies, which cannot be automatically generalized to production. Interestingly, comprehension models do not explicitly incorporate purely syntactic lemma nodes, which play such an important role in the model by Levelt et al. (1999). Syntactic features of words are stored with the lexical representation of a word, but it is often not spelled out whether this information is hooked up to form representations, to semantic representations or to more abstract lexical nodes.[1] This has consequences for the potential locus of morphological effects derived from paradigms which rely on both comprehension and production, as we will discuss.

Initially, speech production models took their data from sources other than experiments. Evidence from linguistics, speech errors, and language disorders motivated a separate role for morphemes in production (cf. Garrett, 1975; Levelt, 1989). Speech errors that involve the misordering of morphemic units (e.g., *slicely thinned* instead of *thinly sliced*, Stemberger, 1985) indicate that speakers use morphemes as processing units in speech production. Data from aphasic patients who, when in search of existing words, produce novel combinations of morphemes (e.g., *poorless*) also support this (Badecker & Caramazza, 1991). In general, all of us are able to create and understand new words composed of familiar parts – usually morphemes. This competence draws on knowledge of the internal morphological structure of words. In German, for example, compounding results in a large number of lexical items. Often, linking elements have to be inserted in compounds, e.g., *Rindfleisch* (beef) vs. *Rinderfilet* (roast beef). Linking elements are phonologically motivated, but take morphemes as relevant units. Native speakers know which linking element belongs to which combination, and also, which combinations of compound constituents and linking elements are in principle acceptable. They use this knowledge to construct novel compounds, such as *Rücktrittsangebot* (offer to resign one's position).

Without diminishing the value of data of the type mentioned above, experiments are necessary to corroborate models developed on their basis. The experimental investigation of morphological structure in speech production poses quite some problems. First, it is generally difficult to elicit specific spoken utterances under controlled conditions. Second, it is particularly intricate to separate effects of morphological structure from those due to semantic relatedness and phonological similarity. Whereas it is difficult enough to find materials suitable for an interesting contrast of

---

[1] Allen and Badecker (2002) propose a lemma level in comprehension which encompasses both semantic and syntactic information.

morphological, semantic, or form similarity, and to present them for comprehension, it is a major feat when speaking is at issue. Only two paradigms have been used so far: implicit priming and picture-word interference, the data of which we will summarize below. Given this scarcity of tasks, we tested the suitability of another speech production paradigm: the word translation task, from L2 (English) into L1 (German). Research has shown that this task taps into semantic and lexical knowledge (La Heij, Kuipers, & Costa, 2006; Vigliocco, Lauer, Damian, & Levelt, 2002; Wheeldon & Levelt, 1995). In particular, we employed the variant which combines targets for translation with distractor words (La Heij, de Bruyn, Elens, Hartsuiker, Helaha, & van Schelven, 1990).

As stated before, investigations of morphological processing in speaking are rare. With a paradigm known as implicit priming (Meyer, 1990, 1991), Roelofs investigated morphological planning in speech production (Roelofs, 1996, 1998). In this paradigm, speakers first have to learn a set of prompt-response pairs such as *keyboard – input, knowledge – insight, air – inflow*. During a subsequent test phase they have to produce a learned response as fast as possible when a prompt (e.g., *knowledge*) is shown. The same response words occur in two sets. In a homogeneous set, the response words share part of their form (e.g., *input, insight, inflow*), whereas response words in heterogeneous sets are unrelated (e.g., *input, misprint, uptake*). The overlap in homogeneous sets enables the speaker to prepare part of the response before prompts are presented, which is not possible in heterogeneous sets. Studies have shown that production latencies (i.e., the interval between prompt onset and speech onset) are smaller in homogeneous than in heterogeneous sets. Meyer (1990, 1991) observed preparation effects for monomorphemic words with word-initial form overlap (e.g., *weaver, weasel, wheedle*). Roelofs (1996, 1998) found that the size of the preparation effect was larger when the overlapping first syllable constituted a morpheme (e.g., *input*) than when it did not (e.g., *Indian*).

Zwitserlood, Bölte, and Dohmes (2000, 2002) used picture-word interference to investigate morphological processing in speech production. In this paradigm, pictures that are to be named are combined with distractor words which have to be ignored (cf. Glaser & Düngelhoff, 1984; Lupker, 1982). Distractor words were morphologically, phonologically, or semantically related to the picture name. Morphological similarity in German, as in many languages, is naturally confounded with semantic and phonological relatedness (e.g., *flowery* is semantically, phonologically, and morphologically related to the picture name *flower*). To prove that morphological complexity has a separate representational status, it is essential to disentangle effects due to phonological, semantic, and morphological similarity. With a delayed variant of picture-word interference (word and picture were separated by a lag of 7–10 intervening trials) Zwitserlood et al. could separate morphological from semantic and phonological effects. No impact of semantic or phonological relatedness was evident with long lags between distractor and picture, but morphological facilitation survived.

An interesting opportunity to test for the independence of morphological and semantic representations is provided by morphologically complex words that are semantically opaque. The meaning of a morphologically complex word is often not straightforwardly related to the meaning of its constituent morphemes. Whereas the meaning of a semantically transparent compound (e.g., *butter knife*) is derivable from the meaning of its constituent morphemes, this does not hold for semantically opaque compounds (e.g., *butterfly*). Effects of semantic transparency can be observed in comprehension studies (see Feldman, 2000, for an overview). Feldman suggests that if a particular paradigm or task is sensitive to semantic effects, differences are observed between semantically opaque and semantically transparent words that are both morphologically related to the target word. No differences between transparent and opaque prime words are observed with long-lagged priming, a paradigm which is insensitive to semantic effects in comprehension. Small but mostly reliable differences in the amount of priming caused by transparent and opaque words are reported when primes and targets are presented in close temporal vicinity (Bentin & Feldman, 1990, for Hebrew; Feldman, Soltano, Pastizzo, & Francis, 2004, for English; Zwitserlood, 1994, for Dutch). To take the Zwitserlood study as an example, morphologically related opaque compounds (drankorgel, drunkard) produced about 40 ms of priming to their target (e.g., orgel, organ), compared with an unrelated control. Morphologically and semantically related primes (kerkorgel, church organ) showed a larger effect (54 ms). Thus, an additional semantic relationship adds to the facilitation, but this facilitation cannot be reduced to semantic relatedness. Clearly, the bulk of the effect is purely morphological.

In contrast, production experiments comparing morphological effects with effects of shared meaning do not reveal effects of semantic transparency. Roelofs and Baayen (2002) examined the status of morphological constituents of opaque complex words with implicit priming. They compared the preparation effect for transparent (e.g., *input*), opaque (e.g., *invoice*), and morphologically simple nouns (e.g., *Indian*). Again, a larger preparation effect was found when the shared initial segment constituted a morpheme than when it did not. Interestingly, the morphological preparation effect for opaque nouns was almost the same as for transparent nouns. The authors argue that morphemes are planning units in the production of complex words, but that semantic transparency is not essential for morphological preparation.

Similar issues were addressed by Dohmes, Zwitserlood, and Bölte (2004) with picture-word interference. They investigated whether semantically transparent (e.g., *Buschrose*, bush rose) and semantically opaque compounds (e.g., *Gürtelrose*, shingles) differ in their efficiency as distractor words in picture naming (e.g., picture of a rose). In addition, monomorphemic words such as *Neurose* (neurosis) which completely contain the target were used to evaluate the contribution of mere form overlap. Dohmes et al. found a robust morphological effect in the standard, immediate variant of picture-word interference (in which pictures and distractors are presented in close temporal vicinity) as well as in the delayed variant. The presence of a morphologically complex word facilitated the subsequent production of one of its constituents: the picture name. Again, as with implicit priming, facilitation was almost identical for semantically transparent and opaque compounds, corroborating the independence of morphology from semantics. Form-related distractors facilitated picture naming only in the immediate variant, and to a lesser degree than morphologically related distractors.

In sum: The available data from two speech production tasks provide evidence for a role of morphology separate from semantics and phonology. Compared with the wealth of data from language comprehension, the evidence is still scarce. As pointed out earlier, this is mainly due to the lack of suitable paradigms. Implicit priming and picture-word interference both have their drawbacks. Implicit priming allows for only very small material sets, because participants can only learn a limited amount of pairs during the learning phase. Moreover, preparation effects are only observed when the overlap is at word onset. No facilitation is found for overlap of non-initial morphemes (e.g., *handbook, cookbook*) or prefixed verbs (e.g., *indoen - uitdoen*, put in – take off; Roelofs, 1996). The picture-word interference paradigm fares better here, showing facilitation with non-initial overlap between distractors and picture names (e.g., *cookbook* – picture of a book; Dohmes et al., 2004; Zwitserlood et al., 2000, 2002).

Picture-word interference looks at any issue in word production, including morphology, in an indirect manner. The distractor is morphologically complex, while the target for speaking is morphologically simple. Such an indirect approach is typical for the paradigm, which intrinsically relies on the interface of comprehension and production and, more or less explicitly stated, on shared or connected representations. But the picture-word interference paradigm also has its limitations. Obviously, it can only be applied to words that can be depicted. In the published literature on morphology in speaking, only pictures of concrete objects have been used. Alternative tasks that can elicit spoken utterances for a wide range of concepts, not only those that can be presented as pictures, would be useful for many questions and for morphology in particular. For this reason, we investigated the suitability of word translation for the issues at hand.

Word translation has been frequently employed in studies on bilingualism. In this task, a word is presented in one language and its word-translation equivalent must be expressed in another language (cf. De Groot, 1992; Kroll & Stewart, 1994). The word-translation task can be modified into a task comparable to picture-word interference by adding distractor words (La Heij et al., 1990). The rationale is the same: As the picture in picture-word experiments, the probe word (in L2) that has to be translated should result in the activation of the intended target word (in L1). The fate of this target word can be influenced by simultaneously presenting a distractor (cf. Bloem & La Heij, 2003; La Heij et al., 1990).

It is not entirely clear whether translation of the probe word into the target word is conceptually mediated or takes place via lexical connections (which represent word-form information in most models of bilingualism). Sholl, Sankaranarayanan, and Kroll (1995) argue for an asymmetry: Only translation from the more dominant to the less dominant language is sensitive to conceptual-level processing. In contrast, La Heij, Hooglander, Kerling and van der Velden (1996) argue that translation in both directions is largely conceptually mediated.

For our purposes, it is largely irrelevant whether target-word activation is conceptually or lexically mediated, because evidence converges on the idea that morphological complexity is lexically coded, most probably at the form level (Levelt et al., 1999; Roelofs & Baayen, 2002; Zwitserlood et al., 2002). As with picture-word interference the morphologically complex distractor words are processed by the 'native' comprehension system, on all relevant dimensions, from orthography via morphology to semantics. We expect translation latencies to be influenced by distractor words in the same way as picture naming latencies in picture-word interference.

As argued before, word translation has advantages over both picture-word interference and implicit priming, because it allows for larger sets of more diverse stimuli. We also expect the paradigm to be sensitive to non-initial overlap between target and distractor, for which implicit priming is not sensitive. To assess the suitability of the paradigm for morphology and to add to a meagre database on the role of morphology in speaking, we tested conditions for which data from picture-word interference were already available. As in Dohmes et al. (2004), we tested for effects of non-initial morphological relatedness between target words and distractors in the presence and in the absence of semantic transparency. We compared effects for semantically transparent distractors such as *Handtasche* (hand bag) and semantically opaque distractors such as *Plaudertasche* (chatter-box, target: *Tasche*, bag), in Experiment 1. We also contrasted data from conditions of morphological similarity to those with mere form overlap between targets and distractors (Experiment 2), with morphologically related distractors such as *Stadttor* (town gate) and phonologically related distractors such as *Reaktor* (reactor, target: *Tor*, gate). Here, we expected morphological effects to be larger than phonological effects. If results are broadly similar to those obtained with picture-word interference, this constitutes important corroborating evidence for morphological units in speaking and establishes that word-translation is a useful tool in the study of morphological processing and representation.

EXPERIMENT 1

Method

Participants.   The experiment was conducted with 18 native speakers of German from the University of Münster, who received course credit for participation.

Materials.   Forty-five English monomorphemic nouns[2] served as targets. All target words were non-cognates, except for one (Nudel – noodle). Each target was combined with three German compounds that served as distractors. Target and distractor were either morphologically and semantically related (*Handtasche*, hand bag), morphologically related but semantically opaque (*Plaudertasche*, chatterbox) or unrelated (*Sündenbock*, scapegoat) to the German translation of the English noun (*bag* → Tasche), see Appendix B. The unrelated condition served as a baseline to evaluate size and direction of priming effects. Distractors were matched for word frequency and word length. According to the Leipziger Wortschatz – Lexikon, mean frequency class for semantically related distractors was 17.5 (mean word length was 10.1 letters), for semantically opaque distractors 17.8 (mean word length was 10.1 letters) and for unrelated control distractors 17 (mean word length was 9.91 letters). This online-lexicon reports categories of frequency for each word, based on the frequency of the German word 'der', which is the most frequent word in German. High values indicate low frequencies. In a pretest, 45 morphologically and semantically related compounds, 45 morphologically related and semantically opaque compounds and 45 unrelated control compounds were presented together with the German translation of the corresponding English noun. Six participants rated the semantic related-ness of each item pair on a five-point scale (1 – not related at all, 5 – strongly related). The mean relatedness score was 4.37 ($SD = 0.42$) for the

---

[2] There were two morphologically complex English words, one in Experiment 1 and another in Experiment 2. Their German translation was morphologically simple.

semantically transparent pairs, 2.1 ($SD = 0.52$) for the semantically opaque condition, and 1.02 ($SD = 0.08$) for the unrelated condition. The 45 targets were distributed across three lists, using a Latin Square design. Each target appeared only once per list but with a different distractor on each list. Of the 45 compounds on each list, 30 compounds had morphologically related targets, 15 compounds had unrelated targets. To decrease the relatedness proportion, 45 filler compounds were added which were in all aspects unrelated to the German translation of their target. Nine practice trials preceded each list. There were two different sequences of trials within each list. Participants saw all lists, in one of three presentation orders (1-2-3, 2-3-1, 3-1-2).

Procedure. Prior to the experiment, participants were trained to produce the intended translation for the English nouns using a vocabulary trainer (Langenscheidt Vokabeltrainer Englisch, CD-ROM Version 2.0).

Participants were tested individually in a quiet room, sitting in front of a computer screen (CTX 1785 XE). They were instructed to translate the English nouns as quickly and accurately as possible. Latencies were measured with the aid of a voice-key (Sennheiser HME 25-1). All stimuli appeared as white characters against a black background. The structure of each trial was as follows. First, participants saw a warning signal (an asterisk) for 252 ms. Next, the screen was cleared for 252 ms, followed by the display of the distractor for 398 ms, centred on the screen. The target was presented 120 pixels below distractor position 106 ms after Distractor onset (SOA −106) for a duration of 398 ms. Reaction time was measured from target word onset and time-out was set to 1900 ms. The experiment lasted about 30 minutes.

Results

The overall error rate for erroneous answers was 4.9%. Erroneous answers, disfluencies, triggering of the voice-key by non-speech sounds and latencies less than 200 ms or greater than 1900 ms were discarded from the analyses. Latencies were averaged over participants (F_1) or items (F_2) and submitted to separate ANOVAs. Degrees of freedom were adjusted with the conservative lower bound procedure in all ANOVAs. We first analysed the results with Distractor Type (semantically transparent, semantically intransparent, and unrelated) and Presentation (first, second, and third) as factors. Table 1 lists reaction times and error percentages as a function of Distractor Type and Presentation. We controlled whether translation latencies changed over the time-course of the experiment and whether there was any interaction with the factor Distractor Type. The main effect of Presentation was not significant for $F_1(1, 17) < 1$, but for $F_2(1, 44) =$

TABLE 1

Experiment 1: Mean RTs in ms, standard deviations (in parentheses) and error percentages as a function of Distractor Type and Presentation

	Presentation							
	First		Second		Third		Mean	
Distractor Type	RT	% Error	RT	% Error	RT	% Error	RT	% Error
Transparent	864.3	6.9	861.7	2.3	851.6	2.3	859.2	3.8
	(31.7)		(21.9)		(28.7)		(21.5)	
Opaque	900.3	4.7	848	2.4	854.1	3.1	867.4	3.4
	(29.2)		(28.6)		(30.4)		(25.39)	
Control	929.1	7.9	915.4	5.3	920.9	2.8	921.8	5.3
	(39.1)		(32.3)		(32.1)		(31.63)	

4.678, $p < .001$. Paired t-tests showed that word-translation latencies decreased from the first (917 ms) to the second presentation, 885 ms, $t_2(44) = 2.702, p = .01$, but not from the second to the third presentation, 882 ms; $t_2(44) = 0.282, p = .78$. We found no significant interaction between Distractor Type and Presentation, $F_1 < 1; F_2 < 1$). Therefore the remaining analyses are presented collapsed across this factor.

The main effect of Distractor Type was significant, $F_{1(1,17)} = 11.000$, $p < .001; F_2(1, 44) = 12.070, p = .001$. The two morphologically related distractors showed nearly identical effects. Planned comparisons revealed that compared with unrelated distractors (922 ms), English nouns were translated significantly faster when a semantically transparent (859 ms) or opaque compound (867 ms) was presented (see Appendix A). The difference of 8 ms between the two distractor types was not significant. The ANOVA on the mean error proportions revealed no further information.

Thus, morphologically related distractors facilitated translation, regardless of the degree of semantic transparency. Moreover, we again obtained evidence that non-initial morphological overlap can facilitate word production (cf. Dohmes et al., 2004).

Discussion

The data of Experiment 1 clearly show that morphological overlap facilitates word-translation. The facilitation effect was of similar size for semantically transparent and opaque distractors, suggesting that morphology plays a role that is largely independent of semantic compositionality. This finding is in line with the model of Levelt et al. (1999) as well as with the theory of autonomous morphology proposed by Aronoff (1994). We will postpone an evaluation of all potential explanations for the effects observed here to the general discussion. Before doing so, we have to assess another potential confound: between morphology and phonological overlap. This is the purpose of Experiment 2, in which we investigate and compare effects of morphological overlap with those of pure form overlap.

EXPERIMENT 2

Method

Participants.   The experiment was conducted with 21 native speakers of German from the University of Münster, who received course credit for participation.

Materials and procedure.   Forty-five English nouns served as targets. Each target was combined with three German distractors. Distractor words were morphologically and semantically related (*Faltenrock*, pleated skirt), monomorphemic and form-related (*Barock*, baroque), or unrelated (*Flugzeug*, plane) to the German translation of the English noun (*skirt* → Rock). The form-related distractors accidentally happen to contain the string which constitutes the translation equivalent (e.g., *Barock* – Rock; *Insekt* – Sekt), see Appendix B. The unrelated condition served as a baseline to evaluate size and direction of priming effects. Mean frequency class according to the Leipziger Wortschatz – Lexikon was 17.2 for semantically related distractors (mean word length was 9.2 letters), 13.5 for form-related distractors (mean word length was 7.1 letters) and for unrelated control distractors this was 16.5 (mean word length was 8.6 letters).

As in Experiment 1, semantic relatedness was pretested. Forty-five morphologically and semantically related compounds, 45 form-related words and 45 unrelated control compounds were presented together with the German translation of the corresponding English noun. Mean semantic relatedness, in a 5-point scale, was 4.07 ($SD = 0.59$) for the semantically transparent condition, 1.16 ($SD = 0.25$) for the form-related condition, and 1.03 ($SD = 0.09$) for the unrelated condition. The procedure was the same as in Experiment 1.

Results

The overall error rate was 5% for erroneous answers. We applied the same type of pre-processing and data analysis as in Experiment 1. Again, results were first analysed with Distractor Type (morphologically related, form-related and unrelated) and Presentation (first, second and third) as factors. Table 2 lists reaction times and error percentages as a function of

Distractor Type and Presentation. The main effect of Presentation was significant for $F_1(1, 20) = 5.567, p = .029$ and $F_2(2, 44) = 17.625, p < .001$. Paired t-tests showed that word-translation latencies decreased from the first (954 ms) to the second presentation (906 ms), $t_1(20) = 2.683, p = .014$, $t_2(44) - 4.447, p < .001$, but not from second to third presentation (902 ms), $t_1(20) = 0.277, p = .785, t_2(44) = 0.282, p < .779$. We found no significant interaction between Distractor Type and Presentation, $F_1 < 1$; $F_2 < 1$. Therefore the remaining analyses are presented collapsed across this factor.

The ANOVA on the averaged latencies yielded a significant main effect of Distractor Type $F_1(1, 20) = 5.238, p = .033; F_2(1, 44) = 5.5852, p = .02$. Planned comparisons revealed that English nouns paired with a morphologically (and semantically) related distractor (895 ms) were translated significantly faster than those paired with either a form-related (930 ms) or an unrelated distractor (939 ms). The difference between form-related and unrelated distractor latencies (9 ms) was not significant (see Appendix A). Again, the ANOVA on the mean error proportions revealed no further information.

So, as in Experiment 1, morphologically related distractors facilitated word-translation latencies. This facilitation is not due to form overlap because form overlap alone does not result in significant facilitation. Such a pattern of results is compatible with what was found earlier. Both Roelofs (1996, 1998) and Dohmes et al. (2004) observed reliable differences between the impact of morphological similarity and of pure form overlap.

TABLE 2

Experiment 2: Mean RTs in ms, standard deviations (in parentheses) and error percentages as a function of Distractor Type and Presentation

	Presentation							
	First		*Second*		*Third*		*Mean*	
Distractor Type	*RT*	*% Error*	*RT*	*% Error*	*RT*	*% Error*	*RT*	*% Error*
Transparent	914.9 (32.5)	6.0	887.6 (33.0)	2.8	882.8 (33.8)	2.4	895.1 (29.5)	3.3
Form-related	972.7 (33.4)	9.2	914.3 (36.6)	2.4	903.9 (36.6)	2.4	930.3 (33.3)	4.7
Control	975.5 (40.5)	11.5	918.9 (35.4)	6.4	921.9 (41.8)	2.8	938.8 (37.0)	6.6

GENERAL DISCUSSION

We presented data from two experiments on the impact of morphological relatedness, semantic transparency, and form overlap on word-translation performance for morphologically simple words. The data are easily summarised: First, morphologically related distractors produced facilitation irrespective of the semantic transparency of their relation to the relevant target word. The size of the effect was almost identical for semantically transparent and opaque compounds. On the other hand, form-related distractors did not reliably affect target-word production. Thus, facilitation in the morphological conditions does not simply result from form overlap. We will address three issues in the remainder of this discussion: (1) the locus of effects from our morphological conditions in comprehension and production, (2) whether and how models can accommodate the data, and (3) differences and commonalities between picture-word interference and word-translation.

Morphological effects at the production/ comprehension interface

Considered in isolation, there are many potential explanations for the particular effects obtained here. To decide in favour of one or the other interpretation, we will also draw on results from earlier studies in production, as well as on data and models for the role of morphology in comprehension. A first question concerns the locus of effects that we labelled 'morphological'. Our favoured explanation, here and elsewhere, is in terms of shared morphemes between production and comprehension. Alternatively, effects could be due to shared meaning, to shared lemmas, or to shared form. We will consider the merits and problems of each of these explanations in sequence.

Let us first consider what happens with the stimuli in this particular translation study (and in many of our picture-word experiments, for that matter). The words which participants produce are actually morphologically simple, so their lexical representation is quite straightforward: One lemma, and one word form or lexeme. The distractor words are morphologically complex. On the basis of good evidence, we assume that the comprehension system parses the distractors into constituent morphemes (e.g., Baayen & Schreuder, 1999; Drews & Zwitserlood, 1995; Marslen-Wilson et al., 1994). These morphemes activate their syntactic ('lemma') and semantic properties ('concept'). Is the complexity of words lost after parsing, in other words, does it suffice to have individual morphemes to understand the meaning of words? This might hold for semantically fully transparent complex words, by combining the meanings of constituent morphemes. But for opaque words, such a process would clearly fail (e.g., *blackguard, bluestocking*). Consider also that fully transparent words are rare gems, and that semantic transparency is not an all-or-none phenomenon. The meaning of many seemingly transparent complex words is not readily derivable from the meanings of their morphemes (e.g., *blackboard, bluebell, lazy chair*). In fact, some of our transparent distractors were of this type (e.g., *Fliegenpilz*, lit. 'fly mushroom', toadstool). Thus, to understand the meaning of complex words, morphological parsing needs to be accompanied by combinatorial information specific to the morphemes involved. Although complex words are parsed into morphemes during language comprehension, the particular combination must percolate to the semantic level. In linguistic theories, this is sometimes implemented as a kind of bracketing around constituent morphemes.

Whatever the exact nature of meaning processing in comprehension is, the positive impact of morphologically related distractors, both in translation and picture-word interference, cannot be solely explained in terms of semantic facilitation. Both here and in earlier research, we observe identical effects from semantically transparent and opaque distractors, in situations in which we can be sure that distractors are semantically processed (Dohmes et al., 2004). Even if the individual morphemes of a complex word (e.g., *blue* and *stocking*) activate their meaning at a conceptual level, the concept belonging to the complete, opaque word (e.g., *bluestocking*) surely must be most highly activated. Otherwise, comprehension would go astray. In contrast to a transparent case such as *nylon stocking*, the concept of *bluestocking* is clearly not related to the concept of *stocking*, which is needed for picture naming. Thus, whereas *nylon stocking* would also semantically activate the concept *stocking*, *bluestocking* would not. Still, we find no differences between transparent and opaque distractors, where a conceptual locus of the facilitation would predict one.

If not at a conceptual level, can effects be located at the 'lemma' level of speech production? As mentioned earlier, most comprehension models do not explicitly incorporate a lemma level. But of course, distractor words are believed to activate their lemmas – whole generations of picture-word studies rely on lemmas to explain negative effects of certain types of semantic similarity between targets and distractors. As argued above, individual morphemes, which are the product of morphological parsing through comprehension, could activate their lemmas, the lemma needed for target production being among them. So, facilitatory effects are possibly not only due to shared morphemes; they may also reflect repeated access to a common representation at the lemma level. On the basis of our results, we can not decide about facilitation that occurs at the lemma level. A lemma explanation can account for many aspects of the data. For reasons given below, we believe, however, that the influence of shared morphemes is more decisive.

First, even if distractor words are parsed and the lemmas of their constituents are activated, we believe that the lemma of the complete compound must be activated as well. As argued earlier, the reason lies in the fact that the meaning of compounds can rarely be derived by combining the meanings of their constituents. If only constituent lemmas are active, it is hard to see how these relate to the concept of the complete compound in ways that are superior to the mapping of the two individual lemmas onto their individual concepts. This holds for both directions: from concept to lemma and from lemma to concept. Of course, it is vital to see an implementation of such dynamics. But if a 'compound' lemma of a semantically transparent compound is active, it holds the same type of semantic relation to the target lemma (e.g., Querflöte – Flöte: traverso – flute) as is the case for stimuli that produce interference in picture-word experiments. It is a categorical relation. La Heij et al. (2006) have shown that semantically related distractors induce semantic interference not only in a basic level picture naming task but also in word translation. Still, we did not find interference but facilitation.

Second, given the dynamics of selection at the lemma level, we would expect some difference between distractors that *only* activate the lemma needed for picture naming, and distractors that activate more than one lemma, keeping morphological overlap constant. This is not what we observe. Inflected (plural) distractors (e.g., *Blum*en, flowers) do not have a separate lemma, and thus activate the (singular) target lemma only (the target being the picture of a flower). Derived words (e.g., *blumig*, flowery) might also activate the target lemma after parsing. But they crucially also need their own lemma, since they have different syntactic properties (e.g., word class) as the target lemma. Even if the target lemma is active after parsing, the derived word's lemma surely must be more strongly activated. Since derived and inflected distractors had the exact same facilitatory impact on picture naming, facilitation cannot readily be explained as a mere consequence of multiple accesses to the same lemma (Zwitserlood et al., 2000).

Third, as stated before, identical or inflected distractors activate only one lemma. But compounds activate (minimally!) two: The lemmas of their constituent morphemes. Although the first constituent specifies the second, it is often unrelated to the target lemma (e.g., *Glasauge*, with 'glass' to the picture of an eye; *Blumentopf*, with 'pot' to the picture of a flower). As a consequence, compared to inflected and identical cases, an additional lemma is in the race in the case of compound words. Although empirical evidence is lacking, theoretically an additional lemma should cause more problems for the selection process.

If the 'morphological' facilitation effect is located at the lemma level, picture naming should benefit more from inflected or identical distractors that only activate the target lemma than from compounds, which activate an additional lemma. However, we found clear facilitation from all distractor types, with no differences between identical, inflected, and compounded distractors (Zwitserlood et al., 2000; Bölte, Zwitserlood, & Dohmes, 2004). Such data are more in line with the view that compounds possess only one lemma (Levelt et al., 1999). Currently, undisputable evidence for the locus of the 'morphological' effects at either lemma or lexeme level is lacking. Further experiments on the contributions of shared/different lemmas (as well as of shared/different concepts) on potential interactions of sources of similarity are desperately needed to evaluate their impact on morphological effects.

Together with the speech error and aphasic speech evidence and with the linking element argument cited above, and with evidence to the contrary lacking, we believe that the data thus far can best be explained in terms of shared morphemes between distractors and targets for production. The fact that morphological facilitation is obtained independent of semantic transparency and of phonological overlap argues for morphological representations that are separate from semantics and phonology. The morphologically complex distractor is decomposed into its constituent morphemes, and this holds equally for semantically transparent and opaque words. The morpheme shared between the distractor and the to-be produced target benefits from repeated access, thus facilitating the production of the translated word. Keeping in mind that effects emerge from 'crosstalk' between comprehension (of distractors) and production (of the translated words), we argue that (1) morphological units exist in speech production, and (2) morphological representations could well be shared between the comprehension and production. If they are not, they must at least be closely connected.

Models and data

The absence of an influence of semantic transparency on morphological facilitation corroborates earlier results (Dohmes et al., 2004; Roelofs & Baayen, 2002). At first glance, 'pure' morphological effects seem to conflict with distributed connectionist approaches (e.g., Plaut & Gonnerman, 2000). In such views, 'morphology' derives from learned relationships among surface forms of words, and their meaning. If form and meaning interact, priming effects should be greater for words that are both morphologically and semantically related than for those that are related on only one dimension. However, Plaut and Gonnerman argue that priming in the absence of semantic similarity can be obtained in morphologically rich languages, such as Hebrew. It is an empirical question whether German falls into this category.

Our results fit well with models that assume decomposed word constituents (cf. for production: Dell, 1986; Levelt et al., 1999; for comprehension: Baayen & Schreuder, 1999). In particular, such models can readily explain pure morphological effects, in the absence of semantic similarity. In fact, morphemes are the units of lexical form in many such models, and effects of phonological overlap are often explained at the level of individual phonemes, not of morpheme-sized word forms.

Our present set of data is also compatible with some variants of the 'full-listing' approach, which assume that morphological relations between full forms are in some way represented (e.g., Butterworth, 1983; Colé, Beauvillain, & Segui, 1989). When morphologically related complex words are interconnected in a network of full-word nodes, morphologically related distractor-picture pairs (e.g., *heartily* – heart) should produce facilitation. However, different effects are expected for derived (e.g., *heartily*) and identical distractors (e.g., *heart*). Identical distractors should produce more facilitation because the exact same representation is addressed twice. As stated above, we found equal amounts of facilitation for identical and derived distractors with picture-word interference (Bölte et al., 2004). This result is better explained by morphological (de)composition and representation.

At a more theoretical level, morphological effects independent of semantic similarity agree well with an autonomous level of morphology as suggested by Aronoff (1994). According to this theory, word production is divided into several stages. Aronoff argues that morphology is a separate and autonomous component, not an appendage of syntax or phonology. The main priority after conceptualisation and lemma selection is to produce the proper word form. At this level, meaning is no longer relevant. Therefore, morphological processing should not be influenced by semantics, which is what we found.

Differences and similarities between picture word interference and word translation

Most of the effects reported here, obtained with the translation task, replicated what was found with picture-word interference and with implicit priming. Importantly, we obtained morphological priming even in the absence of semantic similarity between distractors and targets. This was also found with picture-word interference (Dohmes et al., 2004) and implicit priming (Roelofs & Baayen, 2002). The fact that we did not obtain reliable phonological effects does not fit with what was observed earlier. Zwitserlood et al. (2000) as well as Dohmes et al. (2004) obtained reliable priming due to mere form overlap with the immediate picture-word interference paradigm. This effect disappeared when a lag between distractor and picture was introduced.

Why did pure form-overlap not facilitate the production of target words in the immediate word-translation task? Bloem & La Heij (2003, 2004) and La Heij et al. (1990) obtained phonological word-translation effects at various SOAs (−250, 0 or +140 ms). Phonological relatedness was defined as word-initial overlap between distractor and target (e.g., cat – cap). In the present study we used distractor – target pairs with non-initial overlap, such as *Insekt – Sekt*. There is evidence that initial and non-initial distractors differ in the onset of the facilitatory effect. Meyer and Schriefers (1991) found that the onset of the effect in the onset-related condition was at SOA −150 ms, whereas it emerged at SOA = 0 ms in the end-related condition. We used a SOA of −106 ms that might not be the most favourable SOA for end overlap. Admittedly, the same SOA was used in Dohmes et al. (2004). But reaction times were about 180–200 ms longer in the translation task than in the picture-word study, so that the same SOA potentially has a different impact.

Yet another reason could be the different size of effects. Compared with Dohmes et al. (2004), who found priming effects of 100 ms and more for transparent and opaque compounds, effects in the word-translation task are reduced nearly by half. The phonological effect amounted to 70 ms in immediate picture-word interference; this was reduced to a non-significant 12 ms in word-translation. So, the overall reduction in effect size in word-translation, compared with picture-word interference, may have severely reduced form-overlap effects. Thus, word-translation and picture-word interference seem to differ in the sensitivity to form overlap and in the development of such effects over time.

To summarize: our experiments show that the word-translation task yields a pattern of morphological priming effects which is similar to what is obtained with picture-word interference. First, the presence of morphologically related distractors facilitates word production. Second, this effect is not modified by semantic transparency. Distractors speed up word translation as long as the German target word and the distractor share a morpheme. We argue that this is indeed a morphological effect, and that it cannot be reduced to semantics, lemma activation, or pure form overlap. The overall similarity of results obtained with the two paradigms clearly shows that the word-translation task is a good method to investigate morphological processing and representation in speech production. Experiments on speech production rely on paradigms that provide good control over the speakers' responses, which is what this paradigm allows. Moreover, to draw general conclusions about mechanisms involved in language production, it is indispensable to use stimuli from a large and varied set of materials. The word-translation task complies with these requirements and can thus make a substantial contribution to experimental speech production research.

REFERENCES

Allen, M., & Badecker, W. (2002). Inflectional regularity: Probing the nature of lexical representation in a cross-modal priming task. *Journal of Memory and Language, 46*, 705–722.

Aronoff, M. (1994). *Morphology by itself.* Cambridge, MA: MIT Press.

Baayen, H., & Schreuder, R. (1999). War and peace: Morphemes and full forms in a noninteractive activation parallel dual-route model. *Brain and Language, 68*, 27–32.

Badecker, W., & Caramazza, A. (1991). Morphological composition in the lexical output system. *Cognitive Neuropsychology, 8*, 335–367.

Bentin, S., & Feldman, L. B. (1990). The contribution of morphological and semantic relatedness to repetition priming at short and long lags: Evidence from Hebrew. *Quarterly Journal of Experimental Psychology, 42A*, 693–711.

Bloem, I., & La Heij, W. (2003). Semantic facilitation and semantic interference in word translation: Implications for models of lexical access in language production. *Journal of Memory and Language, 48*, 468–488.

Bloem, I., & La Heij, W. (2004). Semantic facilitation and semantic interference in language production: Further evidence for the conceptual selection model of lexical access. *Journal of Memory and Language, 51*, 307–323.

Bölte, J., Zwitserlood, P., & Dohmes, P. (2004). Morphology in experimental speech production research. In T. Pechmann & C. Habel (Eds.), *Trends in linguistics: Multidisciplinary approaches to language production* (pp. 431–471). Berlin: Mouton de Gruyter.

Butterworth, B. (1983). Lexical representation. In B. Butterworth (Ed.), *Language production* (pp. 257–294). London: Academic Press.

Colé, P., Beauvillain, C., & Segui, J. (1989). On the representation and processing of prefixed and suffixed derived words: A differential frequency effect. *Journal of Memory and Language, 28*, 1–13.

Caramazza, A., Laudanna, A., & Romani, C. (1988). Lexical access and inflectional morphology. *Cognition, 28*, 297–332.

Chialant, D., & Caramazza, A. (1995). Where is morphology and how is it represented? The case of written word recognition. In L. B. Feldman (Ed.), *Morphological aspects of language processing.* Hillsdale, NJ: Lawrence Erlbaum Associates Inc.

De Groot, A. M. B. (1992). Determinants of word translation. *Journal of Experimental Psychology: Learning, Memory and Cognition, 18*, 1001–1018.

Dell, G. S. (1986). A spreading-activation theory of retrieval in sentence production. *Psychological Review, 93*, 283–321.

Dohmes, P., Zwitserlood, P., & Bölte, J. (2004). The impact of semantic transparency of morphologically complex words on picture naming. *Brain and Language, 90*, 203–212.

Drews, E., & Zwitserlood, P. (1995). Morphological and orthographic similarity in visual word recognition. *Journal of Experimental Psychology: Human Perception and Performance, 21*, 1098–1116.

Feldman, L. B. (2000). Are morphological effects distinguishable from the effects of shared meaning and shared form? *Journal of Experimental Psychology: Learning, Memory, and Cognition, 26*, 1431–1444.

Feldman, L. B., Soltano, E. G., Pastizzo, M. J., & Francis, S. E. (2004). What do graded effects of semantic transparency reveal about morphological processing? *Brain and Language, 90,* 17–30.

Frauenfelder, U. H., & Schreuder, R. (1992). Constraining psycholinguistic models of morphological processing and representation: The role of productivity. In G. Booij & J. van Marle (Eds.), *Yearbook of morphology* (pp. 165–183). Amsterdam: Kluwer.

Garrett, M. F. (1975). The analysis of sentence production. In G. H. Bower (Ed.), *The psychology of learning and motivation,* (pp. 133–177). New York: Academic Press.

Glaser, W. R., & Düngelhoff, F.-J. (1984). The time course of picture-word interference. *Journal of Experimental Psychology: Human Perception and Performance, 10,* 640–654.

Kroll, J. F., & Stewart, E. (1994). Category interference in translation and picture naming: Evidence for asymmetric connections between bilingual memory representations. *Journal of Memory and Language, 33,* 149–174.

Kuipers, J.-R., La Heij, W., & Costa, A. (2006). A further look at semantic context effects in language production: The role of response congruency. *Language and Cognitive Processes, 21,* 892–919.

La Heij, W., de Bruyn, E., Elens, E., Hartsuiker, R., Helaha, D., & van Schelven, L. (1990). Orthographic facilitation and categorical interference in a word-translation variant of the Stroop task. *Canadian Journal of Psychology, 44,* 76–83.

La Heij, W., Hooglander, A., Kerling, R., & van der Velden, E. (1996). Nonverbal context effects in forward and backward word translation: Evidence for concept mediation. *Journal of Memory and Language, 35,* 648–665.

Levelt, W. J. M. (1989). *Speaking: From intention to articulation.* Cambridge, MA: MIT Press.

Levelt, W. J. M., Roelofs, A., & Meyer, A. (1999). A theory of lexical access in speech production. *Behavioral and Brain Sciences, 22,* 1–75.

Lupker, S. J. (1982). The role of phonetic and orthographic similarity in picture-word interference. *Canadian Journal of Psychology, 36,* 349–367.

Manelis, L., & Tharp, D. (1977). The processing of affixed words. *Memory and Cognition, 5,* 690–695.

Marslen-Wilson, W., Tyler, L. K., Waksler, R., & Older, L. (1994). Morphology and meaning in the English mental lexicon. *Psychological Review, 101,* 3–33.

Meyer, A. S. (1990). The time course of phonological encoding in language production: The encoding of successive syllables of a word. *Journal of Memory and Language, 29,* 524–545.

Meyer, A. S. (1991). The time course of phonological encoding in language production: The phonological encoding inside a syllable. *Journal of Memory and Language, 30,* 69–89.

Meyer, A. S., & Schriefers, H. (1991). Phonological facilitation in picture-word interference experiments: Effects of stimulus onset asynchrony and types of interfering stimuli. *Journal of Experimental Psychology: Learning, Memory, and Cognition, 17,* 1146–1160.

Plaut, D. C., & Gonnerman, L. M. (2000). Are non-semantic morphological effects incompatible with a distributed connectionist approach to lexical processing? *Language and Cognitive Processes, 15,* 445–485.

Roelofs, A. (1996). Serial order in planning the production of successive morphemes of a word. *Journal of Memory and Language, 35,* 854–876.

Roelofs, A. (1998). Rightward incrementality in encoding simple phrasal forms in speech production: Verb-particle combinations. *Journal of Experimental Psychology, 24,* 904–921.

Roelofs, A., & Baayen, R. H. (2002). Morphology by itself in planning the production of spoken words. *Psychonomic Bulletin and Review, 9,* 132–138.

Sholl, A., Sankaranarayanan, A., & Kroll, J. F. (1995). Transfer between picture naming and translation: A test of asymmetries in bilingual memory. *Psychological Science, 6,* 45–49.

Schreuder, R., & Baayen, R. H. (1995). Modelling morphological processing. In L. B. Feldman (Ed.), *Morphological aspects of language processing* (pp. 131–156). Hillsdale, NJ: Lawrence Erlbaum Associates Inc.

Stemberger, J. P. (1985). An interactive activation model of language production. In W. A. Ellis (Ed.), *Progress in the psychology of language* (pp. 143–186). Hove, UK: Lawrence Erlbaum Associates Ltd.

Vigliocco, G., Lauer, M., Damian, M. F., & Levelt, W. J. M. (2002). Semantic and syntactic forces in noun phrase production. *Journal of Experimental Psychology: Learning, Memory and Cognition, 28*, 46–58.

Wheeldon, L. R., & Levelt, W. J. M. (1995). Monitoring the time course of phonological encoding. *Journal of Memory and Language, 34*, 311–334.

Zwitserlood, P. (1994). The role of semantic transparency in the processing and representation of Dutch compounds. *Language and Cognitive Processes, 9*, 341–368.

Zwitserlood, P., Bölte, J., & Dohmes, P. (2000). Morphological effects on speech production: Evidence from picture naming. *Language and Cognitive Processes, 15*, 563–591.

Zwitserlood, P., Bölte, J., & Dohmes, P. (2002). Where and how morphologically complex words interplay with naming pictures. *Brain and Language, 81*, 358–367.

APPENDIX A

t-test values for Participant and Item analyses Experiment 1

	Analysis	
	Participant	Item
Semantically transparent vs. control	$t_1(17) = 3.625, p < .001$	$t_2(44) = 3.758, p < .001$
Opaque vs. control	$t_1(17) = 4.157, p < .001$	$t_2(44) = 3.820, p < .001$
Semantically transparent vs. opaque	$t_1(17) = 0.411, p = .686$	$t_2(44) = 0.378, p = .707$

t-test values for Participant and Item analyses Experiment 2

	Analysis	
	Participant	Item
Semantically transparent vs. control	$t_1(20) = 2.911, p = .009$	$t_2(44) = 3.066, p = .004$
Form-related vs. control	$t_1(20) = 0.578, p = .570$	$t_2(44) = 0.618, p = .540$
Semantically transparent vs. form-related	$t_1(20) = 2.457, p = .023$	$t_2(44) = 2.851, p = .007$

APPENDIX B

Material Experiment 1 (English translation in parentheses)

	Distractor Type		
Semantically transparent	Semantically opaque	Control word	Target word
Aasgeier (vulture)	Pleitegeier	Taufpate (godfather)	Geier (vulture)
Abendstern (evening star)	Augenstern	Ruderboot (rowing boat)	Stern (star)
Auerhahn (mountain cock)	Wasserhahn (water tap)	Blütenkelch (calyx)	Hahn (cock)
Autoschlüssel (car key)	Notenschlüssel (clef)	Feuerzunge	Schlüssel (key)
Bandnudel (ribbon noodles)	Ulknudel	Erzengel (archangel)	Nudel (noodle)
Bratapfel (baked apple)	Adamsapfel (Adam's apple)	Rasierklinge (razor blade)	Apfel* (apple)
Brotkorb (bread basket)	Brustkorb (chest)	Lebertran (cod-liver oil)	Korb (basket)
Kordhose (corduroys)	Windhose whirlwind	Hufeisen (horseshoe)	Hose* (trousers)
Edelschimmel mould	Amtsschimmel (red tape)	Reispflanze	Schimmel (mould)
Fliegenpilz (fly agaric)	Glückspilz (lucky devil)	Hafendamm (mole)	Pilz (mushroom)
Frachtschiff (cargo ship)	Kirchenschiff (nave)	Modenschau (fashion show)	Schiff* (ship)
Glasauge (glass eye)	Bullauge (porthole)	Dampfwalze (steam roller)	Auge (eye)
Grundschule (primary school)	Baumschule (tree nursery)	Lichthupe (headlamp flasher)	Schule (school)
Haarbürste (hairbrush)	Kratzbürste (crosspatch)	Fahrrinne (fairway)	Bürste (brush)
Haarkamm (hair comb)	Wellenkamm (wave peak)	Kniestrumpf (knee-length sock)	Kamm* (comb)
Hammerhai (shovelhead)	Kredithai (loan shark)	Dornenhecke (thorn hedge)	Hai (shark)
Handtasche (handbag)	Plaudertasche (chatterbox)	Sündenbock (scapegoat)	Tasche* (bag)
Hemdkragen (collar of a shirt)	Geizkragen (tightwad)	Gipfeltreffen (summit conference)	Kragen (collar)
Holzschraube (woodscrew)	Schreckschraube (boot)	Fischkonserve (canned fish)	Schraube* (screw)
Jagdhund (hound)	Seehund (seal)	Grundstück (realty)	Hund (dog)
Kirschbaum (cherry tree)	Purzelbaum (somersault)	Damenwahl (ladies' choice)	Baum (tree)
Korbstuhl (cane chair)	Dachstuhl (truss)	Kinnbart (chin-beard)	Stuhl* (chair)
Küchenherd (kitchen stove)	Eiterherd (suppurative focus)	Tannenwald	Herd (stove)

Distractor Type			
Semantically transparent	*Semantically opaque*	*Control word*	*Target word*
Kugelblitz	Geistesblitz	Datenbank	Blitz
(ball lightning)	(brainstorm)	(databank)	(flash)
Kupferkessel	Talkessel	Türklingel	Kessel
(cauldron, cupreous)	(basin)	(doorbell)	(cauldron)
Laubfrosch	Knallfrosch	Parkbucht	Frosch*
(greenback)	(firecracker)	(lay-by)	(frog)
Maulesel	Drahtesel	Kochlöffel	Esel
(hinny)		(wooden spoon)	(donkey)
Mittagspause	Blaupause	Kneifzange	Pause
(lunch break)	(blueprint)	(nippers)	(break)
Nadelstich	Eierstich	Tafelwein	Stich
(pinprick)	(royale)	(table wine)	(stitch)
Querflöte	Sektflöte	Strafzettel	Flöte
(transverse flute)	(champagne glass)	(ticket)	(flute)
Regenschirm	Bildschirm	Stallknecht	Schirm*
(umbrella)	(screen)	(stableman)	(umbrella)
Rhesusaffe	Lackaffe	Steinpilz	Affe
(rhesus monkey)	(smoothy)	(cep)	(monkey)
Schinkenwurst	Hanswurst	Jutesack	Wurst
(ham sausage)	(tomfool)	(gunnysack)	(sausage)
Schneehase	Angsthase	Weltkarte	Hase
(arctic hare)	(scaredy-cat)	(world map)	(hare)
Siamkater	Muskelkater	Nagelfeile	Kater*
(Siamese cat)	(muscle ache)	(nail file)	(tomcat)
Singvogel	Galgenvogel	Tauchermaske	Vogel*
(songbird)	(hangdog)	(diving mask)	(bird)
Sonnenkönig	Zaunkönig	Kontaktlinse	König
(Sun King)	(wren)	(contact lens)	(king)
Sportangel	Türangel	Heuboden	Angel*
	(door hinge)	(hayloft)	(fishing rod)
Tabakspfeife	Backpfeife	Ofenkachel	Pfeife*
(pipe)	(a slap in the face)	(stove tile)	(pipe)
Trittleiter	Reiseleiter	Bügelfalte	Leiter
(ladder)	(tour guide)	(crease)	(ladder)
Vogelschnabel	Grünschnabel	Brillenfassung	Schnabel
(beak)	(greenhorn)	(glasses frame)	(beak)
Vorderbein	Elfenbein	Perlhuhn	Bein
(foreleg)	(ivory)	(guinea fowl)	(leg)
Wandspiegel	Meeresspiegel	Tautropfen	Spiegel*
(pier glas)	(sea level)	(dewdrop)	(mirror)
Wildente	Zeitungsente	Pappnase	Ente*
(wild duck)	(canard)	(cardboard nose)	(duck)
Zuchthengst	Bürohengst	Seidenraupe	Hengst
(stallion, for breeding)	(pencil pusher)	(silkworm)	(stallion)

Note: Some of the German material loses its morphological complexity in the English translation. In addition, we were not able to find appropriate translations for all stimuli. Targets that were used in the study by Dohmes, Zwitserlood, & Bölte (2004) are marked by an asterisk.

Material Experiment 2

| Distractor Type | | | |
Semantically transparent	Semantically opaque	Control word	Target word
Aussicht (outlook)	Gesicht (face)	Anfall (attack)	Sicht (view)
Bauchtanz (belly dance)	Distanz (distance)	Treibnetz (drift net)	Tanz (dance)
Bergsee (mountain lake)	Odyssee (odyssey)	Ladendieb (shop lifter)	See* (lake)
Dauerlauf (endurance run)	Auflauf (casserole)	Lagerplan	Lauf (run)
Edelstahl (stainless steel)	Diebstahl (theft)	Raufaser (wood-chip)	Stahl (steel)
Ehegatte (spouse)	Fregatte (frigate)	Hainbuche	Gatte (spouse)
Expertenrat	Heirat (marriage)	Gewitter (thunderstorm)	Rat (advice)
Fahrplan (timetable)	Kaplan (chaplain)	Hartgeld (hard cash)	Plan (schedule)
Faltenrock (pleated skirt)	Barock (baroque)	Flugzeug (air plane)	Rock* (skirt)
Filzhut (fedora)	Vorhut (vanguard)	Eisfach	Hut* (Hat)
Fischfang (fishing)	Empfang (reception)	Kalkstein (limestone)	Fang (catch)
Glasschale	Pauschale (lump sum)	Stirnlocke (forelock)	Schale* (bowl)
Glockenschall	Marschall	Kuchenstück (piece of cake)	Schall (sound)
Grönland (greenland)	Heiland (redeemer)	Frackhemd (dress shirt)	Land* (country)
Hauswand (house wall)	Gewand (robe)	Briefblock (writing pad)	Wand (wall)
Heldenmut (prowess)	Armut (poverty)	Bierfass (beer barrel)	Mut (courage)
Herbstlaub (autumn foliage)	Urlaub (vacation)	Chefkoch (chef)	Laub (foliage)
Holztisch (wooden table)	Fetisch (fetish)	Volkslied (country song)	Tisch (table)
Kleidermotte (clothes moth)	Klamotte (rag)	Bindfaden (string)	Motte* (moth)
Königskrone (royal crown)	Makrone (macaroon)	Turnhalle (gymnasium)	Krone* (crown)
Krimsekt	Insekt (insect)	Fernrohr (telescope)	Sekt* (sparkling wine)
Landgraf (landgrave)	Paragraf (paragraph)	Lehrbuch (textbook)	Graf (earl)
Märchenfee	Kaffee (coffee)	Waschbär (raccoon)	Fee* (fairy)

| Distractor Type | | | |
Semantically transparent	Semantically opaque	Control word	Target word
Mauseloch	Moloch	Stehplatz	Loch
(mouse hole)	(moloch)	(standing room)	(hole)
Neukunde	Sekunde	Frostbeule	Kunde
(prospect)	(second)	(frostbite)	(customer)
Nusstorte	Retorte	Tarnkappe	Torte*
	(retort)	(magic-cap)	(gateau)
Obstmade	Pomade	Stichsäge	Made*
	(pomade)	(jigsaw)	(maggot)
Patentante	Resultante	Leibwache	Tante
(godmother)	(resultant)	(bodyguard)	(aunt)
Plattfuß	Beifuss	Lastkran	Fuß*
(flat foot)	(mugwort)		(foot)
Reisepass	Kompass	Dorfteich	Pass*
(passport)	(compass)		(passport)
Saftpresse	Zypresse	Drehwurm	Presse
(juice squeezer)	(cypress)		(squeezer)
Schnellzug	Anzug	Rotkohl	Zug*
(express train)	(suit)	(red cabbage)	(train)
Schublade	Schokolade	Sandwüste	Lade
(drawer)	(chocolate)	(sandy dessert)	(drawer)
Schulzeugnis	Erzeugnis	Rostbraten	Zeugnis
(school certificate)	(product)	(roast)	(certificate)
Senklot	Pilot	Rebstock	Lot*
(plumb-line)	(pilot)	(vine)	(plumb)
Stadttor	Reaktor	Grashalm	Tor*
(city gate)	(reactor)	(blade of grass)	(gate)
Strommast	Damast	Sanduhr	Mast*
(power pole)	(damask)	(hour glass)	(pylon)
Verbandswatte	Krawatte	Heimorgel	Watte
	(tie)		(cotton wool)
Viehweide	Eingeweide	Poststempel	Weide
(meadow)	(bowels)	(post mark)	(meadow)
Wagenrad	Kamerad	Rehkitz	Rad
(cart wheel)	(fellow)	(fawn)	(wheel)
Wertsache	Ursache	Kopfkissen	Sache
(article of value)	(cause)	(pillow)	(thing)
Zeittakt	Kontakt	Kurort	Takt
(clock pulse)	(contact)	(health resort)	(beat)
Zopfband	Proband	Maulwurf	Band*
(bow ribbon)	(subject)	(mole)	(ribbon)
Zwischenruf	Beruf	Druckknopf	Ruf
(interjection)	(profession)	(push button)	(call)

Some of German material loses their morphological complexity in the English translation. In addition, we were not able to find appropriate translations for all stimuli. Targets that were used in the study by Dohmes, Zwitserlood, & Bölte, 2004 are marked by an asterisk.

LANGUAGE AND COGNITIVE PROCESSES
2006, 21 (7–8), 945–973

Grammatical gender selection and the representation of morphemes: The production of Dutch diminutives

Niels O. Schiller

Leiden Institute for Brain and Cognition, Leiden, Maastricht University, Maastricht, and Max Planck Institute for Psycholinguistics, Nijmegen, The Netherlands

Alfonso Caramazza

Harvard University, Cambridge, MA, USA

In this study, we investigated grammatical feature selection during noun phrase production in Dutch. More specifically, we studied the conditions under which different grammatical genders select either the same or different determiners. Pictures of simple objects paired with a gender-congruent or a gender-incongruent distractor word were presented. Participants named the pictures using a noun phrase with the appropriate gender-marked determiner. Auditory (Experiment 1) or visual cues (Experiment 2) indicated whether the noun was to be produced in its standard or diminutive form. Results revealed a cost in naming latencies when target and distractor take different determiner forms independent of whether or not they have the same gender. This replicates earlier results showing that congruency effects

Correspondence should be addressed to Niels O. Schiller, Department of Cognitive Neuroscience, Faculty of Psychology, Maastricht University, P.O. Box 616, 6200 MD Maastricht, The Netherlands. E-mail: n.schiller@psychology.unimaas.nl

The research was supported in part by NIH grant DC04542 to Alfonso Caramazza. Niels O. Schiller is supported by the Royal Netherlands Academy of Arts and Sciences (KNAW) and by the Netherlands Organisation for Scientific Research (NWO; grant no. 453-02-006). The authors would like to thank Suzan Kroezen and Marcel van Gerven (Max Planck Institute for Psycholinguistics, Nijmegen, The Netherlands) for running the participants.

This paper benefited from discussion at the 45th TeaP conference in Kiel, Germany (March, 2003), the XIIIth ESCoP conference in Granada, Spain (September, 2003), the 44th Annual Meeting of the Psychonomic Society in Vancouver, Canada (November, 2003), and the 9th NVP winter congress in Egmond aan Zee, The Netherlands (December, 2003). For discussion and helpful comments the authors wish to thank the members of the Utterance Encoding group at the Max Planck Institute for Psycholinguistics, Nijmegen, The Netherlands, Xavier Alario (CNRS & Université de Provence) and Albert Costa (Universitat de Barcelona).

http://www.psypress.com/lcp   DOI: 10.1080/016909600824609

are due to competition during the selection of determiner forms rather than gender features. The overall pattern of results supports the view that grammatical feature selection is an *automatic* consequence of lexical node selection and therefore not subject to interference from incongruent grammatical features. Selection of the correct determiner form, however, is a competitive process, implying that lexical node and grammatical feature selection operate with distinct principles.

The basic question addressed in this study is whether or not the retrieval of grammatical gender in speech production can be delayed by presenting distractor words differing in gender from the target. Noun phrase (NP) production requires the retrieval of different forms of lexical information from long-term memory such as semantic, grammatical, and phonological. Semantic information refers to the meaning of a word (e.g., is it animate or inanimate, natural or man-made, etc.) while phonological information has to do with the actual form of a word (e.g., its phonemes, syllables, stress pattern, etc.). Grammatical information is necessary for constructing agreement between words. For example, in Dutch NPs, adjectives and nouns agree in number and gender, e.g., *groen boek*$_{(neu)}$ ('green book') vs. *groene boeken*$_{(neu)}$ ('green books') vs. *groene tafel*$_{(com)}$ ('green table') vs. *groene tafels*$_{(com)}$ ('green tables'). The Dutch word *boek* has neuter (neu) gender while *tafel* has common (com) gender. In order to be able to produce the correct form of the adjective in Dutch (*groen* or *groene*) the gender (and number) features of the noun have to be retrieved (for an alternative view see Mirković, MacDonald, & Seidenberg, 2005). Once the target gender node is selected, it can be used to activate the appropriate gender-marking suffix for the adjective.

Gender is a lexical property of nouns (Corbett, 1991). Thus, the study of gender feature retrieval provides a window into the mechanisms that govern the selection of lexical grammatical features and their role in determiner and inflectional morphology processing. Recent interest in grammatical feature processing is in part due to the development of methods proposed by Schriefers (1993). His procedure provides a window on NP processing in speech production. For example, he used the picture-word interference paradigm to investigate the syntactic processes involved in selecting the definite article and the adjective's inflection in NP production by Dutch speakers. In this paradigm, participants are instructed to name a picture while ignoring a simultaneously presented distractor word. This task is a variant of the Stroop (1935) paradigm and it has been used successfully to investigate various aspects of lexical access in language production (for reviews see Glaser, 1992; MacLeod, 1991). Schriefers (1993) presented his participants with coloured line drawings and asked them to name the objects by producing a determiner (Det)-adjective (Adj) NP (e.g., **het groene boek**$_{neu}$ 'the green book' vs. **de groene tafel**$_{com}$ 'the green table', Experiment 1) or a plain adjective NP (e.g., *groen boek*$_{neu}$ 'green book' vs. *groene tafel*$_{com}$ 'green table', Experiment 2). Distractor words that were either of the same or different gender as the picture name were presented visually. On the assumption that noun lexical nodes automatically activate their gender information, gender incongruence between target picture and distractor word could delay the selection of the correct gender information if one assumed that selection of gender nodes is a competitive process – the *gender selection interference hypothesis* (GSIH).

Schriefers (1993) obtained faster reaction times in both experiments when target picture and distractor word had the same gender than when they had different genders. Van Berkum (1997), La Heij, Mak, Sander, and Willeboordse (1998), Schiller and Caramazza (2003) as well as Starreveld and La Heij (2004) replicated the gender congruency effect in Dutch. Similar results were obtained in German by Schriefers and Teruel (2000) and Schiller and Caramazza (2003) and in Croatian by Costa, Kovacic, Fedorenko, and Caramazza (2003), but not in Romance languages such as Italian (Miozzo & Caramazza, 1999; Miozzo, Costa, & Caramazza, 2002), Spanish, Catalan (Costa, Sebastián-Gallés, Miozzo, & Caramazza, 1999), and French (Alario & Caramazza, 2002). An overview and account of all of these results can be found in Caramazza, Miozzo, Costa, Schiller, and Alario (2001). Schriefers (1993) interpreted this *gender congruency effect* as reflecting competition in the selection of a word's syntactic features. He argued that the activation of the gender feature of the distractor word interferes with the naming of the picture in those cases where the distractor's gender is different from that of the target noun. This is because two different gender specifications compete for selection in the gender-incongruent condition, whereas only one gender is activated in the gender-congruent condition. The gender congruency effect was absent, however, when nouns were named *without* determiners (La Heij et al., 1998; Starreveld & La Heij, 2004; but see Cubelli, Lotto, Paolieri, Girelli, & Job, 2005). Levelt, Roelofs, and Meyer (1999) interpreted this latter result as follows: When no determiner is needed in speech production, no gender feature is selected. Therefore, there is no gender feature competition in the bare noun naming condition, and hence a gender congruency effect does not occur in such a situation.

Although the method proposed by Schriefers is useful for addressing grammatical feature selection during NP production, the specific locus of the gender effect is not obvious. For instance, the putative gender congruency effect observed in Dutch might in fact be a determiner selection interference effect as noted by Miozzo and Caramazza (1999). In Dutch, the determiner form in an NP can be selected on the basis of the noun's gender alone. The determiner for common gender singular nouns is *de* and for neuter gender singular nouns it is ***het*** in *all* contexts (in contrast to Romance languages where the actual form of the determiner often depends on the phonological context of the following word). Once the noun's gender has been selected, its associated determiner form can be immediately selected for production. However, if gender selection were a non-competitive process in Dutch, the locus of the effect could theoretically be at the level of determiner selection and not at the level of gender feature selection. That is, if we assume that determiner form selection is a competitive process, we might expect slower determiner selection when target and distractor nouns have different genders. This is because the activation of a competing determiner (through the activation of the gender of the distractor noun) would interfere with the selection of the target determiner – the *determiner selection interference hypothesis* (DSIH).

The work on gender/determiner congruency is important because it allows the explicit formulation of assumptions about specific aspects of lexical access. Certainly, this is the case with respect to whether grammatical feature selection is a competitive process or whether grammatical features are accessed automatically as part of lexical node selection. Schiller and Caramazza (2003) provided experimental evidence from Dutch (and German) in support of this latter possibility. Dutch distinguishes two genders in the noun system, i.e. common and neuter. In the standard (singular) form, the determiner *de* is used for common gender and ***het*** for neuter gender, as for instance in *de tafel* ('the table', com) or *het boek* ('the book', neu). In a series of experiments, Schiller and Caramazza (2003) found gender congruency effects in the singular conditions where Dutch (and German) nouns take different determiners, but not in the plural conditions where the determiners are the same for all genders (e.g., *het boek* 'the book' – *de boeken* 'the books' and *de tafel* 'the table' – *de tafels* 'the tables'). If the gender congruency effect is caused by interference at the level of gender feature selection, we should have observed the effect in the production of both singular and plural NPs. This is because according to the GSIH the interference effect is independent of determiner form properties. However, if the gender congruency effect is caused by interference at the level of determiner selection (DSIH), we should not observe such an effect when the target and the distractor word, independently of whether or not the two nouns have the same gender, require the same determiner form. This latter hypothesis was supported by the results of the Schiller and Caramazza (2003) study.

Further evidence for determiner competition during NP naming came from a study by Janssen and Caramazza (2003). In this study, the authors demonstrated that during the naming of Dutch plural NPs (e.g., *de boeken* 'the books') the determiner of the singular form (e.g., ***het*** *boek* 'the book') is also activated. This was reflected in longer naming latencies when the singular and plural determiners were not the same (e.g., *het boek* 'the book' – *de boeken* 'the books') than when they were the same (e.g., *de kerk* 'the church' – *de kerken* 'the churches'). Schriefers, Jescheniak, and Hantsch (2002) replicated this effect in German (see also Schriefers, Jescheniak, & Hantsch, 2005; but see Schiller & Costa, in press). Bare noun (e.g., *boek* 'book' – *boeken* 'books' and *kerk* 'church' – *kerken* 'churches') and quantifier + noun naming (e.g., *een boek* 'one book' – *twee boeken* 'two books' and *een kerk* 'one church' – *twee kerken* 'two churches'), i.e., conditions that do not require the selection of gender-marked determiners, did not show the same competition costs. Therefore, Janssen and Caramazza (2003) argued, 'the selection of the determiner *de* in *de boeken* competes for selection with the determiner *het*, but no such competition occurs in the case of *de kerken*' (p. 640), supporting their interpretation that these results reflect determiner selection processes. In a second experiment Janssen and Caramazza (2003) showed that diminutive NP naming was faster for neuter gender nouns (e.g., *het boekje* 'the little book') than for common gender nouns (e.g., *het kerkje* 'the little church') relative to their corresponding base forms (i.e., *het boek* or *de kerk*). Interestingly, this effect disappeared when no determiner selection was necessary (bare noun naming) or when the gender-unmarked indefinite determiner was used to name the NPs. The authors interpreted these results as demonstrating that the gender feature of the base noun is visible to the determiner selection process and that the base form of a diminutive noun is active during morphological processing in diminutive NP production in Dutch.

Recently, Spalek and Schriefers (2005) replicated and extended Janssen and Caramazza's (2003) data by demonstrating that the determiner competition effect is modulated by the relative dominance of the morphological forms (standard vs. diminutive). Spalek and Schriefers (2005) used words that occurred dominantly in the diminutive in Dutch (e.g., *lepel* 'spoon' or *blik* 'can') and words that occurred dominantly in the base form (e.g., *fakkel* 'torch' or *paleis* 'palace'). For base-form dominant words they replicate Janssen and Caramazza (2003), i.e., *de*-words were named slower in the diminutive (*het fakkeltje*) than in the base form (*de fakkel*) and for *het*-words the reverse pattern emerged (*het paleis* faster than *het paleisje*). Moreover, even for diminutive-dominant words there was an interaction between gender and format of the target words reflecting the fact that *het*-words were produced significantly faster than their corresponding base forms but for *de*-words no such difference occurred. Spalek and Schriefers (2005) concluded that 'the form of the interaction for diminutive-dominant items implies that the gender of the base form becomes activated, even in the case of words with a strong diminutive preference' (p. 110).

The investigation of diminutive production in Dutch may also provide another way of disentangling the DSIH and the GSIH. Dutch has the interesting linguistic property that all diminutives take the determiner **het** whether or not the base word has neuter gender (e.g., **het** *boek* 'the book' – **het** *boekje* 'the little book' vs. *de kerk* 'the church' **het** *kerkje* – 'the little church'). Thus, in Dutch, different determiners are selected for common and neuter gender nouns when used in the standard form (*de* and **het**), but in the diminutive form always the same determiner is used for both genders (**het**). However, the formulation of specific hypotheses about diminutive production depends on the assumptions made about the representation of diminutives. There are at least two possibilities how to represent diminutives: (a) a whole word representation such as *kerkje* or (b) a separate morpheme representation such as ($kerk_{com}$)*je*. In the latter representation the gender feature of the base word is visible to the determiner selection process, while in the former it is not. Dutch diminutives are treated as 'neuter' and always take the determiner *het*. That is, there is a strong correlation in Dutch between the grammatical feature 'neuter' and a phonological property of diminutives, i.e. the suffix *–tje* (or predictable allomorphs such as *–je* or *–pje*). Therefore, the gender feature 'neuter' of diminutives can be conceived of as an emergent property from phonological (and semantic) information of the diminutive word form (see Mirković et al., 2005). An explicit connection between the suffix *–tje* and a neuter gender feature is not required.

If (a) were the case, DSIH and GSIH would make the same predictions with respect to a potential gender/determiner congruency effect but the underlying causes of the effects are different. According to the GSIH the gender congruency effect is caused at the level of gender feature selection, i.e., when incongruent gender features such as *common* and *neuter* compete for selection. Therefore, we should observe the effect in the production of both standard (*de* $kerk_{com}$ – *het* $glas_{neu}$ 'the glass' vs. *de* $kerk_{com}$ – *de* jas_{com} 'the jacket'; the first noun of each pair refers to the target picture name, the second to the printed distractor word) and diminutive (*het* $kerkje_{neu}$ – *het* $glas_{neu}$ vs. *het* $kerkje_{neu}$ – *de* jas_{com}) NPs. The DSIH would make the same prediction but for a different reason. According to the DSIH, gender features are selected automatically in the course of lexical access; the congruency effect occurs due to determiner competition when incongruent determiners compete for selection at the phonological form level. The conditions of determiner mismatch would be the same as those of grammatical feature mismatch both in standard (*de* $kerk_{com}$ – **het** $glas_{neu}$ vs. *de* $kerk_{com}$ – *de* jas_{com}) and diminutive (**het** $kerkje_{neu}$ – **het** $glas_{neu}$ vs. **het** $kerkje_{neu}$ – *de* jas_{com}) NP production.

However, data provided by Janssen and Caramazza (2003) and by Spalek and Schriefers (2005) make possibility (a) quite unlikely: Their data suggest that the gender feature (e.g., *common*) and determiner (e.g., *de*) of the base form of a noun (e.g., *kerk*) become activated when its diminutive form (*het kerkje*) needs to be produced (see above). Furthermore, the assumption that diminutives are represented as separate morphemes and that the gender feature of the base word is visible to the determiner selection process is at least plausible for transparently derived diminutives. Transparently derived diminutives are words like *kerkje* ('small church') where the diminutive predominantly expresses a size relation between the base word *kerk* ('church') and its diminutive form. However, there are also diminutives for which this does not hold. In colloquial Dutch, a diminutive form does not necessarily mean that the object being referred to with a diminutive form is physically small, but often there is a connotation of 'cuteness' carried by the diminutive. Examples are *kopje* ('cup'; not 'small cup'), *bloemetje* ('bunch of flowers'; 'small flower' is *bloempje*; Booij, 2002), *flensje* ('thin pancake'; where the base word *flens* ['flange'] has no semantic relationship with the diminutive form), and *meisje* ('girl'; where the base word 'meis' does not exist [anymore] – only the form *meid* ['maid'] occurs in contemporary Dutch). In those opaque diminutives it is at least questionable whether or not the gender of the base word – if available at all – is visible to the determiner selection process. Therefore, the materials used in this study were carefully selected such that only transparently derived diminutives that refer to the (small) size of objects were included. Formally, this was done by making sure that the diminutive form referred primarily to the smaller size of the referent relative to its base form referent and by including only those diminutives, which were of lower frequency of occurrence than their base words.

If (b) were the case, however, GSIH and DSIH would make different predictions. According to the DSIH we should observe a congruency effect when target and distractor word require different determiner forms, independent of whether or not the two nouns have the same gender. This condition is met in the diminutive NP production for common nouns (**het** *kerk*$_{com}$*je* – **de** *jas*$_{com}$ vs. **het** *kerk*$_{com}$*je* – **het** *glas*$_{neu}$). The GSIH makes the opposite prediction in this case since congruency effects are accounted for at the level of grammatical feature selection (*het kerk*$_{com}$*je* – *de jas*$_{com}$ vs. *het kerk*$_{com}$*je* – *het glas*$_{neu}$). This latter contrast between the GSIH and the DSIH forms the basis for the research reported here.

Thus, we test complex hypotheses, which combine assumptions about the representation of diminutives with assumptions about the way in which distractor words affect the access of properties required for target NP production. Implicit in the predictions we have derived for the production of standard and diminutive NPs from the two hypotheses under consideration here is the assumption that the processing of a distractor word influences the production system in certain ways. Specifically, it is assumed that the distractor word activates its corresponding lexical node and associated grammatical features in the production network. The general plausibility of this assumption has been confirmed by the studies showing a gender congruency effect in NP production (Costa et al., 2003; La Heij et al., 1998; Schriefers, 1993; Schriefers & Teruel, 2000; Schiller & Caramazza, 2003; Schiller & Costa, in press; Starreveld & La Heij, 2004; Van Berkum, 1997). That is, the gender congruency effect can be taken to indicate that the gender feature of the distractor word is activated in the picture-word interference task when NPs are produced.

EXPERIMENT 1: STANDARD AND DIMINUTIVE NP PRODUCTION IN DUTCH (WITH AUDITORY CUES)

In our first experiment, we attempted to replicate and extend the determiner congruency effect in Dutch with a different linguistic structure in order to provide further evidence that the effect occurs at the level of determiner selection. Native Dutch participants were required to name a set of pictures. Each picture was paired with a gender-congruent distractor word and with a gender-incongruent distractor word. Additionally, we added semantically related and phonologically related distractor words as control conditions to check whether or not distractor words were processed. Pictures appeared as single objects and were preceded by a low (standard condition) or a high tone (diminutive condition). Participants were asked to name the picture with the appropriate determiner in the NP format indicated by the tone, e.g., *de kerk* ('the church') or *het kerkje* ('the small church'). The Det + N naming task is equivalent to the task employed by Costa et al. (1999), La Heij et al. (1998), Miozzo and Caramazza (1999), Schiller and Caramazza (2003), and Schriefers and Teruel (2000). The GSIH and DSIH make different predictions in naming standard and diminutive NPs. The GSIH predicts a gender congruency effect independently of whether production involves standard or diminutive NPs. The DSIH predicts different effects for standard and diminutive NPs. More specifically, this latter hypothesis predicts a three-way interaction between the format of the NP (standard or diminutive), the gender of the target (common or neuter), and the congruency condition between the target gender and the distractor gender (congruent or incongruent).

Method

Participants.   Experiment 1 included 28 participants. All participants were native Dutch speakers recruited from the pool of participants of the Max Planck Institute for Psycholinguistics in Nijmegen (mostly students from Nijmegen University in the Netherlands). They were paid for their participation.

Materials.   Forty-eight target pictures corresponding to monomorphemic Dutch nouns were selected for naming. The diminutive is extremely productive in Dutch and some forms may already have lexical status (e.g., *een kopje koffie* 'a cup of coffee' and not 'a small cup of coffee' or *een toetje* 'a desert' and not 'a small desert'). There were equally many common and neuter gender picture names (e.g., *de kerk* 'the church', com; *het boek* 'the book', neu). The mean frequency of occurrence per one million word forms was similar for the common and the neuter gender picture names. Each picture was paired with a gender-congruent, a gender-incongruent, a semantically related, and a phonologically related distractor word. The distractor words had similar frequency characteristics as the picture names. Mean length in syllables and segments was matched between the gender-congruent and incongruent distractor words. Gender-congruent and incongruent distractor words were semantically and phonologically unrelated to the picture names. Semantically and phonologically related distractors had the same gender as the target. Therefore, the ratio of gender-congruent to gender-incongruent trials was three to one. This means that the unequal distribution between these two conditions might have an impact on the results. However, this objection was addressed in a study by Schriefers et al. (2002) who obtained similar interaction patterns independent of whether the distribution of grammatical features or the distribution of determiner forms was controlled. Therefore, this argument could be empirically refuted.

The complete list of target pictures and distractor words can be found in Appendix A. Pictures were simple black line drawings of everyday objects presented on a white background. They were taken from the pool of pictures of the Max Planck Institute for Psycholinguistics in Nijmegen. Distractor words were displayed without their determiners in their singular form in black characters (font type and size: Geneva, 30 pts) in or across the object. Pictures appeared in the centre of the screen with the distractor words appearing at slightly different positions around fixation to prevent participants from ignoring the distractors. For an individual picture, however, the position of all four distractor words was the same.

Procedure.   Participants were tested individually in a dimly lit testing booth. They sat in front of a computer screen at a viewing distance of approximately 80 cm. The experimenter scored potential errors via headphones in a separate room. The computer screen was a NEC MultiSync M500 monitor. On each trial, a fixation point appeared for 500 ms followed by the picture and the distractor word. After 300 ms, participants heard a tone via headphones indicating whether the target was to be produced in the standard format (low tone) or in the diminutive (high tone). Depending on the tone (low or high) they were required to name the object with the appropriate determiner in the standard or in the diminutive format. Since participants only knew 300 ms *after* target and distractor onset whether a standard or a diminutive NP had to be produced, they could not prepare the appropriate determiner in the diminutive format upon perceiving the pictures. However, 300 ms is long enough to allow them to recognise and process the word.

Participants were instructed to fixate the fixation point and to name the target picture as quickly and as accurately as possible with the appropriate determiner in Dutch. At picture onset, a voice key connected to a microphone was activated to measure the naming latencies. As soon as a response was given and the voice key was triggered, picture and distractor word disappeared from the screen and after a short pause of one second the next trial started. If no response was recorded within 2 s, the next trial started automatically. The Nijmegen Experimental Set-Up (NESU) controlled the presentation of the trial sequences. A response was considered invalid when it exceeded the response deadline of 2 s, when it included a speech error, when a wrong determiner or picture name was produced, or when the voice key was triggered incorrectly. Invalid responses were excluded from the reaction time analyses.

Design. The experiment consisted of three parts. First, participants were engaged in a familiarisation phase. They saw each picture once on the computer screen to become familiarised with the pictures and learn the designated picture names (in case alternative names were preferred by the participants). Each picture appeared on the screen and after 2 s the designated name was added below the picture. Both remained in view until the participants pressed a button. Participants were asked to use the designated name for each picture. After the familiarisation phase, participants received a practice phase during which each picture was presented once as single objects in the centre of the screen preceded by a fixation point. A row of Xs was presented where the distractor word would appear in the naming phase (see below). Participants' task was to name the picture as quickly and as accurately as possible using the appropriate determiner and picture name, e.g., *de kerk* ('the church'). This procedure was adopted to make sure that participants knew the correct determiner for each picture name. After completion of the practice phase, the experimenter corrected participants in case they did not use the designated name for a given picture.

The naming phase began immediately after the practice phase. Stimuli were presented in 4 blocks of 96 trials each (48 items × 4 conditions × 2 formats = 384 trials). Target pictures and distractor words appeared at the same time (i.e., the SOA was 0 ms). Twelve times during the naming phase, feedback was given on the screen about the mean naming latencies, which participants were required to write down. This procedure had the purpose of speeding participants up. In each block, each target occurred twice, once accompanied by a low and once by a high tone in different conditions. Blocks were randomised individually for each participant with the following constraints: (a) Before the same object or distractor word was presented again, at least one other object or distractor word appeared in between; (b) targets could have the same format or the same gender on no more than two consecutive trials; (c) the same condition could not appear more than twice in a row. Tones could be of the same type no more than three times in a row. Finally, the order of the blocks was varied across participants. The experiment lasted approximately one hour.

Results

Naming latencies shorter than 350 ms and longer than 1500 ms (4.7% of the data) were counted as outliers. The mean naming latencies and error rates are summarised in Table 1. Analyses of variance were run with Format of Target (standard or diminutive), Gender of Target (common or neuter), and Congruency (gender-congruent vs. gender-incongruent) as independent variables. Separate analyses were carried out with participants (F_1) and items (F_2) as random variables. Variability is reported with 95% confidence intervals (CIs).

Naming latencies. The effect of Format of Target was highly significant, $F_1(1, 27) = 49.61$, $CI = 13.6$ ms, $p < .01$; $F_2(1, 46) = 47.23$, $CI = 9.1$ ms, $p < .01$. Naming latencies to diminutive NPs (578 ms) were 47 ms faster than naming latencies to standard NPs (625 ms). Furthermore, neuter gender targets were named slightly faster (598 ms) than common gender targets (605 ms), but this 7 ms effect of Gender of Target was not significant, $F_1(1, 27) = 2.12$, $CI = 10.1$ ms, *ns*; $F_2(1, 46) < 1$. Gender of Target and Format of Target interacted significantly, $F_1(1, 27) = 16.12$, $CI = 13.3$ ms, $p < .01$; $F_2(1, 46) = 8.37$, $CI = 12.9$ ms, $p < .01$, reflecting the fact that the diminutive form (566 ms) was named 65 ms faster than the standard form (631 ms) for neuter gender targets but the same contrast led only to a 29 ms difference for the common gender targets (591 ms and 620 ms for diminutive and standard forms, respectively).

The effect of Congruency was not significant, $F_1(1, 27) = 3.75$, $CI = 8.4$ ms, *ns*; $F_2(1, 46) = 2.24$, $CI = 7.8$ ms, n.s. However, Congruency interacted significantly with Format of Target, $F_1(1, 27) = 12.24$, $CI = 8.0$ ms, $p < .01$; $F_2(1, 46) = 4.20$, $CI = 10.1$ ms, $p < .05$. This interaction is

TABLE 1

Mean naming latencies (in ms) and percentage errors (in parentheses) in Experiment 1
(Dutch Det + Noun naming with auditory cues)

Format of target	Condition	Gender of Target		Mean
		Common	Neuter	
Standard		(e.g., de kerk)	(e.g., het boek)	
	Gender-congruent	607 (5.4)	625 (3.1)	616 (4.2)
	Gender-incongruent	632 (5.7)	636 (3.9)	634 (4.8)
	Semantically related	623 (4.8)	637 (3.1)	630 (3.9)
	Phonologically related	600 (6.1)	633 (3.3)	616 (4.7)
	Differences			
	Congruency effect	+25 (+0.3)	+11 (+0.8)	+18 (+0.6)
	Semantic effect	+16 (−0.6)	+12 (0.0)	+14 (−0.3)
	Phonological effect	−7 (+0.7)	+8 (+0.2)	0 (+0.5)
Diminutive		(e.g., het kerkje)	(e.g., het boekje)	
	Gender-congruent	602 (5.1)	556 (1.8)	579 (3.4)
	Gender-incongruent	580 (5.1)	575 (2.2)	578 (3.6)
	Semantically related	615 (6.3)	564 (4.3)	590 (5.3)
	Phonologically related	606 (5.4)	563 (2.7)	585 (4.0)
	Differences			
	Congruency effect	−22 (0.0)	+19 (+0.4)	−1 (+0.2)
	Semantic effect	+13 (+1.2)	+8 (+2.5)	+11 (+1.9)
	Phonological effect	+4 (+0.3)	+7 (+0.9)	+6 (+0.6)

due to an 18 ms gender congruency effect in the standard format, while in the diminutive format there was a 2 ms difference in the reverse direction. Congruency did not interact with Gender of Target, $F_1(1, 27) = 2.71$, $CI = 11.7$ ms, *ns*; $F_2(1, 46) = 1.31$, $CI = 11.1$ ms, *ns*. Most importantly, however, the three-way interaction between Congruency, Gender of Target, and Format of Target was significant, $F_1(1, 27) = 13.46$, $CI = 15.2$ ms, $p < .01$; $F_2(1, 46) = 7.05$, $CI = 14.6$ ms, $p < .05$, reflecting the fact that for common gender nouns in the diminutive format the gender-incongruent (but determiner-congruent) condition (580 ms) produced faster naming latencies than the gender-congruent condition (602 ms). In contrast, common gender nouns in the standard format as well as neuter gender nouns in both formats yielded faster naming latencies in the gender-congruent than in the gender-incongruent condition. This interesting three-way interaction is visualised in Figure 1.

The differences between the gender-congruent and the gender-incongruent conditions were assessed by paired *t*-tests. For common gender targets in the standard format (*de kerk*) the 25 ms difference between the gender-congruent (607 ms) and the gender-incongruent

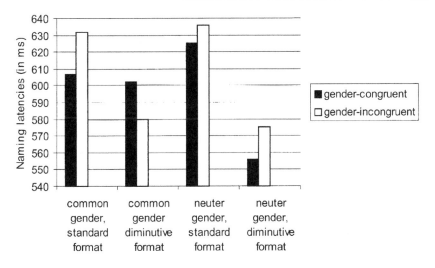

Figure 1. Naming latencies (in ms) for gender-congruent and gender-incongruent conditions in Experiment 1.

condition (632 ms) was significant, $t_1(27) = 3.33, p < .01; t_2(23) = 2.56, p < .05$. In the diminutive format (*het kerkje*) the corresponding 22 ms difference (602 ms vs. 580 ms, respectively) was marginally significant, $t_1(27) = 2.93, p < .01; t_2(23) = 1.80, p = .08$. For neuter gender targets in the standard form (*het boek*) the 11 ms difference between the gender-congruent (625 ms) and the gender-incongruent condition (636 ms) was not significant $t_1(27) = 1.20, ns; t_2(23) = 1.16, ns$. However, in the diminutive format (*het boekje*) the corresponding 19 ms difference (556 ms vs. 575 ms, respectively) was marginally significant, $t_1(27) = 3.42, p < .01; t_2(23) = 1.75, p = .09$.

The semantically related condition (610 ms) was produced significantly slower than the gender-congruent condition, $t_1(27) = 2.77, SD = 24.75, p < .01; t_2(47) = 3.02, SD = 29.88, p < .01$, showing that distractor words were processed and influenced the naming of the target pictures. Phonological relatedness (600 ms) did not have an effect, $t_1(27) < 1; t_2(47) = 1.11, SD = 26.40, ns$, possibly due to the SOA of 0 ms applied in this experiment. Phonological effects were mostly reported for positive SOAs, i.e., the distractor being presented after picture onset (see Schriefers, Meyer, & Levelt, 1990; but see also Starreveld, 2000 and Jescheniak & Schriefers, 2001).

Error rates. The effect of Form of Target was not significant, $F_1(1, 27) = 1.84, CI = 0.4\%, ns; F_2(1, 46) = 2.87, CI = 0.2\%, ns$. The effect of Target Gender, however, was significant, $F_1(1, 27) = 12.78, CI = 0.3\%$,

$p < .01$; $F_2(1, 46) = 15.85$, $CI = 0.3\%$, $p < .01$, reflecting the fact that more errors were made on common gender targets than on neuter gender targets. However, there was no interaction between Form of Target and Target Gender, $F_1(1, 27) < 1$; $F_2(1, 46) < 1$. The effect of Congruency was not significant, either $F_1(1, 27) < 1$; $F_2(1, 46) < 1$, nor did it interact with Form of Target or Target Gender.

Discussion

The results of Experiment 1 are interesting for several reasons. First, the experiment demonstrates that the gender congruency effect is a stable phenomenon in Dutch. Schriefers (1993) obtained the original gender congruency effect in Dutch. More recently, Van Berkum (1997), La Heij et al. (1998), and Schiller and Caramazza (2003) replicated this effect in Dutch. As can be seen in Table 1, the gender congruency effect in the standard format was similar for both genders, as reflected by the absence of an interaction between Gender of Target and Congruency.

Second, our results go beyond earlier results because they show that the gender congruency effect is reversed when pictures with common gender names are named with the appropriate determiner in the diminutive format. Thus, our results support the claim that the putative gender congruency effect may actually be a determiner congruency effect, as suggested by Miozzo and Caramazza (1999) and empirically supported by Schiller and Caramazza (2003). According to this account, the interference effect does not occur in selecting the gender of the target noun but in selecting its appropriate determiner form.

How does the determiner form actually become selected? Lexical representations activate their corresponding determiners via features. According to Alario and Caramazza (2002), activation is collected in a determiner frame. Features of relevance for determiner selection in Dutch are Gender of Target (common or neutral) and Format of Target (standard or diminutive). The features definiteness and number also affect determiner selection in Dutch, but since we did not manipulate these features in the current study, we will not discuss them here. Each activated feature or combination of features in a frame activates a corresponding determiner (see also Spalek & Schriefers, 2005). Specifically, the gender feature *common* activates the determiner *de*, *neuter* activates the determiner *het*, and the feature *diminutive* activates the determiner *het*. The format feature *standard* does not activate a specific determiner as this depends on the gender of the referent. The combination of the features *common* + *standard* activates the determiner *de*, *common* + *diminutive* activates the determiner *het*, as well as *neuter* + *standard* and *neuter* + *diminutive*. Following Spalek and Schriefers (2005), we assume that combination of features weight more in determiner selection than individual features because it is the combination of features that eventually governs the selection of the determiner.

Common gender nouns (e.g., *de kerk*) activate the determiner *de* by virtue of the features *common* and *common + standard*. A gender-congruent distractor word (e.g., *de jas* 'the jacket') also activates the determiner *de*, whereas a gender-incongruent distractor word (e.g., *het glas* 'the glass') activates the determiner *het*. This forms the basis of the classic gender/determiner congruency effect. In the diminutive format (e.g., *het kerkje*), the target activates the determiner *de* by virtue of the feature *common* and to a larger extent the determiner *het* by virtue of the feature *diminutive* and the feature combination *common + diminutive*. A gender-congruent distractor word (e.g., *de jas*), however, activates the determiner *de* via its gender feature *common* and the feature combination *common + standard*. In other words, the gender-congruent common gender distractor word becomes determiner-incongruent in this special situation (e.g., target: *het kerkje*, distractor: *de jas*). Therefore, before the correct determiner *het* can be selected, relatively more competition between *de* and *het* must be resolved than in the gender-incongruent, but determiner-congruent condition (e.g., target: *het kerkje*, distractor: *het glas*), when the distractor word (e.g., *het glas*) activates the target determiner *het* by virtue of the feature *neuter* and the feature combination *neuter + standard*. Therefore, the gender-incongruent, determiner-congruent condition yielded faster naming latencies than the gender-congruent, determiner-incongruent condition. This is exactly what is predicted by the DSIH, but not by the GSIH according to which the effect should have been the reverse of what we found.

Neuter gender nouns (e.g., *het boek*) similarly activate the determiner *het* through the features *neuter* and *neuter + standard*. A gender-congruent word (e.g., *het glas*) will do the same, while a gender-incongruent distractor word (e.g., *de jas*) activates the competing determiner de via the feature *common* and the feature combination *common + standard*. In the diminutive format (e.g., *het boekje*), the target activates the determiner *het* by the features *neuter* and *diminutive* as well as by the feature combination *neuter + diminutive*. A gender-congruent distractor word (e.g., *het glas*) will again activate the determiner *het*, while a gender-incongruent distractor word (e.g., *de jas*) will activate the competing determiner *de*. Therefore, for neuter gender targets, there is no difference in determiner competition between standard and diminutive format, whereas for common gender targets there is.

One might argue, however, that the determiner congruency effect should be larger for diminutives than for standard forms because in the former condition the determiner *het* receives more activation than in the latter. This difference is actually reflected numerically in a (marginally) significant difference between the gender-congruent and the gender-incongruent condition for neuter gender diminutives while the same difference is not significant for neuter gender targets in standard format. However, the interaction between Congruency and Format of Target is not significant for neuter gender targets (both $Fs < 1$).

The results obtained for Dutch in Experiment 1 do not support the GSIH. Instead, the experimental outcome so far supports the alternative DSIH. However, although the outcome of the experiment was exactly as predicted by the DSIH, it resides on one crucial comparison (common gender nouns with gender-congruent vs. gender-incongruent distractor words in diminutive format). The other conditions (i.e., common gender nouns in standard format and neuter gender nouns in both standard and diminutive format) do not allow us to distinguish between the GSIH and the DSIH because both hypotheses make identical predictions for these conditions. Therefore, it is important to replicate the effect to exclude the possibility that the outcome of Experiment 1 is due to Type I error. In Experiment 2, we set out to replicate the determiner congruency effect in Dutch with a slightly different methodology. Instead of auditory signals (low vs. high tones) that cued participants about the utterance format (standard vs. diminutive NP) we manipulated the relative size of the objects. A relatively large object indicated that a standard NP was to be used (*de kerk* or *het boek*) and a relatively small object indicated that a diminutive NP had to be used (*het kerkje* or *het boekje*).

EXPERIMENT 2: STANDARD AND DIMINUTIVE NP PRODUCTION IN DUTCH (WITH VISUAL CUES)

In this experiment, native Dutch participants were asked to name a set of pictures paired with a gender-congruent and a gender-incongruent distractor word. Pictures appeared as single objects but varied in size: A relatively large picture would indicate that participants should produce a standard Det+N NP, whereas a relatively small picture would indicate that they were required to name the target using a diminutive Det+N NP. Thus, Experiment 2 is a replication of Experiment 1 with a slightly different procedure.

There is, however, one potential problem with Experiment 2. It could be argued that as soon as participants detected that an object was presented in its smaller variant they automatically selected the determiner **het** (without further consideration of the target's gender) and started to produce their response. By doing so, the gender-incongruent distractor would not get a chance to interfere with the selection of the picture's name gender specification in the diminutive condition. According to this scenario, there should not be a difference between the gender-congruent and the gender-incongruent condition in the diminutive format. However, if we replicate the outcome of our first experiment, we can be sure that participants processed the distractor words also in the diminutive condition. Furthermore, we again included a semantically related and a phonologically related control condition in order to obtain additional positive evidence that the distractor words are being processed and affect the selection/production of the target noun.

Method

Participants.   Nineteen Dutch students from the same population as described for Experiment 1 took part in Experiment 2. All participants were paid for their participation and none of them had also taken part in Experiment 1.

Materials, procedure, and design.   Materials, procedure, and design were the same as in Experiment 1 except the NP format was no longer cued by a tone but by a visual cue. Pictures appeared in two sizes, a relatively large one and a relatively small one. A large picture indicated the use of a standard NP such as *de kerk* or *het boek*. A relatively small picture indicated that a diminutive NP was to be used as, for instance, *het kerkje* or *het boekje*. Large pictures fitted into a 12-cm by 12-cm frame, small pictures were no bigger than 5 cm by 5 cm, and participants could easily discriminate between the two picture sizes.

Results

Using the same criteria as in the first experiment 1.3% of the data was counted as outliers. The mean naming latencies and error rates are summarised in Table 2.

Naming latencies.   The effect of Format of Target was again highly significant, $F_1(1, 18) = 11.41$, $CI = 16.6$ ms, $p < .01$; $F_2(1, 46) = 39.90$, $CI = 6.2$ ms, $p < .01$. Naming latencies to diminutive NPs (658 ms) were 26 ms faster than naming latencies to standard NPs (684 ms). Furthermore, neuter gender targets were named slightly faster (665 ms) than common gender targets (676 ms), but this 11 ms effect of Gender of Target was not significant, $F_1(1, 18) = 3.99$, $CI = 11.9$ ms, *ns*; $F_2(1, 46) < 1$. Gender of Target and Format of Target did not interact, $F_1(1, 18) < 1$; $F_2(1, 46) < 1$.

The effect of Congruency was significant $F_1(1, 18) = 13.00$, $CI = 6.7$ ms, $p < .01$; $F_2(1, 46) = 4.56$, $CI = 9.0$ ms, $p < .05$. Pictures were named 11 ms faster in the gender-congruent (665 ms) than in the gender-

TABLE 2

Mean naming latencies (in ms) and percentage errors (in parentheses) in Experiment 2
(Dutch Det + Noun naming with visual cues)

| Format of target | Condition | Gender of Target | | Mean |
		Common	Neuter	
Standard		(e.g., de kerk)	(e.g., het boek)	
	Gender-congruent	671 (3.9)	674 (4.2)	672 (4.1)
	Gender-incongruent	706 (8.6)	686 (3.5)	696 (6.0)
	Semantically related	691 (5.3)	685 (3.1)	688 (4.2)
	Phonologically related	673 (4.4)	667 (4.6)	670 (4.5)
	Differences			
	Congruency effect	+35 (+4.7)	+12 (−0.7)	+24 (+1.9)
	Semantic effect	+20 (+1.4)	+11 (−1.1)	+16 (+0.1)
	Phonological effect	+2 (+0.5)	−17 (+0.4)	−2 (+0.4)
Diminutive		(e.g., het kerkje)	(e.g., het boekje)	
	Gender-congruent	676 (5.7)	640 (5.3)	658 (5.5)
	Gender-incongruent	654 (5.5)	659 (5.0)	657 (5.3)
	Semantically related	681 (6.8)	654 (6.1)	667 (6.5)
	Phonologically related	654 (7.0)	635 (4.8)	644 (5.9)
	Differences			
	Congruency effect	−22 (−0.2)	+19 (−0.3)	−1 (−0.2)
	Semantic effect	+5 (+1.1)	+14 (+0.8)	+9 (+1.0)
	Phonological effect	−22 (+1.3)	−5 (−0.5)	−14 (+0.4)

incongruent condition (676 ms). Congruency did not interact with Gender of Target $F_1(1, 18) = 2.43$, $CI = 8.4$ ms, *ns*; $F_2(1, 46) < 1$, but the interaction between Congruency and Format of Target was significant, $F_1(1, 18) = 13.09$, $CI = 10.6$ ms, $p < .01$; $F_2(1, 46) = 6.62$, $CI = 9.0$ ms, $p < .05$, reflecting the fact that the gender-congruency effect was 24 ms in the standard format, but 1 ms in the reverse direction when a diminutive NP was produced. Most importantly, the three-way interaction between Condition, Gender of Target, and Format of Target was again significant, $F_1(1, 18) = 17.79$, $CI = 15.8$ ms, $p < .01$; $F_2(1, 46) = 10.34$, $CI = 12.7$ ms, $p < .01$, due to the fact that for common gender nouns in the diminutive format – but not for the other three Congruency conditions the gender-incongruent (but determiner-congruent) condition produced faster naming latencies (654 ms) than the gender-congruent condition (676 ms). This important three-way interaction is visualised again in a graph (see Figure 2).

The differences between the gender-congruent and the gender-incongruent conditions were again assessed by paired *t*-tests. For common gender targets in the standard format (*de kerk*) the 35 ms difference

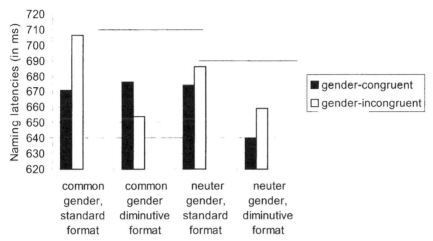

Figure 2.   Naming latencies (in ms) for gender-congruent and gender-incongruent conditions in Experiment 2.

between the gender-congruent (671 ms) and the gender-incongruent condition (706 ms) was significant, $t_1(18) = 4.57, p < .01; t_2(23) = 2.88, p < .01$. In the diminutive format (*het kerkje*) this difference (22 ms; 676 ms vs. 654 ms, respectively) was marginally significant, $t_1(18) = 4.11, p < .01$; $t_2(23) = 1.91, p = .07$. For neuter gender targets in the standard form (*het boek*) the 12 ms difference between the gender-congruent (674 ms) and the gender-incongruent condition (686 ms) was not significant, $t_1(18) = 1.63$, *ns*; $t_2(23) = 1.20$, *ns*. However, in the diminutive format (*het boekje*) the corresponding 19 ms difference (640 ms vs. 659 ms, respectively) was significant by participants but not by items, $t_1(18) = 3.37, p < .01; t_2(23) = 1.51$, *ns*.

The semantically related condition (678 ms) yielded a significant inhibition effect relative to the gender-congruent condition (665 ms); $t_1(18) = 2.73, SD = 20.68, p < .05; t_2(47) = 2.08, SD = 41.27, p < .05$, demonstrating that distractor words were processed and influenced the naming of the target pictures. The effect of phonological relatedness (657 ms) was again negligible, $t_1(18) = 1.55, SD = 22.02$, *ns*; $t_2(47) = 1.21$, $SD = 35.47$, *ns*, possibly due to the same reasons discussed in Experiment 1.

Error rates.   The effect of Form of Target was not significant, $F_1(1, 18) = 2.93, CI = 0.5\%$, *ns*; $F_2(1, 46) = 3.11, CI = 0.2\%$, *ns*. The effect of Target Gender, however, was significant by participants but not by items, $F_1(1, 18) = 4.58, CI = 0.4\%, p < .05; F_2(1, 46) = 1.85, CI = 0.4\%$, *ns*. However, there was no interaction between Form of Target and Target Gender,

$F_1(1, 18) < 1; F_2(1, 46) < 1$. The effect of Congruency was not significant, either $F_1(1, 18) < 1; F_2(1, 46) < 1$, nor did it interact with Form of Target or Gender of Target.

Discussion

The results of Experiment 2 are very similar to those of Experiment 1. The effect of a gender-incongruent distractor word in Dutch only yielded an interference effect when the determiner was also incongruent with the determiner of the target – just as in Experiment 1. However, when the gender-incongruent distractor word had the same determiner as the target, whereas the gender-congruent distractor word had a different determiner, which was the case for common gender nouns in the diminutive format (e.g., *het kerkje*), the gender congruency effect was reversed. This effect is not in agreement with the GSIH but it was predicted by the DSIH.

In Dutch, there are two different determiners in the standard utterance format, which mark the gender of a noun (i.e., *de* for common gender or *het* for neuter gender). In the diminutive format, however, there is only one determiner for both genders (i.e., *het*). If the gender congruency effect obtained in Experiment 2 genuinely reflected competition in selecting gender features, it should have been obtained independently of whether an object is named in the standard or in the diminutive utterance format. However, Experiments 1 and 2 showed that gender-incongruent distractors only yielded a competition effect when the determiners were also incongruent. No gender congruency effect was obtained in naming common gender diminutive NPs where the same determiner is used for both the target and the gender-incongruent distractor. In this condition, a genuine determiner congruency effect occurred. Together with the results obtained in Experiment 1, the outcome of Experiment 2 strongly suggests that the gender congruency effect may be better characterised as a determiner congruency effect as suggested by Miozzo and Caramazza (1999) and Schiller and Caramazza (2003).

GENERAL DISCUSSION

The GSIH (Gender Selection Interference Hypothesis) predicts that a gender congruency effect should be observed irrespective of the type of NP that must be produced, under the assumption that the gender feature of the base word of the diminutive form is specified. In contrast, the DSIH (Determiner Selection Interference Hypothesis) predicts that a gender congruency effect should be obtained only for certain types of NPs – those involving the selection of different determiner forms. Earlier experimental evidence by Schiller and Caramazza (2003) supported the DSIH but not the GSIH. A gender congruency effect was found only for Dutch and

German singular NP production (when different determiners compete for selection) and not for plural NP production (when only one determiner form could be selected). These results suggest that grammatical feature selection is a non-competitive process. That is, grammatical features automatically become available as part of the lexical node selection process (Caramazza et al., 2001). However, if the phonological realisation of grammatical features results in different *lexical forms*, there is interference due to competition at the level of form selection.

The present results are important for at least two reasons: First, they show that the gender/determiner congruency effect is robust. Second, the present results support earlier results by Schiller and Caramazza (2003) and provide additional evidence for the DSIH from Dutch. As we noted earlier, the gender feature *neuter* of diminutives is an emergent property of phonological features of diminutive forms since all diminutives in Dutch end in the suffix *tje* (or predictable allomorphs of *–tje*) (see Mirković et al., 2005). Therefore, it is possible to contrast the GSIH and the DSIH in Dutch. If the GSIH is correct, effects of gender congruency should occur for common gender nouns in standard as well as in diminutive NPs. If, in contrast, the DSIH is correct, common gender nouns should exhibit a gender congruency effect in standard NPs and a reversed gender congruency effect in diminutive NPs. This is exactly what was found in both experiments reported in the present study.

It is important to note that the only possible way to account for the data presented above is by assuming a combination of the DSIH and the hypothesis of a separate (decomposed) representation of diminutives. A decomposed representation of diminutives would, for instance, assume one lexical entry for the noun (e.g., *kerk* 'church'), which is connected to a specific gender node (e.g., *com*). When the diminutive *kerkje* is to be produced, two concepts must be activated: the concept for TABLE and the concept for DIMINUTIVE. These two concepts activate (a) the lexical entry *kerk* (with its gender node *com*) and (b) the lexical entry for diminutive form, i.e., the appropriate allomorph of *tje*. Together these two forms are combined to yield the derived morpheme *kerkje*, i.e., the desired diminutive form. Our data support the view that the gender node *com* of the base word (i.e., *kerk*) is activated and selects its corresponding determiner. The plausibility of a decomposed representation of morphemes is further supported by data from Janssen and Caramazza (2003) as well as Spalek and Schriefers (2005). However, ultimately we will need to carry out further work to more precisely establish how diminutives are represented before a firmer interpretation of our results is possible.

If the DSIH is the correct account of the gender congruency effect observed in Dutch, German (Schiller & Caramazza, 2003; Schiller & Costa, in press), and Croatian (Costa et al., 2003), the effect has a further important implication for theories of speech production. The DSIH implies that the determiner *form* of the distractor word is activated even though the distractor lexical node itself is not selected for production (since it is never produced); otherwise there could not be interference at the level of determiner selection. That is, interference arises because of the following set of events: (1) the distractor noun's gender feature is activated, (2) it sends activation to its determiner form, and (3) the activated form competes for selection with the determiner form activated by the target noun. However, this scenario of how determiner selection interference arises presupposes *cascaded processing of information* from the level where grammatical features are specified to the level of word form encoding. Discrete serial stage models (e.g., Levelt et al., 1999), which claim that only the word forms of the *selected* lexical nodes are encoded, are not compatible with the DSIH. Hence, they cannot account for the pattern of determiner selection interference in NP production in Dutch reported in this study – or for NP production in German (Schiller & Caramazza, 2003; Schiller & Costa, in press) or pronoun production in Croatian (Costa et al., 2003).

In both experiments reported in this study, the determiner interference effect was weakest for neuter gender nouns in the standard utterance format. Although the effect pointed into the expected direction – according to the DSIH – in all conditions in both experiments, the individual differences were not always significant. This may have to do with the fact that the two genders are not equally distributed in Dutch. There are more than twice as many *de*-words than *het*-words in Dutch. This marginal occurrence of *het*-words (relative to *de*-words) may be responsible that *het*-words behave somewhat different from *de*-words. For instance, Van Berkum (1997) only considered *de*-words in his gender congruency experiment. Note, however, that in our experiments reported here, the common gender nouns in the diminutive format formed the most important condition. This crucial condition always behaved as predicted by the DSIH, but not as the GSIH predicts. Also note that diminutive response times were consistently faster than response times to nouns in standard format – contrary to what one would have expected, for instance, on the basis of the word frequencies (diminutive forms were always of lower frequency than their corresponding standard forms). This may have been due to the tone pitch in Experiment 1 or the absolute size of the pictures in Experiment 2, but in any case, it does not compromise our primary conclusion, that these data support the DSIH, but not the GSIH.

One may argue, however, that the present results contradict the results of Schiller and Caramazza (2003) in certain respects. In that study, we claimed that in plural conditions the plural target forces the selection of an

NP frame specifying *plural*. For that reason, neuter gender singular distractors (e.g., *het boek* 'the book') did not show more interference than common gender distractors (e.g., *de tafel* 'the table') – although the latter but not the former did not have the same determiner as the plural targets. This is presumably because all singular distractors receive a plural interpretation (*de boeken/de tafels* – target: *de poezen* 'the cats'), hence leading to determiner congruency. The same argument might be put forward here: In the diminutive condition, an NP frame marked for *diminutive* might be selected, and hence the distractors might receive a diminutive interpretation and consequently neuter gender might get activated independently of the distractor word's original gender. If this were the case, distractors in the diminutive condition would activate the determiner *het* no matter what their original gender was. This should have led to a situation in which no difference should have been visible between the gender-congruent and the gender-incongruent condition for diminutive targets.

However, this is not what we found in our experiment. We did find significant differences in the diminutive condition, which were contingent on whether or not the distractor was gender-congruent with the target. Therefore, it might be the case that no diminutive NP frame is imposed on the determiner selection process by diminutive targets. One reason why an NP frame is imposed in the case of *plural* but not in the case of *diminutive* might be that *plural* is a grammatical feature while *diminutive* is a semantic feature. In some cases, i.e. opaque diminutives, the diminutive derivation process can lead to rather dramatic changes in meaning. Therefore, imposing a diminutive frame might not always be desirable. *Plural*, however, being a grammatical feature, changes the meaning of the base word only minimally and in a predictable way. Although it is beyond the scope of the current study, further research on this topic is needed.

Another reason might be that a *diminutive* and a *plural* frame are qualitatively different: An NP frame marked for plural may just specify N + plural, without specifying the gender of the noun. The whole plural frame would then be assigned the determiner *de*, i.e., the only determiner used in plural NPs in Dutch. One reason for such a frame structure might be that noun plurals are often irregular in Dutch (and especially in German; see Schiller & Caramazza, 2002). Concatenating the base word's singular form with some sort of plural suffix cannot generate irregular plurals. Therefore, activating the base word to form the plural would often be useless. In contrast, diminutive derivation is a rather regular morphophonological computation. Therefore, a diminutive NP frame might not only specify N + diminutive, but it might consist of the actual noun including its gender, e.g., $kerk_{com}$ + diminutive or $boek_{neu}$ +

diminutive – at least in the case of transparently derived diminutives (opaque diminutives might not even appear in a diminutive NP frame since their meaning does not include any diminutive semantic features). Since the gender feature would be visible to the determiner selection process in those diminutive NP frames, it might activate its determiner and cause competition in determiner selection. Here, we cannot decide between these two and maybe other possibilities. However, our data show that the gender of the base word in transparently derived diminutives is most likely visible to the determiner selection process either because no diminutive NP frame is selected or because gender is visible in the frame.

In conclusion, this study has produced evidence in support of the hypothesis that grammatical feature selection is an automatic, non-competitive process (Caramazza et al., 2001). Word-specific grammatical features automatically become available as part of the selection of a lexical node. These grammatical features activate their associated form representations when the information cascades down to the level of phonological encoding. However, when two different determiner forms compete for selection, a determiner congruency effect is found – independent of the nouns' genders. Consistent with the DSIH, interference effects from gender-incongruent distractors were reversed in the diminutive format for common gender nouns but not in the standard format. This result suggests that the gender congruency effect first observed by Schriefers (1993) is a misnomer. A more appropriate name for the phenomenon is *determiner congruency effect*. The determiner congruency effect observed in Dutch reflects competition at the level of determiner form selection. Effects of determiner congruency between a target picture name and a distractor word are only found in languages where the selection of the determiner depends on the gender (and number) of the noun alone and thus can occur very early in the NP production process.

REFERENCES

Alario, F.-X., & Caramazza, A. (2002). The production of determiners: Evidence from French. *Cognition, 82*, 179—223.

Baayen, R. H., Piepenbrock, R., & Gulikers, L. (1995). *The CELEX lexical database* (CD-ROM). Linguistic Data Consortium, University of Pensylvania, Philadelphia, PA.

Booij, G. (2002). *The morphology of Dutch*. Oxford: Oxford University Press.

Caramazza, A., Miozzo, M., Costa, A., Schiller, N. O., & Alario, F.-X. (2001). A cross-linguistic investigation of determiner production. In E. Dupoux (Ed.), *Language, brain and cognitive development: Essays in honor of Jacques Mehler* (pp. 209–226). Cambridge, MA: MIT Press.

Corbett, G. (1991). *Gender*. Cambridge: Cambridge University Press.

Costa, A., Sebastián-Gallés, N., Miozzo, M., & Caramazza, A. (1999). The gender congruity effect: Evidence from Spanish and Catalan. *Language and Cognitive Processes*, *14*, 381–391.

Costa, A., Kovacic, D., Fedorenko, E., & Caramazza, A. (2003). The gender congruency effect and the selection of freestanding and bound morphemes: Evidence from Croatian. *Journal of Experimental Psychology: Learning, Memory, and Cognition*, *29*, 1270–1282.

Cubelli, R., Lotto, L., Paolieri, D., Girelli, M., & Job, R. (2005). Grammatical gender is selected in bare noun production: Evidence from the picture-word interference paradigm. *Journal of Memory and Language*, *53*, 42–59.

Glaser, W. R. (1992). Picture naming. *Cognition*, *42*, 61–105.

Janssen, N., & Caramazza, A. (2003). The selection of closed-class words in noun phrase production: the case of Dutch determiners. *Journal of Memory and Language*, *48*, 635–652.

Jescheniak, J. D., & Schriefers, H. (2001). Priming effects from phonologically related distractors in picture-word interference. *Quarterly Journal of Experimental Psychology*, *54A*, 371–382.

La Heij, W., Mak, P., Sander, J., & Willeboordse, E. (1998). The gender-congruency effect in picture-word tasks. *Psychological Research*, *61*, 209–219.

Levelt, W. J. M., Roelofs, A., & Meyer, A. S. (1999). A theory of lexical access in speech production. *Behavioral and Brain Sciences*, *22*, 175.

MacLeod, C. M. (1991). Half a century of research on the Stroop effect: An integrative review. *Psychological Bulletin*, *109*, 163–203.

Miozzo, M., & Caramazza, A. (1999). The selection of determiners in noun phrase production. *Journal of Experimental Psychology: Learning, Memory, and Cognition*, *25*, 907–922.

Miozzo, M., Costa, A., & Caramazza, A. (2002). The absence of a gender congruency effect in Romance languages: A matter of stimulus onset asynchrony? *Journal of Experimental Psychology: Learning, Memory, and Cognition*, *28*, 388–391.

Mirković, J., MacDonald, M. C., & Seidenberg, A. S. (2005). Where does gender come from? Evidence from a complex inflectional system. *Language and Cognitive Processes*, *20*, 139–167.

Schiller, N. O., & Caramazza, A. (2002). The selection of grammatical features in word production: The case of plural nouns in German. *Brain and Language*, *81*, 342–357.

Schiller, N. O., & Caramazza, A. (2003). Grammatical feature selection in noun phrase production: Evidence from German and Dutch. *Journal of Memory and Language*, *48*, 169–194.

Schiller, N. O., & Costa, A. (in press). Different selection principles of free-standing and bound morphemes in language production. *Journal of Experimental Psychology: Learning, Memory, and Cognition*.

Schriefers, H. (1993). Syntactic processes in the production of noun phrases. *Journal of Experimental Psychology: Learning, Memory, and Cognition*, *19*, 841–850.

Schriefers, H., Jescheniak, J. D., & Hantsch, A. (2002). Determiner selection in noun phrase production. *Journal of Experimental Psychology: Learning, Memory, and Cognition*, *28*, 941–950.

Schriefers, H., Jescheniak, J. D., & Hantsch, A. (2005). Selection of gender-marked morphemes in speech production. *Journal of Experimental Psychology: Learning, Memory, and Cognition*, *31*, 159–168.

Schriefers, H., Meyer, A. S., & Levelt, W. J. M. (1990). Exploring the time course of lexical access in language-production: Picture-word interference studies. *Journal of Memory and Language*, *29*, 86–102.

Schriefers, H., & Teruel, E. (2000). Grammatical gender in noun phrase production: The gender interference effect in German. *Journal of Experimental Psychology: Learning, Memory, and Cognition, 26*, 1368–1377.

Spalek, K., & Schriefers, H. (2005). Dominance affects determiner selection in language production. *Journal of Memory and Language, 52*, 103–119.

Starreveld, P. A. (2000). On the interpretation of onsets of auditory context effects in word production. *Journal of Memory and Language, 42*, 497–525.

Starreveld, P. A., & La Heij, W. (2004). Phonological facilitation of grammatical gender retrieval. *Language and Cognitive Processes, 19*, 677–711.

Stroop, J. R. (1935). Studies of interference in serial verbal reactions. *Journal of Experimental Psychology, 18*, 643–662.

Van Berkum, J. J. A. (1997). Syntactic processes in speech production: The retrieval of grammatical gender. *Cognition, 64*, 115–152.

APPENDIX A

Stimulus materials in Experiments 1 and 2

Target picture name		Gender	Distractor word conditions	
Standard	Diminutive		Gender-congruent	Gender-incongruent
appel ('apple')	appeltje	common	kat ('cat')	lint ('ribbon')
auto ('car')	autootje	common	magneet ('magnet')	podium ('stage')
bezem ('broom')	bezempje	common	sleutel ('key')	stuur ('steering wheel')
bijl ('ax')	bijltje	common	mond ('mouth')	gewei ('antlers')
boom ('tree')	boompje	common	muur ('wall')	kompas ('compass')
dolfijn ('dolphin')	dolfijntje	common	gitaar ('guitar')	graf ('tomb')
draak ('dragon')	draakje	common	vork ('fork')	gras ('grass')
emmer ('bucket')	emmertje	common	muis ('mouse')	tapijt ('carpet')
fakkel ('torch')	fakkeltje	common	zoon ('son')	loket ('counter')
fiets ('bike')	fietsje	common	taart ('cake')	kuiken ('chicken')
hand ('hand')	handje	common	boot ('boat')	vuur ('fire')
harp ('harp')	harpje	common	fles ('bottle')	wiel ('wheel')
jurk ('dress')	jurkje	common	kers ('cherry')	zadel ('saddle')
kerk ('church')	kerje	common	jas ('jacket')	glas ('glas')
klomp ('wooden shoe')	klompje	common	ladder ('ladder')	wapen ('weapon')
koffer ('suitcase')	koffertje	common	helm ('helmet')	ei ('egg')
maan ('moon')	maantje	common	zak ('bag')	touw ('rope')
muts ('cap')	mutsje	common	lamp ('lamp')	rooster ('scheme')
pijp ('pipe')	pijpje	common	hengel ('fishing-rod')	brood ('bread')
raket ('rocket')	raketje	common	pleister ('band aid')	bureau ('desk')
robot ('robot')	robotje	common	staart ('tail')	blad ('leaf')
stoel ('chair')	stoeltje	common	cactus ('cactus')	anker ('anker')
vis ('fish')	visje	common	bank ('bank')	masker ('mask')
wortel ('carrot')	worteltje	common	das ('tie')	gordijn ('curtain')
bad ('bath')	badje	neuter	gewei ('antlers')	mond ('mouth')
been ('leg')	beentje	neuter	kompas ('compass')	muur ('wall')
boek ('book')	boekje	neuter	ei ('egg')	helm ('helmet')
bord ('plate')	bordje	neuter	graf ('tomb')	gitaar ('guitar')
bot ('bone')	botje	neuter	gras ('grass')	vork ('fork')
fornuis ('stove')	fornuisje	neuter	loket ('counter')	zoon ('son')
geweer ('rifle')	geweertje	neuter	kuiken ('chicken')	muis ('mouse')
harnas ('armor')	harnasje	neuter	wiel ('wheel')	fles ('bottle')
hek ('fence')	hekje	neuter	vuur ('fire')	boot ('boat')
kasteel ('castle')	kasteeltje	neuter	podium ('stage')	magneet ('magnet')
konijn ('rabbit')	konijntje	neuter	glas ('glas')	jas ('jacket')
kruis ('cross')	kruisje	neuter	stuur ('steering wheel')	sleutel ('key')
nest ('nest')	nestje	neuter	tapijt ('carpet')	taart ('cake')
oor ('ear')	oortje	neuter	lint ('ribbon')	kat ('cat')
orgel ('organ')	orgeltje	neuter	wapen ('weapon')	ladder ('ladder')
paard ('horse')	paardje	neuter	brood ('bread')	hengel ('fishing-rod')
pak ('suit')	pakje	neuter	zadel ('saddle')	kers ('cherry')
raam ('window')	raampje	neuter	bureau ('desk')	pleister ('band aid')
spook ('ghost')	spookje	neuter	anker ('anker')	cactus ('cactus')
varken ('pig')	varkentje	neuter	masker ('mask')	bank ('bank')
vergiet ('sieve')	vergietje	neuter	touw ('rope')	zak ('bag')
vlot ('raft')	vlotje	neuter	blad ('leaf')	staart ('tail')
web ('web')	webje	neuter	gordijn ('curtain')	das ('tie')
zwaard ('sword')	zwaardje	neuter	rooster ('scheme')	lamp ('lamp')

(continued)

Appendix A

Stimulus materials in Experiments 1 and 2; continued

Target picture name		Gender	Distractor word conditions	
Standard	Diminutive		Semantically Related	Phonologically Related
appel ('apple')	appeltje	common	peer ('pear')	abdij ('abbey')
auto ('car')	autootje	common	trein ('train')	aula ('auditorium')
bezem ('broom')	bezempje	common	hark ('rake')	beer ('bear')
bijl ('ax')	bijltje	common	zaag ('saw')	bijbel ('bible')
boom ('tree')	boompje	common	plant ('plant')	boog ('bow')
dolfijn ('dolphin')	dolfijntje	common	haai ('shark')	dolk ('dagger')
draak ('dragon')	draakje	common	heks ('witch')	draad ('wire')
emmer ('bucket')	emmertje	common	gieter ('bucket')	engel ('angel')
fakkel ('torch')	fakkeltje	common	kaars ('candle')	fabriek ('factory')
fiets ('bike')	fietsje	common	brommer ('scooter')	finale ('final')
hand ('hand')	handje	common	voet ('foot')	halte ('stop')
harp ('harp')	harpje	common	viool ('violin')	hals ('neck')
jurk ('dress')	jurkje	common	trui ('sweater')	juf ('miss')
kerk ('church')	kerje	common	tempel ('temple')	ketting ('chain')
klomp ('wooden shoe')	klompje	common	laars ('boot')	klok ('clock')
koffer ('suitcase')	koffertje	common	tas ('bag')	koffie ('coffee')
maan ('moon')	maantje	common	ster ('star')	maag ('stomach')
muts ('cap')	mutsje	common	pet ('cap')	mus ('sparrow')
pijp ('pipe')	pijpje	common	sigaar ('cigar')	pijl ('arrow')
raket ('rocket')	raketje	common	tank ('tank')	radijs ('radish')
robot ('robot')	robotje	common	computer ('computer')	rotonde ('rotunda')
stoel ('chair')	stoeltje	common	tafel ('table')	stoep ('pavement')
vis ('fish')	visje	common	eend ('duck')	vinger ('finger')
wortel ('carrot')	worteltje	common	tomaat ('tomato')	wurm ('worm')
bad ('bath')	badje	neuter	toilet ('toilet')	balkon ('balcony')
been ('leg')	beentje	neuter	hoofd ('head')	beest ('animal')
boek ('book')	boekje	neuter	schilderij ('painting')	boeket ('bouquet')
bord ('plate')	bordje	neuter	mes ('knife')	bos ('forest')
bot ('bone')	botje	neuter	skelet ('skeleton')	bont ('fur')
fornuis ('stove')	fornuisje	neuter	servies ('dinner-set')	fossiel ('fossile')
geweer ('rifle')	geweertje	neuter	kanon ('cannon')	gewicht ('weight')
harnas ('armor')	harnasje	neuter	schild ('shield')	hart ('heart')
hek ('fence')	hekje	neuter	gaas ('wire-netting')	hemd ('shirt')
kasteel ('castle')	kasteeltje	neuter	huis ('house')	kado ('gift')
konijn ('rabbit')	konijntje	neuter	schaap ('sheep')	koord ('cord')
kruis ('cross')	kruisje	neuter	vierkant ('square')	kruid ('herb')
nest ('nest')	nestje	neuter	hol ('whole')	net ('net')
oor ('ear')	oortje	neuter	gezicht ('face')	orakel ('oracle')
orgel ('organ')	orgeltje	neuter	klavier ('keyboard')	object ('object')
paard ('horse')	paardje	neuter	hert ('deer')	paleis ('palace')
pak ('suit')	pakje	neuter	vest ('waistcoat')	palet ('palette')
raam ('window')	raampje	neuter	luik ('shutter')	ravijn ('canyon')
spook ('ghost')	spookje	neuter	monster ('monster')	spoor ('track')
varken ('pig')	varkentje	neuter	kalf ('calf')	vat ('barrel')
vergiet ('sieve')	vergietje	neuter	bestek ('cover')	verkeer ('traffic')
vlot ('raft')	vlotje	neuter	schip ('ship')	vlies ('membrane')
web ('web')	webje	neuter	rag ('cobweb')	werk ('work')
zwaard ('sword')	zwaardje	neuter	speer ('spear')	zwijn ('hog')

(continued)

Note to Appendix A. The mean frequency of occurrence per one million word forms of the 48 base words used in this study was 76.0 (according to CELEX; Baayen, Piepenbrock, & Gulikers, 1995). Only 10 diminutive forms of these words were actually listed in CELEX, with a mean frequency of 7.3 per million. The average overall frequency of all diminutives (assuming a frequency of zero for those that were not listed) was 1.5 per million. That means that the difference in frequency of occurrence between base words and diminutives is more than a factor of 50.

LANGUAGE AND COGNITIVE PROCESSES
2006, 21 (7–8), 974–1010

The role of local and global syntactic structure in language production: Evidence from syntactic priming

Holly P. Branigan, Martin J. Pickering and
Janet F. McLean,
University of Edinburgh, Edinburgh, Scotland

Andrew J. Stewart
University of Manchester, Manchester, UK

Experimental research has provided evidence for an autonomous stage of syntactic processing during language production. We report eight syntactic priming experiments that investigated whether this stage uses the same procedures to produce phrases with a particular structure when they appear in different syntactic contexts. Experiments 1–3 demonstrated syntactic priming for verb phrase structure in main clauses, irrespective of whether the global structure of the prime and target sentences varied. Experiments 4–6 demonstrated syntactic priming for verb phrase structure in subordinate clauses, both when prime and target were both subordinate clauses, and when one was a subordinate clause and the other was a main clause. Experiments 7 and 8 directly compared syntactic priming between main and subordinate clauses with priming between main clauses and priming between subordinate clauses. We interpret these results as evidence that the processor uses the same procedures to build syntactic structure in different syntactic contexts.

When people produce sentences, they must convert a message into a series of sounds. Research on language production suggests that this conversion involves a series of intermediate levels of representation (e.g., Garrett,

Correspondence should be addressed to Holly P. Branigan, Department of Psychology, University of Edinburgh, 7 George Square, Edinburgh EH8 9JZ, UK.
E-mail: Holly.Branigan@ed.ac.uk
Order of the first two authors is arbitrary. We thank Stuart Boutell and Matthew Crocker. This research was supported by a British Academy Postdoctoral Fellowship (awarded to H.B.) and ESRC Grant No. R000237418.

http://www.psypress.com/lcp   DOI: 10.1080/016909600824609

1980; Levelt, 1989). The initial stage, conceptualisation, specifies the idea or message that the speaker wishes to convey. The second stage, formulation, involves converting the message into a series of linguistic representations. In the last stage, articulation, this linguistic structure is realised as a program of motor movements. In this paper, we consider formulation, and in particular the construction of syntactic structure. Specifically, we assume the existence of at least one autonomous level of syntactic representation that is concerned with the grammatical structure of utterances independent of their sound or meaning (e.g., Bock & Levelt, 1994).

But how are such syntactic procedures specified with respect to the part of the sentence to which they make reference? One possibility is that they can be specified with respect to limited information, so that the processor does not make reference to the structure of the whole sentence or some larger expression within a sentence during the production of individual expressions. Other expressions may undergo syntactic processing in parallel, but during normal (error-free) production, they are not relevant to the construction of the target expression. For example, in producing a simple utterance like The man sneezed, it might be that people formulate the man (rather than man the or some other expression entirely) in a way that pays no attention to the production of the verb sneezed. Of course, the verb sneezed may instigate the production of a noun phrase, but it does not play any further role in determining the structure of that noun phrase. Alternatively, syntactic procedures may obligatorily make reference to more information, so that the structure of either the whole sentence or some larger expression within a sentence is relevant in the production of individual expressions.

In this paper, we report eight experiments that exploited the tendency for people to repeat syntactic structure between utterances, in order to see whether the procedures that people use to combine expressions remain constant, irrespective of the role that those expressions play within the sentence as a whole. If these procedures remain constant when the relevant expressions play very different roles, it would suggest that the procedures involved in syntactic processing need not make reference to the structure of the whole sentence or some larger expression within it.

REPRESENTING SYNTACTIC INFORMATION

Speakers must ensure that their utterance accords with the rules of their language's grammar; for example, in English it is grammatical to say The girl gave the boy the puppy (the Double Object, or DO structure) or The girl gave the puppy to the boy (the Prepositional Object or PO structure), but not Gave the girl the boy the puppy. To do this, the speaker must apply procedures that lead to the construction of the appropriate syntactic structure. For example, in constructing the PO structure, the speaker would form the appropriate verb phrase by applying a procedure (or procedures) that combines the verb give, the noun phrase the puppy, and the prepositional phrase to the boy. More generally, the procedure would combine a verb, a noun phrase, and a prepositional phrase (in that order) to produce a verb phrase.

Such procedures may be defined with respect to just those constituents that make up that structure, in what we shall term a *local* account. In this case, the procedure would take as its input the verb, the noun phrase, and the prepositional phrase. On this account, the same procedure would be applied to construct the ditransitive verb phrase gave the puppy to the boy in The girl gave the puppy to the boy and John said that the girl gave the puppy to the boy. In contrast, in a *global* account the procedure would make reference to aspects of the sentence that do not form part of the structure. In this case, different procedures might be used to construct gave the puppy to the boy for the two sentences. Note that the two accounts are not necessarily mutually exclusive: the processor might make use of both locally and globally defined procedures. In this paper our primary concern is with whether it can make use of locally defined procedures, or whether it must obligatorily make use of procedures that make reference to (some aspect of) global structure.

Most research on language production appears to assume a local account (e.g., Bock & Loebell, 1990; Garrett, 1980; Kempen & Hoenkamp, 1987; Pickering & Branigan, 1998). For example, Pickering and Branigan (1998) proposed a network model of lexico-syntactic representation in which individual verbs are associated with combinatorial nodes that specify the expressions with which they can combine to form a larger expression. These nodes make no reference to syntactic context, other than the identity of the verb. Hence in this model, the same combinatorial node is always involved in the production of a verb phrase like gave the puppy to the boy, whether it is part of a sentence like The girl gave the puppy to the boy or John said that the girl gave the puppy to the boy. But what evidence is there for the assumption that syntactic processing in production can be local in this sense?

A large body of work concerned with the building of syntactic structure has drawn on data from syntactic priming, or the tendency for people to repeat syntactic structure across utterances. Studies of naturally occurring speech suggest that people tend to repeat grammatical structure (Schenkein, 1980; Tannen, 1989). For example, interviewees were more likely to use a passive if a passive had recently been employed in the interview (Weiner & Labov, 1983). Bock (1986) provided a controlled experimental demonstration of this tendency to repeat syntactic structure. Under the guise of a memory test, speakers alternated between repeating prime sentences and describing semantically unrelated target pictures. She manipulated the syntactic forms of the sentences that speakers repeated. For example, the prime sentence might use the PO form of an alternating dative verb in one condition (e.g., A rock star sold some cocaine to an undercover agent) and the DO form in the other condition (e.g., A rock star sold an undercover agent some cocaine). Participants tended to produce a PO description of the target picture after a PO prime and a DO description of the target picture after a DO prime. Active/passive sentences produced comparable effects. This phenomenon is known as *syntactic priming* (or syntactic persistence).

There have been many subsequent demonstrations of syntactic priming with a range of constructions and methods, and in other languages (see Ferreira & Bock, 2006; Pickering & Branigan, 1998). Such research has provided clear evidence that the effects are truly syntactic and are unlikely to be a byproduct of repetition at other levels, such as lexical, semantic, prosodic, or focus structure (Bock, 1989; Bock & Loebell, 1990; Hartsuiker & Westenberg, 2000). They occur in the absence of closed class and open class lexical repetition (Bock, 1989); when the prime and target sentences share syntactic structure but not event structure (e.g., locative sentences prime passive sentences; Bock & Loebell, 1990); and for structural alternations that do not differ in focus structure (e.g., main/auxiliary verb word order in Dutch; Hartsuiker & Westenberg, 2000). A focus-based account is also excluded by Scheepers (2003), who found no priming for sentences that shared focus structure (in terms of which entity was modified by a subordinate clause) but did not share syntactic structure. We can also exclude prosodic explanations, as grammatically distinct sentences with similar prosodic structure do not prime each other (Bock & Loebell, 1990).

Bock and Loebell (1990) argued that the repetition of sentence structure therefore provides evidence for hierarchical constituent representations in language production, which are not associated with conceptual, phonological, or metrical information. On the basis of evidence for syntactic priming between verb phrases that differed in detailed syntactic structure, Pickering and Branigan (1998) argued explicitly for the existence of processes and representations in language production that make reference to only immediate syntactic structure (i.e., do not make reference to aspects of syntactic structure other than the identity of the verb and the immediate expressions with which it combines to form a larger expression). More specifically, they found reliable priming when the prime and target verb phrase differed with respect to the internal structure of complement noun phrases. Hence it appears that speakers recognise relationships between sentences that have the same constituent structure at one level (in this case, at the level of the verb and its complements) but not at another level (in this case, the internal structure of the complements). Pickering and Branigan explained syntactic priming in terms of combinatorial nodes. When a prime sentence is processed, it activates the relevant combinatorial nodes; these nodes subsequently retain activation, facilitating their re-use. Alternative accounts explain priming as the result of implicit learning of syntax (Bock & Griffin, 2000; Chang, Dell, Bock, & Griffin, 2000).

But in all of the experiments described above, prime and target sentences had the same global structure (i.e., structure above the level of the verb phrase). Hence these experiments are equally compatible with the possibility that the processor obligatorily makes reference to (some aspect of) global syntactic structure when constructing a phrase like gave the puppy to the boy. Certainly there is evidence that speakers are able to process more than one clause at a time. For example, speech error data show that speakers may simultaneously process more than one clause (Bock & Cutting, 1992; Garrett, 1980) and Smith and Wheeldon (1999) demonstrated that speakers take longer to initiate utterances involving two clauses than one clause. These results suggest that some aspect of the second clause can be processed prior to articulation of the second clause. However, they do not necessarily mean that speakers make reference to global syntactic structure when constructing local syntactic structures.

Scheepers (2003) reported data that suggest that syntactic priming may not straightforwardly reflect the repetition of local syntactic structure. He investigated (the German translation of) sentences such as The assistant announced the score of the candidate, which was unexpectedly poor. Such sentences are globally ambiguous: The relative clause which was unexpectedly poor might modify the first noun phrase the score or the second noun phrase the candidate. He found that prior production of a German sentence with a high-attached relative clause (RC) such as (the German translation of) The assistant announced the score of the candidate, which was unexpectedly poor increased the likelihood of subsequently producing another high-attached relative clause, whereas prior production of a low-attached relative clause such as The assistant announced the score of the candidate, who had performed very well increased the likelihood of producing a low-attached relative clause. Both types of sentence involve the same local syntactic structure ([NP RC]), but they differ in the noun phrase to which this structure applies. In the high-attached case, it applies to the first noun phrase (in which the second noun phrase is embedded); in the low-attached case, it applies to the second noun phrase (which is embedded in the first noun phrase). Hence, Scheepers' results cannot be explained in terms of the increased activation of one structure over another; instead the priming effect is associated with the same syntactic structure in two different global syntactic structures. A straightforward explanation of his results is that the processor makes reference to global syntactic structure when constructing local syntactic structures.

Thus although most research seems to have implicitly assumed that syntactic processing in production makes reference to just those constituents that immediately make up a structure, there is little evidence to support this claim, and some evidence which may argue against it. It is therefore an open question whether syntactic activation obligatorily makes references to global syntactic structure. To test this, we would need to see whether priming occurs when prime and target involve different global structures, for example if the prime contains a dative-alternating construction embedded in a complex sentence whereas the target involves a simple main-clause dative.

EXPERIMENTS

We now report a series of experiments that investigated whether people construct syntactic structure using procedures that obligatorily make reference to (some aspect of) global structure. The experiments employed syntactic priming to investigate the conditions under which people tend to repeat syntactic structure between sentences. In all experiments, we manipulated the syntactic structure of a verb phrase in the prime sentence, and examined whether this primed the production of the same verb phrase structure in an immediately following target sentence. We will refer to the manipulated verb phrase as the experimental verb phrase and the verb as the experimental verb. Hence, the prime and target sentences always involved verb phrases with the same local structure, meaning that they had the same constituents in the same order. Additionally, we manipulated whether the verb phrase appeared in sentences that had the same or different global structure, meaning that the sentences were the same or different with respect to the syntactic structure of those parts of the sentence that did not form part of the verb phrase.

In all experiments, the experimental verb was a dative-alternating verb like give, lend, or show, which meant that the experimental verb phrase could occur in one of two forms with very similar meanings. For example, the verb show is compatible with the PO form the patient showed his injury to the doctor or the DO form the patient showed the doctor his injury. Prior research has made extensive use of this construction, and it provides some of the clearest evidence that priming is truly syntactic in origin (Bock, 1986, 1989; Bock & Loebell, 1990; Branigan, Pickering, &

Cleland, 2000a; Pickering & Branigan, 1998; Pickering, Branigan, & McLean, 2002). Priming of such structures occurs both when the verb is repeated between prime and target (e.g., Branigan et al., 2000a; Pickering & Branigan, 1998; Cleland & Pickering, 2006), and when it is not (e.g., Bock, 1986, 1990), but is stronger when the verb is repeated (Branigan et al., 2000a; Pickering & Branigan, 1998; Cleland & Pickering, 2006); for this reason our experiments used the same verb in prime and target.

In Experiments 1–6, we examined whether syntactic priming occurred in the absence of shared global structure. Experiment 1 established that syntactic priming occurred when prime and target sentences were both simple main clause sentences comprising a subject noun phrase and the experimental verb phrase. In Experiments 2 and 3, we introduced an additional phrase at the beginning of the prime sentences, so that the global structure ceased to be identical between prime and target. Experiments 4, 5, and 6 introduced a potentially more important manipulation of global structure, by using a complex sentence for either prime or target sentence or both. Specifically, we manipulated whether the experimental verb phrase appeared in a main clause or in a subordinate clause. If syntactic processing in production makes use of locally defined procedures, as many accounts of production implicitly assume, then syntactic priming should occur under all of these conditions, as the local syntactic structure associated with the experimental verb phrase remained constant. However, if syntactic processing does not make use of locally defined procedures and obligatorily makes reference to global structure, then priming should occur in Experiments 1 and 4, where the prime and target sentences had the same global structure, but not necessarily in the other experiments.

EXPERIMENT 1: PRIMING FROM 'SIMPLE' MAIN CLAUSE TO MAIN CLAUSE

Method

Participants.   Eighteen participants from the University of Glasgow community were paid to participate. The participants in this experiment and in all the subsequent experiments were native speakers of English.

Items.   We constructed 18 sets of items. Each comprised two sentence fragments (see Appendix):

1a. The racing driver shows the torn overall . . . (PO-inducing prime)
1b. The racing driver shows the helpful mechanic . . . (DO-inducing prime)
2. The patient shows . . . (target)

The prime fragments (1a-b) contained a subject noun phrase followed by a present-tense verb that could appear in the PO or DO construction, and a post-verbal noun phrase that was compatible with a PO (1a) or DO completion (1b). The target fragment (2) contained a subject noun phrase followed by the same verb as the prime fragments. We employed six verbs which previous work had shown to reliably induce PO and DO completions (e.g., Pickering & Branigan, 1998). Noun phrases comprised a determiner followed by a noun, a noun compound, or an adjective and a noun. We also constructed 72 filler fragments: 36 were noun phrases (of varying types), 18 comprised a subject noun phrase and a verb, and 18 comprised a subject noun phrase, a verb, and a post-verbal noun phrase.

Procedure.   The experimental items were placed into two lists, each comprising nine items from each condition, such that one version of each item appeared in each list. The 108 fragments (18 prime fragments, 18 target fragments, and 72 filler fragments) were individually randomised, with the constraints that each prime fragment immediately preceded its associated target fragment, and at least 3 filler fragments intervened between experimental items. Each fragment was presented as an individual trial; participants were not informed of any relationship between prime and target fragments.

Participants were told that we were interested in seeing what sorts of sentences people produce. They were asked to read each fragment, then to complete it with the first grammatical completion that came to mind, saying the entire sentence aloud.

The experimental files were presented using PsyScope software (Cohen, MacWhinney, Flatts, & Provost, 1993). First, a fixation point ('+') appeared in the centre of the screen for 1000 ms. This was then replaced with a sentence fragment, with the first letter appearing in the location where the fixation point had been presented. After 5000 ms, the fragment was replaced with a blank screen for 1000 ms, then a beep sounded. The screen remained blank for a further 1000 ms, and then the next trial began. Participants' responses were recorded. The experiment began with a practice session of 10 further filler fragments. The experiment took about 20 minutes and contained two breaks whose duration was under participants' control.

Scoring.   Participants' responses to each experiment fragment were scored as PO, DO, or Other. A completion of a PO-inducing prime fragment was scored as a PO prime response if it contained a goal noun phrase which was the object of the preposition to. A completion of a DO-inducing prime fragment was scored as a DO prime response if it contained a patient or theme noun phrase. To be scored as either a PO or a

DO response, the verb provided in the fragment could not be part of a phrasal verb (e.g., <u>The architect hands the latest plan over to the builder</u>). All other prime completions were scored as Others. Note that if a participant completed a DO-inducing prime fragment as a PO (e.g., completing <u>The mother gives the baby . . . with . . . to her husband</u>), or completed a PO-inducing fragment as a DO, the completion was scored as an Other.

A completion of a target fragment was scored as a PO target completion if the verb provided in the fragment was immediately followed by a noun phrase which acted as the patient or theme and then by a prepositional phrase beginning with <u>to</u> which acted as the recipient/goal. A completion of a target fragment was scored as a DO target completion if the verb was immediately followed by a noun phrase which acted as the recipient/goal and then by a noun phrase which acted as the patient or theme. To be scored as either a PO or DO response, it had to have a grammatical alternative in the other category, where the order of the patient and recipient/goal was reversed. Additionally, the verb provided in the fragment could not form part of a phrasal verb. All other target completions were scored as Others.

Design and data analysis. Each participant completed 18 target fragments, nine in each of the two priming conditions defined by the Prime Completion factor (PO vs. DO prime response). Each experimental item was presented to all 18 participants, with 9 participants seeing any one version of an item.

We analysed the results by treating the PO, DO, and Other target completions separately. Our first set of results, the *PO target analyses*, was performed over the proportion of PO target completions following PO prime completions and the proportion of PO target completions following DO prime completions. We calculated proportions because participants may have produced different numbers of Other completions in the different prime completion conditions.

We computed the relevant proportions by dividing the number of PO target completions that were produced after the prime had been completed as a PO (we term these *PO-PO completions*, with the first PO referring to the structure of the prime completion and the second PO referring to the structure of the target completion) by the total number of PO prime completions (i.e., PO-PO completions / (PO-PO + PO-DO + PO-OTHER completions)); and the number of PO target completions that were produced after the prime had been completed as a DO (DO-PO completions) by the total number of DO prime completions (i.e., DO-PO target completions / (DO-PO + DO-DO + DO-OTHER completions)).

Similarly, we computed the *DO target analyses* using the equivalent formulae: PO-DO completions / (PO-PO + PO-DO + PO-OTHER completions); and DO-DO completions / (DO-PO + DO-DO + DO-OTHER completions). We conducted analyses for both PO and DO target completions because it would be arbitrary to choose one rather than the other. We can be more confident about any conclusions if both sets of analyses are significant. A final set of analyses, the Other target analyses, was performed over the proportions of Other target completions following PO prime completions, and over the proportion of Other target completions following DO prime completions. If there are no differences in the Other analyses, it suggests that the effects of priming relate to choice of which syntactic structure to use to describe a particular message, rather than influencing choice of which message to convey.

These proportions were calculated for each participant and for each item. Analyses of variance were performed on these data, with separate analyses treating participants (F_1s) and item (F_2s) as random effects. Prime completion was the within-participants and within-items factor.

Results and discussion

Participants completed prime fragments on 324 trials, of which 292 were completed as either a PO or a DO prime response (90% of all responses). Of these, 49% were completed as PO prime responses and 51% as DO prime responses. In these 292 trials, participants produced 124 (42%) PO target completions, 104 (36%) DO target completions, and 64 (22%) Other target completions.

Table 1 shows the proportions of PO, DO, and Other target completions in the two experimental conditions. Inspection of Table 1 shows a priming effect for both the PO and DO target responses. Priming, the mean of the difference between the PO prime-PO target and DO prime-PO target, and the difference between DO prime-DO target and PO prime-DO target, was 28% in both cases. For the PO target analyses, one-way ANOVAs revealed significant differences between the prime conditions, $F_1(1, 17) = 31.7, p < .001, MSe = 0.025; F_2(1, 17) = 18.8, p < .001, MSe = 0.035$: there were more PO target completions after a PO prime than a DO prime. Similarly, for the DO target analyses, one-way ANOVAs revealed significant differences between the Prime Completion conditions, $F_1(1, 17) = 24.0, p < .001, MSe = 0.028; F_2(1, 17) = 23.4, p < .001, MSe = 0.029$: there were more DO target completions after a DO prime than a PO prime. There was no difference for the Other target completions ($Fs < 1$).

An additional set of analyses was performed on the arcsine-transformed proportions of responses for both participants and items. Since the results of these additional analyses showed the same pattern of effects as those on

TABLE 1

Proportion of PO, DO, and Other target completions produced in each condition in Experiments 1–6 (using participant means)

Experiment	PO targets	DO targets	Other targets
Experiment 1: Priming from simple main clause to simple main clause			
PO Prime	.56	.22	.22
DO Prime	.28	.50	.23
Priming effect	.28	.28	
Experiment 2: Priming from main clause with preceding adverbial phrase to simple main clause			
PO Prime	.53	.28	.19
DO Prime	.35	48	.17
Priming effect	.18	.20	
Experiment 3: Priming from main clause with preceding subordinate clause to simple main clause			
PO Prime	.51	.28	.21
DO Prime	.34	.47	.19
Priming effect	.17	.19	
Experiment 4: Priming from subordinate clause to subordinate clause			
PO Prime	.57	.10	.33
DO Prime	.37	.33	.29
Priming effect	.20	.23	
Experiment 5: Priming from main clause to subordinate clause			
PO Prime	.49	.16	.34
DO Prime	.39	.26	.35
Priming effect	.10	.10	
Experiment 6: Priming from subordinate clause to main clause			
PO Prime	.57	.18	.25
DO Prime	.43	.32	.25
Priming effect	.14.	.14	
Experiments 1–6: Combined analysis:			
Same-Clause-Type PO Prime	.54	.22	.24
Same-Clause-Type DO Prime	.34	.45	.22
Different-Clause-Type PO Prime	.53	.17	.30
Different-Clause-Type DO Prime	.12	.29	.30
Priming effect (Same-Clause-Type)	.20	.23	
Priming effect (Different-Clause-Type)	.12	.12	

Note: PO = Prepositional Object; DO = Double Object.

the raw proportions, we have omitted them from this Experiment and Experiments 2–6 and 8.

These effects are consistent with accounts of syntactic priming in which priming arises from activation of processes or representations that make no reference to constituents other than those that immediately make up the relevant structure (i.e., V, NP, NP comprising a VP, in the case of DO structures; V, NP, PP comprising a VP, in the case of PO structures). However, because the global structure was the same in prime and target, we cannot rule out the possibility that priming relies upon the repetition of global syntactic structure.

EXPERIMENT 2: PRIMING FROM MAIN CLAUSE WITH INITIAL ADVERBIAL PHRASE TO MAIN CLAUSE

In Experiment 2, we conducted an initial test of whether priming occurred between sentences that differed in global structure, by investigating whether syntactic priming effects occur between main clauses that differ in their overall structure. Participants completed the same prime fragments as in Experiment 1, but this time as part of a main clause containing an initial adverbial prepositional phrase (e.g., On Friday, the racing driver showed the torn overall . . .). Target fragments were as in Experiment 1. For this experiment, all verbs were presented in the past tense, because it sounded more natural to combine past-tense verbs with the initial adverbials. If priming occurs between sentences that differ in global syntactic structure, then the structure of the prime completion should reliably affect the structure of the target completion.

Method

Participants.   Eighteen participants from the University of Glasgow community were paid to participate.

Items.   We constructed 18 sets of items. Each comprised two sentence fragments (see Appendix):

3a. On Friday, the racing driver showed the torn overall . . . (PO-inducing prime)
3b. On Friday, the racing driver showed the helpful mechanic . . . (DO-inducing prime)
4. The patient showed . . . (target)

The items were the same as Experiment 1, except that the prime fragment included an initial adverbial phrase, and the verbs were in the past tense.

The fillers were the same as in Experiment 1, except that the verbs were in the past tense, and the subject noun phrase was replaced by a proper name in the 18 fillers containing a subject noun phrase, verb, and post-verbal noun phrase.

Procedure, scoring, design, and data analysis.   All sentence fragments were presented for 7000 ms rather than 5000 ms, as the prime fragments were longer than in Experiment 1. In other respects, procedure, scoring, design, and data analysis were as in Experiment 1.

Results and discussion

Participants completed 304 trials as either a PO or a DO prime response (94% of all responses); 48% of these were completed as PO primes and 52% as DO primes. In these 304 trials, participants produced 134 (44%) PO target completions, 115 (38%) DO target completions, and 55 (18%) Other target completions.

Table 1 shows the proportions of PO, DO, and Other target completions in the two experimental conditions. It reveals a priming effect for both the PO and DO target responses, with the mean being 19%. For the PO target analyses, one-way ANOVAs revealed significant differences between the Prime Completion conditions, $F_1(1, 17) = 6.73, p < .05, MSe = 0.047$; $F_2(1, 17) = 20.8, p < .001, MSe = 0.019$: there were more PO target completions after a PO prime than a DO prime. Similarly, for the DO target analyses, one-way ANOVAs revealed significant differences between the Prime Completion conditions, $F_1(1, 17) = 8.57, p < .01$, $MSe = 0.045; F_2(1, 17) = 24.1, p < .001, MSe = 0.019$: there were more DO target completions after a DO prime than a PO prime. There was no difference for the Other target completions ($Fs < 1$).

As in Experiment 1, participants showed strong and reliable priming effects when producing consecutive main clauses. Previous research has demonstrated that priming occurs when the internal structures of the constituents of the verb phrase in prime and target are not identical (Pickering & Branigan, 1998). This experiment demonstrates that priming also occurs when the global structures of the prime and target are not identical. It suggests that the same syntactic procedures are involved in producing a PO or DO structure in two different global structures, and specifically that these procedures do not obligatorily distinguish between a PO or DO structure in a 'simple' main clause that contains a subject noun phrase and a verb phrase, and a PO or DO structure in a main clause that contains an initial adverbial phrase, a subject noun phrase, and a verb phrase.

The results also show that priming is not dependent upon prime and target having the same global prosodic structure (cf. Bock & Loebell, 1990), and that priming effects occur between structures that differ substantially in phonological length. As an indication, the average length of thc prc-verbal elements and verb in the prime fragment was 9 syllables; in the target fragment, it was only 5 syllables.

EXPERIMENT 3: PRIMING FROM MAIN CLAUSE WITH INITIAL SUBORDINATE CLAUSE TO MAIN CLAUSE

In Experiment 2, the difference between prime and target in terms of global syntactic structure was fairly small. Syntactically, prime and target only differed by the presence of a peripheral (adjunct) phrase like On Friday in the prime. The processor might be sensitive to some but not all aspects of the global syntactic structure. Thus it is possible that the difference in global structure between our primes and targets was not relevant to the processor. Stronger evidence that the syntactic processes or representations that underlie priming do not depend upon the repetition of global syntactic structure would be found if priming occurred when prime and target differed more substantially. Given the apparent importance of the clause as a unit in language production (e.g., Bock & Cutting, 1992; Holmes, 1988), a strong candidate for a relevant difference in syntactic structure is the presence or absence of another clause.

In Experiment 3, we therefore employed the same prime fragments as in Experiment 2, but replaced the initial adverbial phrase with an initial subordinate clause, such as As Anne claimed, the racing driver showed the torn overall. This initial clause contained the same number of phonological words and syllables as the corresponding prepositional phrase in Experiment 2. However, it introduced another clause. The target fragments were identical to those used in Experiment 2.

If the same processes or representations are involved in the production of a PO structure such as showed the torn overall to the mechanic, then production of a prime sentence such as As Anne claimed, the racing driver showed the torn overall . . . should be effective in inducing production of a target PO sentence such as The patient showed the doctor his bruises. Notice that the initial clause is unlikely to affect priming of the experimental verb phrase because the initial clause does not contain a dative-alternating verb, and because it precedes the experimental verb phrase (containing showed).

Method

Participants. Eighteen participants from the University of Glasgow community were paid to participate.

Items. We constructed 18 sets of items. Each comprised two sentence fragments (see Appendix):

5a. As Anne claimed, the racing driver showed the torn overall . . . (PO-inducing prime)
5b. As Anne claimed, the racing driver showed the helpful mechanic . . . (DO-inducing prime)
6. The patient showed . . . (target)

The items were identical to Experiment 2 except that the initial adverbial phrase in the prime fragment was replaced by a clause of the form <u>As X verbed</u>, where <u>X</u> was a proper name and <u>verbed</u> was a past tense verb that takes a clausal complement. The fillers were the same as in Experiment 2.

Procedure, scoring, design, and data analysis. These were as in Experiment 2.

Results and discussion

Participants completed 286 trials as either a PO or a DO prime response (88% of all responses). Of these, 47% were completed as PO primes and 53% as DO primes. In these 286 trials, participants produced 118 (41%) PO target completions, 114 (40%) DO target completions, and 54 (19%) Other target completions for the target fragment.

Table 1 shows the proportions of PO, DO, and Other target completions in the two experimental conditions. It reveals a priming effect for both the PO and DO target responses, with the mean being 18%. For the PO target analyses, one-way ANOVAs revealed significant differences between the Prime Completion conditions, $F_1(1, 17) = 10.89$, $p < .01$, $MSe = 0.026$; $F_2(1, 17) = 15.6$, $p < .01$, $MSe = 0.017$: there were more PO target completions after a PO prime than a DO prime. Similarly, for the DO target analyses, one-way ANOVAs revealed significant differences between the Prime Completion conditions, $F_1(1, 17) = 23.5$, $p < .001$, $MSe = 0.015$; $F_2(1, 17) = 10.5$, $p < .01$, $MSe = 0.025$: there were more DO target completions after a DO prime than a PO prime. There was no difference for the Other target completions ($Fs < 1$). Experiment 3 demonstrated strong and reliable syntactic priming effects of comparable magnitude to those found in Experiments 1 and 2. The results provide further evidence that priming effects occur between sentences that share local structure but differ in global structure. Importantly, they show reliable priming for verb phrase structure between sentences that differ in both syntactic complexity (in terms of numbers of clauses), and semantic complexity (in terms of number of propositions and number of entities). Moreover, they demonstrate that priming for a particular verb phrase structure is not eliminated by the production of a verb phrase with a different structure in a clause that precedes the locus of priming.

EXPERIMENT 4: PRIMING FROM SUBORDINATE CLAUSE TO SUBORDINATE CLAUSE

In Experiments 1–3, the experimental verb phrases formed part of the main clause of the sentence. Experiments 1 and 2 employed single-clause sentences; Experiment 3 employed subordinate clauses in the prime, but these clauses were not the locus of priming. Hence, the locus of priming was a set of procedures associated with the construction of the main clause. Experiments 4–6, in contrast, consider priming under conditions where the experimental verb phrase may form part of a subordinate clause. The distinction between main and subordinate clauses is one of particular importance to linguistic theory. However, an account of syntactic processing in which the processor does not need to make reference to aspects of syntax other than the immediate constituents involved in a structure predicts that the same set of representations and processes can be involved in producing subordinate clauses as in producing main clauses. With regard to the dative alternation, the relevant constituents are VP[V NP PP] and VP[V NP NP], irrespective of whether the verb phrase forms part of the main clause or the subordinate clause.

Hence, the account in which the processor does not need to make reference to aspects of syntax other than the immediate constituents involved in a structure predicts that syntactic priming should occur between main and subordinate clauses, because the relevant processes and representations would be the same in each case. We can straightforwardly test priming from subordinate clause to main clause, as the experimental verb phrases in prime and target are adjacent, and because Experiment 3 has shown that an experimental verb phrase preceded by another verb within the same sentence still serves as an effective prime.

However, there is a potential problem with testing priming from main clauses to subordinate clauses in English, because the main clause of the target (e.g., The rumours alleged that in the target The rumours alleged that the patient showed the doctor his wound) intervenes between the experimental verb phrase in the prime and the experimental verb phrase in the target. Evidence from spoken picture description (Bock & Griffin, 2000) and spoken sentence completion (Branigan, Pickering, Stewart, & McLean, 2000b) suggested that intervening material does not cause priming to decay rapidly. But other work suggests that intervening material can reduce or eliminate syntactic priming. Using written sentence completion, Branigan, Pickering, and Cleland (1999) found priming (of main clause sentences) was greatly diminished if a single sentence intervened between prime and target (and was eliminated when four sentences intervened). Rapid decay also occurred in an arguably related study (in Dutch) by Levelt and Kelter (1982) involving question answering. Although it is far from certain that priming would greatly decay 'over' a short main clause in spoken production, we would be unable to determine whether a lack of priming reflected the activation but subsequent decay of locally defined procedures, or alternatively supported a different account of syntactic encoding. It is also conceivable that priming does not occur in subordinate clauses at all, for reasons unrelated to potential differences between main and subordinate clauses. Hence, we first decided to investigate priming between subordinate clauses. If priming did occur, we would then investigate priming between main and subordinate clauses.

One previous study has found evidence for priming between subordinate clauses. In Dutch, main and auxiliary verbs can occur in either order in some subordinate clauses. Hartsuiker and Westenberg (2000) found priming of main and auxiliary verb order using both written and spoken sentence completion. However, priming of word order may represent a different situation from priming of PO versus DO structure in English, which clearly involves two different constructions.

Method

Participants. Eighteen participants from the University of Edinburgh community were paid to participate.

Items. We constructed 18 sets of items. Each comprised two sentence fragments (see Appendix):

7a. The report claimed that the racing driver showed the torn overall . . .
   (PO-inducing prime)
7b. The report claimed that the racing driver showed the helpful mechanic
   . . . (DO-inducing prime)
8. The rumours alleged that the patient showed . . . (target)

The prime fragments were the same as those used in Experiment 3, except that the initial subordinate clause (e.g., <u>As Anne claimed</u>) was replaced by a main clause fragment consisting of a subject noun phrase, a past-tense verb that allowed a clausal complement, and the word <u>that</u> (e.g., <u>The report claimed that</u>). The target fragments consisted of a subject noun phrase, a past-tense verb that allowed a clausal complement, and a subordinate clause that was identical to the target fragment in Experiment 3. The fillers were the same as in Experiment 1, except that the verbs appeared in the past tense.

Procedure, scoring, design, and data analysis.   These were the same as in Experiment 2.

Results and discussion

Application of the scoring criteria yielded 283 trials where the prime fragment was completed as either a PO or as a DO (87% of all responses); 48% of these were completed as PO primes and 52% as DO primes. In these 283 trials, participants produced 132 (47%) PO completions, 62 (22%) DO completions, and 89 (31%) Other completions for the target fragment.

Table 1 shows the proportions of PO, DO, and Other target completions in the two experimental conditions. It reveals a priming effect for both the PO and DO target responses, with the mean being 21.5%. For the PO target analyses, one-way ANOVAs revealed significant differences between the Prime Completion conditions, $F_1(1, 17) = 8.85, p < .01$, $MSe = 0.037; F_2(1, 17) = 11.8, p < .01, MSe = 0.027$: there were more PO target completions after a PO prime than a DO prime. Similarly, for the DO target analyses, one-way ANOVAs revealed significant differences between the Prime Completion conditions, $F_1(1, 17) = 13.3, p < .001, MSe = 0.037; F_2(1, 17) = 14.7, p < .01, MSe = 0.029$: there were more DO target completions after a DO prime than a PO prime. There was no difference for the Other target completions ($Fs < 1$).

Hence there is strong priming from subordinate-clause primes to subordinate-clause targets. This experiment therefore demonstrated that priming occurs for sentences where the locus of priming is the subordinate clause. Moreover, an intervening main clause did not eliminate syntactic priming. But the global structure was of course the same in prime and target. To demonstrate that priming for such constructions occurs when global structure is not the same, it is necessary to show priming from main to subordinate clauses, or from subordinate to main clauses, or both.

EXPERIMENT 5: PRIMING FROM MAIN CLAUSE TO SUBORDINATE CLAUSE

Method

Participants.   Eighteen participants from the University of Edinburgh community were paid to participate.

Items. We constructed 18 sets of items. Each comprised two sentence fragments (see Appendix):

9a. The racing driver showed the torn overall . . . (PO-inducing prime)
9b. The racing driver showed the helpful mechanic . . . (DO-inducing prime)
10. The rumours alleged that the patient showed . . . (target)

Apart from a change to the past tense, prime fragments were identical to those used in Experiment 1. Target fragments were identical to those in Experiment 4. The fillers were identical to those in Experiment 4.

Procedure, scoring, design, and data analysis. These were the same as in Experiment 2.

Results and discussion

Application of the scoring criteria yielded 292 trials where the prime fragment was completed as either a PO or as a DO (90% of all responses); 49% of these were completed as PO primes and 51% as DO primes. In these 292 trials, participants produced 132 (45%) PO completions, 62 (21%) DO completions, and 98 (34%) Other completions for the target fragment.

Table 1 shows the proportions of PO, DO, and Other target completions in the two experimental conditions, and reveals a mean priming effect of 10%. For the PO target analyses, one-way ANOVAs revealed significant differences between the Prime Completion conditions, $F_1(1, 17) = 5.90$, $p < .05$, $MSe = 0.016$; $F_2(1, 17) = 4.61$, $p < .05$, $MSe = 0.029$: there were more PO target completions after a PO prime than a DO prime. For the DO target analyses, one-way ANOVAs revealed a marginal trend by participants only, $F_1(1, 17) = 3.44$, $p = .08$, $MSe = 0.023$; $F_2(1, 17) = 2.87$, $p = .11$, $MSe = 0.034$: Table 1 shows that there were numerically more DO target completions after a DO prime than a PO prime. There was no difference for the Other target completions ($Fs < 1$).

The results therefore suggest that priming occurs from main to subordinate clauses (though the results were only significant for the PO target analyses). This is compatible with an account in which the processor makes use of locally defined procedures and is not necessarily sensitive to differences in global structure related to the presence or absence of an additional clause. To be more confident about this conclusion, we need to determine whether priming also occurs from subordinate to main clauses, as such an account would also predict.

EXPERIMENT 6: PRIMING FROM SUBORDINATE CLAUSE TO MAIN CLAUSE

Method

Participants.   Eighteen participants from the University of Edinburgh community were paid to participate.

Items.   We constructed 18 sets of items. Each comprised two sentence fragments (see Appendix):

11a. The report claimed that the racing driver showed the torn overall . . . (PO-inducing prime)
11b. The report claimed that the racing driver showed the helpful mechanic . . . (DO-inducing prime)
12.   The patient showed . . .

Prime sentences were the same as those in Experiment 4. Target sentences were the same as those in Experiment 2. The fillers were identical to those in Experiment 4.

Procedure, scoring, design, and data analysis.   These were the same as Experiment 2.

Results and discussion

Application of the scoring criteria yielded 270 trials where the prime fragment was completed as either a PO or as a DO (83% of all responses); 47% of these were completed as PO primes and 53% as DO primes. In these 270 trials, participants produced 133 (49%) PO completions, 72 (27%) DO completions, and 65 (24%) Other completions for the target fragment.

Table 1 shows the proportions of PO, DO, and Other target completions in the two experimental conditions. Inspection of Table 1 shows a priming effect for both the PO and DO target responses: priming was 14%. For the PO target analyses, one-way ANOVAs revealed significant differences between the Prime Completion conditions, $F_1(1, 17) = 5.49, p < .05, MSe = 0.035; F_2(1, 17) = 7.61, p < .05, MSe = 0.035$: there were more PO target completions after a PO prime than a DO prime. Similarly, for the DO target analyses, one-way ANOVAs revealed significant differences between the Prime Completion conditions, $F_1(1, 17) = 5.54, p < .05, MSe = 0.031; F_2(1, 17) = 8.58, p < .01, MSe = 0.019$: there were more DO target completions after a DO prime than a PO prime. There was no difference for the Other target completions ($Fs < 1$).

These results show significant priming from subordinate to main clauses. Together with the finding of priming from main to subordinate clauses (Experiment 5), they allow us to conclude that priming occurs between sentences that differ in global structure related to the presence or absence of a subordinate clause. Taken together, the results of Experiments 1–6 indicate that syntactic priming occurs between sentences that differ – in some cases quite substantially – in their global syntactic structure (and additionally in their global prosodic structure). Our results therefore provide empirical evidence to support the implicit assumption of many accounts of syntactic processing in production, that the production of syntactic structure involves processes and representations that are concerned with the constituents immediately making up a particular structure, but do not necessarily make reference to the larger syntactic structure. In other words, they make reference to local structure but do not need to make reference to global structure. They are also in keeping with the empirical evidence reported by Pickering and Branigan (1998) that syntactic processing does not make reference to the lower-level (comple- ment-internal) syntactic structure.

COMBINED ANALYSES OF EXPERIMENTS 1–6: ARE THERE EFFECTS OF GLOBAL STRUCTURE?

Thus far, we have been concerned with the question of whether the syntactic processes and representations used during language production are obligatorily specified in terms of the global syntactic structure. Our results suggest that they are not. But does syntactic processing make any reference to the global syntactic structure? If so, we might expect syntactic priming effects to be stronger when prime and target share global structure than when they do not. Much evidence shows that syntactic priming is enhanced when other linguistic elements are repeated, even though syntactic priming does not require the repetition of such elements. For example, syntactic priming effects are stronger when the head of the primed phrase is repeated than when it is not (Branigan, McLean, & Jones, 2005; Branigan et al., 2000a; Cleland & Pickering, 2003; Pickering & Branigan, 1998). They are even enhanced when prime and target have semantically related heads, compared to when they do not (Cleland & Pickering, 2003). Specifically, the tendency to use a PO construction following another PO construction is greater when prime and target utterances involve the same verb than if they involve different verbs (Branigan et al., 2000a; Cleland & Pickering, 2006; Corley & Scheepers, 2002; Pickering & Branigan, 1998), and in bilingual production when prime and target utterances use verbs that are translation equivalents (Schoonbaert, Hartsuiker, & Pickering, in press). Indeed such effects provide a central motivation for Pickering and Garrod's (2004) account of how interlocutors become aligned in dialogue, with repetition of linguistic structure at one level enhancing repetition at other linguistic levels. Taken together, these results suggest that the lexical and semantic context of syntactic rule activation affects syntactic activation. Hence the repetition of global syntactic structure might enhance syntactic priming in a similar manner.

Taken individually, Experiments 1–6 cannot cast light on this question, as none of these experiments directly compared priming between sentences with the same or different global structures. But priming was numerically greater in Experiments 1–4, where the prime and target appeared in the same type of clause (i.e., main or subordinate), than in Experiments 5 and 6, where they appeared in different types of clause (21.5%, 19%, 18%, and 27.5% vs. 10% and 14% respectively; see Table 1). We therefore carried out a combined (between-participants and within-items) analysis of all six experiments that included the factor Context (Same vs. Different global structure) to compare priming when the experimental verb phrase appeared in the same type of clause in prime and target (same global structure) versus when it appeared in different types of clause in prime and target (different global -structure). Hence we grouped Experiments 1, 2, 3, and 4 as the same-global-structure condition, and Experiments 5 and 6 as the different-global-structure condition. The Prime factor (PO vs. DO) was the same as in previous analyses.

For the PO target analyses, there was a main effect of Prime, $F_1(1, 106)$ = 44.3, $p < .001$, $MSe = 0.030$; $F_2(1, 17) = 42.5$, $p < .001$, $MSe = 0.013$: there were more PO target completions after a PO prime than after a DO prime. There was a trend towards an interaction (by participants only) between Context and Prime, $F_1(1, 106) = 2.91$, $p = .09$, $MSe = 0.030$; $F_2(1, 17) = 2.23$, $p = .15$, $MSe = 0.008$; Table 1 shows that priming was numerically greater when the experimental verb phrase appeared in the same type of clause in prime and target than when it appeared in different types of clause. There was no effect of Context ($Fs < 1$).

For the DO target analyses, there was a main effect of Prime, $F_1(1, 106) = 48.7$, $p < .001$, $MSe = 0.029$; $F_2(1, 17) = 48.9$ $p < .001$, $MSe = 0.011$: there were more DO target completions after a DO prime than after a PO prime. There was also an interaction between Context and Prime, $F_1(1, 106) = 5.17$, $p < .05$, $MSe = 0.029$; $F_2(1, 17) = 7.19$, $p < .05$, $MSe = 0.006$; Table 1 shows that priming was greater when the experimental verb phrase appeared in the same type of clause in prime and target than when it appeared in different types of clause. There was also an effect of Context, $F_1(1, 106) = 6.11$, $p < .05$, $MSe = 0.082$; $F_2(1, 17) = 19.1$ $p < .01$, $MSe = 0.009$: there were more DO targets in the Same Context than in the

Different Context. There was no difference for the Other target completions ($Fs < 1$).

The results of the combined analysis therefore provide some reason to believe that priming may be affected by the repetition of global structure (in terms of clause type). The DO target analyses indicated priming was reliably stronger by participants and by items when the experimental verb phrase appeared in the same type of clause in prime and target. However, the PO target analyses showed only a weak tendency, by participants only, towards the same effect. The failure to find clearly reliable effects might reflect a power problem, because the Context factor was manipulated between participants (who were run at different times and at two different universities), though it was manipulated within items. To be confident about whether there is an effect of global structure repetition on syntactic priming, it is necessary to directly compare the same participants' performance in both the same- and different-structure conditions. We therefore conducted two further (within-participants) experiments, which directly compared main- and subordinate-clause primes of main-clause targets (Experiment 7) and subordinate-clause targets (Experiment 8).

EXPERIMENT 7: PRIMING FROM MAIN AND SUBORDINATE CLAUSES TO MAIN CLAUSE

Method

Participants.   Thirty-two participants from the University of Edinburgh community were paid to participate.

Items.   We constructed 24 sets of items. Each comprised two sentence fragments (see Appendix):

13a. The racing driver showed the torn overall . . .
13b. The racing driver showed the helpful mechanic . . .
14a. The report claimed that the racing driver showed the torn overall . . .
14b. The report claimed that the racing driver showed the helpful mechanic . . .
15. The patient showed . . .

Eighteen of the items were the same ones as in Experiment 1 and 6, and six additional items (one for each verb) were added (see Appendix). The fillers were the same as in Experiment 4.

Procedure, scoring, design, and data analysis.   The experimental items were placed into four lists, each comprising six items from each condition, such that one version of each item appeared in each list. The 120 fragments (24 prime fragments, 24 target fragments, and 72 filler fragments) were individually randomised, with the constraints that each prime fragment immediately preceded its associated target fragment, and at least 2 filler fragments intervened between experimental items. Each fragment was presented as an individual trial; participants were not informed of any relationship between prime and target fragments. The rest of the procedure was the same as in Experiments 1–6, except that the experiment lasted around 30 minutes. There were two within-participants and within-items factors: Sentence Type (main-to-main vs. subordinate-to-main) and Prime Completion (PO vs. DO prime).

The scoring and data analysis was the same as in Experiments 1–6 with the exception that where 3 or fewer Prime Completions had been completed correctly (i.e., PO primes were completed as POs and DO primes were completed as DOs), we replaced the mean proportion of target completions for participants and items with the participant mean and item mean respectively for that condition. This was done because when the number of responses per cell is 3 or fewer, the proportion calculated for that particular participant or item can be skewed by the small sample size and not be a true reflection of the pattern of responses. Note that this method of replacement may increase the likelihood of finding an interaction, against our experimental predictions. Four participants had their subordinate-to-main PO-prime mean replaced and one participant had his or her subordinate-to-main DO-prime mean replaced (3.9% of the data). One item had its main-to-main PO-prime mean replaced and three items had their subordinate-to-main PO-prime mean replaced (4.2% of the data).

Results and discussion

Application of the scoring criteria yielded 690 trials where the prime fragment was completed as either a PO or as a DO (90% of all responses); 47% of these were completed as PO primes and 53% as DO primes. In these 690 trials, participants produced 335 (49%) PO completions, 209 (30%) DO completions, and 146 (21%) Other completions for the target fragment. In the main-to-main conditions, 360 trials were completed as either a PO or a DO (94% of all responses); 45% of these were completed as PO primes and 55% as DO primes. In these 360 trials, participants produced 177 (49%) PO completions, 118 (33%) DO completions, and 65 (18%) Other completions for the target fragment. The combined proportion of PO and DO target completions was comparable in each condition: 40% following PO primes and 42% following DO primes. In the subordinate-to-main conditions, 330 trials were completed as either a PO or a DO (86% of all responses); 45% of these were completed as PO primes and 55% as DO primes. In these 330 trials, participants produced

158 (48%) PO completions, 91 (28%) DO completions, and 81 (25%) Other completions for the target fragment. The combined proportion of PO and DO target completions was comparable in each condition: 36% following PO primes and 39% following DO primes.

Table 2 shows the proportions of PO, DO, and Other target completions for both the main-to-main and subordinate-to-main conditions after the PO- and DO-prime conditions. It reveals a priming effect for both the PO and DO target responses in both the Sentence Type conditions: mean priming was 17.5% for the main-to-main Sentence Type and 12.5% for the subordinate-to-main Sentence Type. For the PO target analyses, two-way ANOVAs revealed a significant difference between the Prime Completion conditions, $F_1(1, 31) = 14.5, p < .01, MSe = 0.066; F_2(1, 23) = 32.3, p < .001, MSe = 0.028$, no interaction ($Fs < 1$), and no effect of Sentence Type ($Fs < 1$). For the DO target analyses, two-way ANOVAs revealed a significant difference between the Prime Completion conditions, $F_1(1, 31) = 10.0, p < .01, MSe = 0.055; F_2(1, 23) = 32.5, p < .001, MSe = 0.017$, no interaction ($Fs < 3$), but a significant effect (by items only) of Sentence Type, $F_1(1, 31) = 1.98$, n.s.; $F_2(1, 23) = 4.44, p = .05, MSe = 0.020$. For the Other target completions, there was a main effect of Sentence Type,

TABLE 2
Proportion of PO, DO, and Other target completions produced in each condition in Experiments 7 and 8 (using participant means)

Experiment	PO targets	DO targets	Other targets
Experiment 7: Priming from subordinate and main clauses to main clause			
MMPO Prime	.59	.24	.17
MMDO Prime	.41	.41	.18
SMPO Prime	.55	.24	.21
SMDO Prime	.39	.33	.29
Priming effect (MM)	.18	.17	
Priming effect (SM)	.16	.09	
Experiment 8: Priming from subordinate and main clauses to subordinate clause			
MSPO Prime	.47	.09	.43
MSDO Prime	.40	.20	.40
SSPO Prime	.58	.09	.32
SSDO Prime	.40	.28	.33
Priming effect (MS)	.07	.11	
Priming effect (SS)	.18	.19	

Note: PO = Prepositional Object; DO = Double Object; MM = main-clause prime, main-clause target; SM = subordinate-clause prime, main-clause target; MS = main-clause prime, subordinate-clause target; SS = subordinate-clause prime, subordinate-clause target.

$F_1(1, 31) = 7.79, p < .01, MSe = 0.021; F_2(1, 23) = 3.77, p = .06, MSe = 0.026$, but no effect of Prime Completion ($Fs < 2$) and no interaction ($Fs < 3$).

Simple main effects showed that there was significant priming for PO target completions in both the Sentence Type conditions: main-to-main, $F_1(1, 31) = 8.85, p < .01; F_2(1, 23) = 27.3, p < .001$; subordinate-to-main: $F_1(1, 31) = 10.0, p < .01; F_2(1, 23) = 13.6, p < .01$. For the DO target completions, there was significant priming for main-to-main, $F_1(1, 31) = 11.02, p < .01; F_2(1, 23) = 14.8, p < .01$; and a marginal effect (significant by items) for subordinate-to-main: $F_1(1, 31) = 3.59, p = .07; F_2(1, 23) = 10.6, p < .01$.

An additional set of analyses was performed on the arcsine-transformed proportions of responses for both participants and items. The results were nearly identical to those for the raw proportions. The only difference of note was that there was a marginal interaction for DO target completions by participants, $F_1(1, 31) = 3.54, p = .07, MSe = 0.029$, but not by items ($F_2 < 1$). Overall, the results of Experiment 7 show no difference between main and subordinate clause in their effectiveness as primes for main clause targets. They therefore provide no reason to assume that syntactic priming is stronger when global structure is repeated than when it is not repeated, and hence that syntactic processing is sensitive to the global syntactic structure.

EXPERIMENT 8: PRIMING FROM MAIN AND SUBORDINATE CLAUSES TO SUBORDINATE CLAUSE

Method

Participants. Thirty-two participants from the University of Edinburgh community were paid to participate.

Items. We constructed 24 sets of items. Each comprised two sentence fragments (see Appendix):

16a. The racing driver showed the torn overall . . .
16b. The racing driver showed the helpful mechanic . . .
17a. The report claimed that the racing driver showed the torn overall . . .
17b. The report claimed that the racing driver showed the helpful mechanic . . .
18. The rumours alleged that the patient showed . . .

Eighteen of the items were the same ones as in Experiment 4 and 5, and six additional items (one for each verb) were added (see Appendix). The fillers were the same as in Experiment 4.

Procedure, scoring, design, and data analysis.   These were the same as Experiment 7, except that the two within-participants and within-items factors were Sentence Type (main-to-subordinate vs. subordinate-to-subordinate) and Prime Completion (PO vs. DO prime). For the participants, we replaced two main-to-subordinate PO-prime means with the participant mean of that condition, and six subordinate-to-subordinate PO-prime means with the participant mean of that condition (6.3% of the data). For the items, we replaced two subordinate-to-subordinate PO-prime means with the item mean of that condition (2.1% of the data).

Results and discussion

Application of the scoring criteria yielded 677 trials where the prime fragment was completed as either a PO or as a DO (88% of all responses); 47% of these were completed as PO primes and 53% as DO primes. In these 677 trials, participants produced 309 (46%) PO completions, 116 (17%) DO completions, and 252 (37%) Other completions for the target fragment. In the main-to-subordinate prime condition, 349 trials were completed as either a PO or a DO (91% of all responses); 48% of these were completed as PO primes and 52% as DO primes. In these 349 trials, participants produced 152 (44%) PO completions, 53 (15%) DO completions, and 144 (41%) Other completions for the target fragment. The combined proportion of PO and DO target completions was comparable in each condition: 28% following PO primes and 31% following DO primes. In the subordinate-to-subordinate prime condition, 325 trials were completed as either a PO or a DO (85% of all responses); 46% of these were completed as PO primes and 54% as DO primes. In these 325 trials, participants produced 157 (48%) PO completions, 63 (19%) DO completions, and 105 (32%) Other completions for the target fragment. The combined proportion of PO and DO target completions was comparable in each condition: 31% following PO primes and 37% following DO primes.

Inspection of Table 2 shows a priming effect for both the PO and DO target responses in both the Sentence Type conditions: mean priming was 9% for the main-to-subordinate prime and 18.5% for the subordinate-to-subordinate prime Sentence Type. For the PO target analyses, two-way ANOVAs revealed a significant difference between the Prime Completion conditions, $F_1(1, 31) = 14.3, p < .01, MSe = 0.039; F_2(1, 23) = 14.2, p < .01, MSe = 0.034$, no effect of Sentence Type ($Fs < 3.5$) and no interaction ($Fs < 2.5$). For the DO target analyses, two-way ANOVAs revealed a significant difference between the Prime Completion conditions, $F_1(1, 31) = 18.1, p < .001, MSe = 0.037; F_2(1, 23) = 19.2, p < .001, MSe = 0.027$, no effect of Sentence Type ($Fs < 3$), and a marginal interaction by participants only, $F_1(1, 31) = 3.44, p = .07, MSe = 0.012; F2 < 1.5$. For the Other target completions, there was a main effect of Sentence Type, $F_1(1, 31) = 7.58, p < .05, MSe = 0.037, F_2(1, 23) = 3.57, p = .07, MSe = 0.048$, but no effect of Prime Completion ($Fs < 1$) or interaction ($Fs < 1$).

Simple main effects showed that there was significant priming for PO target responses for main-to-subordinate primes (by items only), $F_1(1, 31) = 2.44, p = .13; F_2(1, 23) = 7.71, p < .05$; and subordinate-to-subordinate primes: $F_1(1, 31) = 12.4, p < .01; F_2(1, 23) = 7.14, p < .05$. For the DO target completions, there was significant priming for both subordinate-to-subordinate primes, $F_1(1, 31) = 8.94, p < .01; F_2(1, 23) = 12.3, p < .01$; and subordinate-to-subordinate primes: $F_1(1, 31) = 18.9, p < .001; F_2(1, 23) = 15.8, p < .01$. The results demonstrate priming from both main and subordinate clause primes to subordinate clause targets. Although there is a trend toward more priming from subordinate clause than main clause primes, this difference is not significant and does not provide good evidence that syntactic processing makes reference to the global syntactic structure.

To be more confident about this conclusion, we carried out a combined analysis of Experiments 7 and 8. It is possible that the greater power provided by a combined analysis would make it possible to detect any weak effect of the repetition of global syntactic structure. The factors were Prime Clause (main vs. subordinate), Target Clause (main vs. subordinate) and Prime (PO vs. DO). Target Clause was a between-participants but within-items factor (i.e., it corresponded to Experiment 7 vs. Experiment 8). If priming is greater when global structure is repeated than when it is not repeated, we would expect to find a three-way interaction between Prime Clause, Target Clause, and Prime.

For the PO target analyses, there was a main effect of Prime Clause, $F_1(1, 62) = 30.0, p < .001, MSe = 0.052; F_2(1, 23) = 47.5, p < .001, MSe = 0.027$: there were more PO target completions after a PO prime than a DO prime. There was no main effect of Prime Clause or Target Clause ($Fs < 1$). The only interaction that approached significance (by participants only) was Prime Clause * Target Clause, $F_1(1, 62) = 3.71, p = .06, MSe = 0.034; F2 < 1$. For all the other interactions, $Fs < 2$. In particular, there was no three-way interaction.

For the DO target analyses, there was a main effect of Prime Clause, $F_1(1, 62) = 28.0, p < .001, MSe = 0.043; F_2(1, 23) = 69.3, p < .001, MSe = 0.015$: there were more DO target completions after a DO prime than a PO prime. There was a main effect (by participants only) of Target Clause, $F_1(1, 62) = 8.10, p < .01, MSe = 0.142; F2 < 1$: there were more DO targets after a Main-Clause target. There was also an interaction between Prime Clause and Target Clause, $F_1(1, 62) = 5.60, p < .05, MSe = 0.022; F_2(1, 23) = 6.41, p < .05, MSe = 0.031$. There was a three-way interaction (by participants only), $F_1(1, 62) = 4.82, p < .05, MSe = 0.017; F_2(1, 23) = 1.58, p = 0.22, MSe = 0.018$, providing some evidence for an effect of global structure repetition on priming.

For the Other target completions, the only significant effect was for the Prime Clause × Target Clause interaction, $F_1(1, 62) = 16.9, p < .001, MSe = 0.030; F_2(1, 23) = 5.92, p < .05, MSe = 0.047$.

In summary, there was only a weak suggestion (for DO target completions only, and reliable by participants only) that priming was stronger when global structure was repeated than when it was not repeated. Hence the combined analysis does not provide strong support for the hypothesis that syntactic processing is sensitive to global syntactic structure.

GENERAL DISCUSSION

In eight experiments, we have found evidence that the syntactic procedures that people use to combine expressions remain constant, irrespective of the role that those expressions play within the sentence as a whole. Specifically, people showed a consistent tendency to repeat syntactic structure across utterances, even when the relevant structures played very different roles in the prime and target sentences. Experiment 1 found priming between two main clauses that did not differ in overall structure. Experiment 2 showed priming when the prime contained an initial adverbial phrase (e.g., On Friday), thereby demonstrating that identity of global structure was not necessary for priming. Experiment 3 showed priming when the prime contained an initial subordinate clause (e.g., As Anne claimed), thereby demonstrating that priming occurred when production of the prime involved the construction of two different verb phrases. Experiment 4 showed that priming occurred between experimental verb phrases in subordinate clauses. Experiments 5–8 demonstrated that priming occurred between main and subordinate clauses. In contrast, the experiments did not provide strong evidence that repetition of global structure enhanced syntactic priming. A combined (between-participants and within-items) analysis of Experiments 1–6 showed some suggestion of stronger priming with repeated global structure. However, Experiments 7 and 8, which directly compared priming within participants between clauses of the same type (main or subordinate) and clauses of the opposite type, did not find significant effects of global structure repetition. Furthermore, a combined analysis of Experiments 7 and 8 found only a weak suggestion of stronger priming with repeated global structure.

Hence these experiments consistently demonstrated priming for verb phrase structure in consecutive sentences, both when the global structure was repeated and when it was not, although the magnitude of the effects and the overall pattern of responses varied between experiments. The variations in the magnitude of effects (e.g., 28% vs. 18% priming between main clauses in Experiments 1 and 8 respectively) are in keeping with those found in previous studies of syntactic priming for PO/DO structures using sentence completion (e.g., Branigan et al., 1999, 2000b; Corley & Scheepers, 2002; Pickering & Branigan, 1998; Pickering et al., 2002).

Effects of local structure

The results therefore indicate that the experimental verb phrase does not need to occur in the same position in the global structure of the sentence for syntactic priming to occur. For people to be more likely to produce verb phrases of a particular syntactic type in the target sentence, it is only necessary for a verb phrase of that type to occur somewhere in the prime sentence. For example, if people produce a verb phrase comprising a verb followed by two noun phrases when producing the prime sentence, they will be more likely to produce a verb phrase comprising a verb followed by two noun phrases when producing the target sentence. Hence, the results provide evidence that the procedures leading to the construction of individual expressions are to at least some extent autonomous of syntactic context.

These results are consistent with the (largely implicit) assumption of current models of language production that syntactic processing involves procedures that make reference to just those constituents that immediately make up a structure. Thus the same procedures are involved in constructing the verb phrase gave the puppy to the boy in sentences with quite different global structures such as The girl gave the puppy to the boy and John said that the girl gave the puppy to the boy.

The results are compatible with Pickering and Branigan's (1998) model of the lemma stratum (see also Branigan & Pickering, 2004; Hartsuiker, Pickering, & Veltkamp, 2004). Following Levelt, Roelofs, and Meyer (1999), Pickering and Branigan proposed that the lemma stratum is the level of lexical representation that is concerned with the syntactic properties of a word. Each word is represented by a lemma node that is linked to other nodes representing syntactic properties, such as grammatical category, number, and person. In Pickering and Branigan's account, the lemma nodes represent the base forms of words, and are linked to combinatorial nodes that encode combinatorial information, specifying the expressions with which that word can combine to form larger expressions. For example, the verb give can combine with a noun phrase and prepositional phrase, or with two noun phrases, to produce a verb phrase. The lemma give is therefore linked to both the NP,NP combinatorial node and the NP,PP combinatorial node. When the verb is used in a DO construction, the NP,NP node is activated; when it is used in a PO construction, the NP,PP node is activated.

The same NP,PP combinatorial node is activated whenever a PO structure is produced. Hence it is activated during production of the verb phrase gave the puppy to the boy when this phrase appears in a main clause (The girl gave the puppy to the boy) and when it is embedded in a subordinate clause (John said that the girl gave the puppy to the boy). In Pickering and Branigan's (1998) account, syntactic priming arises from residual activation of a combinatorial node, facilitating its subsequent use in any utterance that can be generated using that node. Because the same combinatorial node is activated and subsequently retains residual activation whenever a structure is produced, irrespective of global structure, this model accounts straightforwardly for our finding that production of a PO structure in one global context (e.g., a main clause) primes production of a PO structure in a different global context (e.g., a subordinate clause).

Our results demonstrate further that such activation persists through the application of other, related rules within the same utterance. Specifically, Experiments 4, 5, and 8 showed priming of subordinate clauses when they were preceded by a main clause. Though there have been demonstrations of priming across intervening sentences (e.g., Bock & Griffin, 2000; Branigan et al., 2000b), this is the first demonstration of priming across intervening clauses within the same sentence.

Effects of global structure

As well as effects of local structure, we might have expected to find clear effects of global structure. There is good evidence that semantic and lexical similarity between prime and target enhance syntactic priming (e.g., Cleland & Pickering, 2003; Pickering & Branigan, 1998), with Pickering and Garrod (2004) arguing that such effects are central to the process by which interlocutors align their mental states in dialogue. On this basis, we might have expected that global syntactic similarity (e.g., prime and target both involving or not involving subordinate clauses) would also enhance syntactic priming.

However, our experiments found no strong evidence that syntactic processing in production makes reference to global structure. Syntactic priming was not reliably increased when global syntactic structure was repeated. It is unlikely that this failure to detect reliable effects arises from use of an insufficiently sensitive measure: the experimental method that we used consistently demonstrated strong and reliable syntactic priming effects based on the repetition of local syntactic structure, and analyses on the combined data from multiple experiments (hence substantially increasing the power of the analyses) did not find reliable influences of the repetition of global syntactic structure. Our evidence therefore suggests that any component that makes reference to global structure exerts a weaker influence than the component that is concerned with strictly local syntactic relationships.

Our findings do appear to contrast with Scheepers (2003), whose priming effects can be most straightforwardly explained in terms of procedures that make reference to the global structure. As we have noted, our experiments do not rule out the existence of such procedures. However, Scheepers explained his findings in terms of the order in which rules that make reference to local structure are applied. An alternative explanation that is compatible with our findings is that high and low attachment of prepositional phrases differ in semantic content (high attachment involves modification of the main assertion of the utterance, whereas low attachment does not), and that his effects arise from priming of semantic content (i.e., during conceptualisation). On this account, Scheepers' finding (Experiment 3) that priming did not occur for sentences that shared focus structure (in terms of which entity was modified by a subordinate clause) but did not share syntactic structure presumably results from differences between the realisation of anaphoric and syntactic dependencies.

Our results therefore form part of a body of research that helps determine the stages that take place during grammatical encoding. We assume that speakers construct a functional representation (containing reference to subject, object, and so forth) and then map this to a constituent-structure representation of the utterance (e.g., Bock & Levelt, 1994). Bock, Loebell, and Morey (1992) argued that relation-changing rules (corresponding to some transformations) do not mediate between the functional and constituent-structure representations. Pickering et al. (2002) argued that speakers do not construct an initial unordered constituent-structure representation that they subsequently linearise. Together, these results suggest a direct mapping between functional structure and a fully specified constituent structure representation. The current results suggest that speakers use syntactic procedures that make reference to just those constituents that immediately make up a structure during the construction of this final constituent-structure representation. They do not provide strong evidence that speakers may also use procedures that make reference to constituents that make up the global syntactic structure.

Our distinction between local and global effects has interesting parallels with the linguistic distinction between context-free and non-context-free grammars (Chomsky, 1965; see Partee, ter Meulen, & Wall, 1990, pp. 451–453). Essentially, context-free grammars and the more powerful noncontext-free grammars occupy different points on a hierarchy that categorises grammars according to their generative power (that is, the expressions that they can produce). In both context-free and noncontext-free grammars, complex sentences can be constructed using a set of rules (or principles) that specify components (constituents) of the sentence in a recursive manner. However, they differ with respect to the amount of information to which the rules make reference. Context-free grammars use rules that do not make reference to the broader syntactic context, whereas noncontext-free rules do make reference to the broader syntactic context.

Our results therefore suggest that syntactic processing in production makes use of procedures that largely correspond to context-free rules, though we cannot rule out the possibility that it also makes some use of noncontext-free procedures. This is interesting in the light of the finding that the vast majority of constructions in natural languages such as English can be captured using context-free rules, with the exceptions requiring very modest extensions to the grammar (e.g., Shieber, 1985).

In conclusion, our experiments demonstrated that syntactic priming occurred between utterances containing a critical verb phrase, irrespective of whether the verb phrase appeared in the same position within the global syntactic structures of the utterances. This finding suggests that syntactic processing in language production uses procedures that make reference to local syntactic structure.

REFERENCES

Bock, J. K. (1986). Syntactic persistence in language production. *Cognitive Psychology, 18,* 355–387.

Bock, J. K. (1989). Closed class immanence in sentence production. *Cognition, 31,* 163–186.

Bock, J. K., & Cutting, J. C. (1992). Regulating mental energy: Performance units in language production. *Journal of Memory and Language, 31,* 99–127.

Bock, J. K., & Griffin, Z. M. (2000). The persistence of structural priming: Transient activation or implicit learning? *Journal of Experimental Psychology: General, 129,* 177–192.

Bock, J. K., & Levelt, W. J. M. (1994). Language production: Grammatical encoding. In M. A. Gernsbacher (Ed.), *Handbook of psycholinguistics* (pp. 945–984). San Diego, CA: Academic Press.

Bock, J. K., & Loebell, H. (1990). Framing sentences. *Cognition, 35,* 1–39.

Bock, J. K., Loebell, H., & Morey, R. (1992). From conceptual roles to structural relations: Bridging the syntactic cleft. *Psychological Review, 99,* 150–171.

Branigan, H. P., McLean, J. F., & Jones, M. G. (2005). A blue cat or a cat that is blue? Evidence for abstract syntax in young children's noun phrases. *Proceedings of the Twenty-ninth Boston University Conference on Language Development.* Somerville, MA: Cascadilla Press.

Branigan, H. P., & Pickering, M. J. (2004). Syntactic representation in the lemma stratum: Commentary on Levelt, Roelofs and Meyer. *Behavioral and Brain Sciences, 27,* 296–297.

Branigan, H. P., Pickering, M. J., & Cleland, A. A. (1999). Syntactic priming in written production: Evidence for rapid decay. *Psychonomic Bulletin and Review, 6,* 635–640.

Branigan, H. P., Pickering, M. J., & Cleland, A. A. (2000a). Syntactic coordination in dialogue. *Cognition, 75*, B13–B25.

Branigan, H. P., Pickering, M. J., Liversedge, S. P., Stewart, A. J., & Urbach, T. P. (1995). Syntactic priming: Investigating the mental representation of language. *Journal of Psycholinguistic Research, 24*, 489–506.

Branigan, H. P., Pickering, M. J, Stewart, A. J., & McLean, J. F. (2000b). Syntactic priming in spoken production: Linguistic and temporal interference. *Memory and Cognition, 28*, 1297–1302.

Chang, F., Dell, G. S., Bock, J. K., & Griffin, Z. M. (2000). Structural priming as implicit learning: A comparison of models of sentence production. *Journal of Psycholinguistic Research, 292*, 217–229.

Chomsky, N. (1965). *Aspects of the theory of syntax*. Cambridge, MA: MIT Press.

Cleland, A., & Pickering, M. J. (2003). The use of lexical and syntactic information in language production: Evidence from the priming of noun-phrase structure. *Journal of Memory and Language, 49*, 214–230.

Cleland, A. A., & Pickering, M. J. (2006). Do writing and speaking employ the same syntactic representations? *Journal of Memory and Language, 54*, 185–198.

Cohen, J. D., MacWhinney, B., Flatt, M., & Provost, J. (1993). PsyScope: A new graphic interactive environment for designing psychology experiments. *Behavioral Research Methods, Instruments, and Computers, 25*, 257–271.

Corley. M., & Scheepers, C. (2002). Syntactic priming in English sentence production: Categorical and latency evidence from an Internet-based study. *Psychonomic Bulletin and Review, 9*, 126–131.

Ferreira, V. S., & Bock, J. K. (2006). The functions of structural priming. *Language and Cognitive Processes, 21*, 1011–1029.

Garrett, M. (1980). Levels of processing in speech production. In B. Butterworth (Ed.), *Language production* (Vol. 1, pp. 177–220). London: Academic Press.

Hartsuiker, R. J., Pickering, M. J., & Veltkamp, E. (2004). Is syntax separate or shared between languages? Cross-linguistic syntactic priming in Spanish/English bilinguals. *Psychological Science, 15*, 409–414.

Hartsuiker, R. J., & Westenberg, C. (2000). Persistence of word order in written and spoken sentence production. *Cognition, 75*, B27–B39.

Holmes, V. M. (1988). Hesitations and sentence planning. *Language and Cognitive Processes, 3*, 323–361.

Kempen, G., & Hoenkamp, E. (1987). An incremental procedural grammar for sentence formulation. *Cognitive Science, 11*, 201–258.

Levelt, W. J. M. (1989). *Speaking: From intention to articulation*. Cambridge, MA: MIT Press.

Levelt, W. J. M., & Kelter, S. (1982). Surface form and memory in question answering. *Cognitive Psychology, 14*, 78–106.

Levelt, W. J. M., Roelofs, A., & Meyer, A. (1999). A theory of lexical access in speech production. *Behavioral and Brain Sciences, 22*, 1–75.

Partee, B. H., ter Meulen, A., & Wall, R. E. (1990). *Mathematical methods in linguistics*. Dordrecht: Kluwer.

Pickering, M. J., & Branigan, H. P. (1998). The representation of verbs: Evidence from syntactic persistence in written language production. *Journal of Memory and Language, 39*, 633–651.

Pickering, M. J., & Branigan, H. P., & McLean, J. F. (2002). Constituent structure is formulated in one stage. *Journal of Memory and Language, 46*, 586–605.

Pickering, M. J., & Garrod, S. (2004). Toward a mechanistic psychology of dialogue. *Behavioral and Brain Sciences, 27*, 169–228.

Scheepers, C. (2003). Syntactic priming of relative clause attachments: Persistence of structural configuration in sentence production. *Cognition, 89,* 179–205.

Schenkein, J. (1980). A taxonomy for repeating action sequences in natural conversation. In B. Butterworth (Ed.), *Language production* (Vol. 1, pp. 21–47). London: Academic Press.

Schoonbaert, S., Hartsuiker, R. J., & Pickering, M. J. (in press). Translation equivalence enhances cross-linguistic syntactic priming. *Journal of Memory and Language.*

Shieber, S. M. (1985). Evidence against the context-freeness of natural-language. *Linguistics and Philosophy, 8,* 333–343.

Smith, M., & Wheeldon, L. (1999). High-level processing scope in spoken sentence production. *Cognition, 73,* 205–246.

Tannen, D. (1989). *Talking voices: Repetition, dialogue and imagery in conversational discourse.* Cambridge: Cambridge University Press.

Weiner, E. J., & Labov, W. (1983). Constraints on the agentless passive. *Journal of Linguistics, 19,* 29–58.

APPENDIX

Item list for Experiments 1–6

The first sentence of each item is the prime and the second is the target. The first phrase in the round brackets occurred in the PO-inducing prime conditions; the second phrase occurred in the DO-inducing prime conditions. Experiment 1 employed none of the phrases within the square brackets and used present-tense verbs in both prime and target (e.g., <u>shows</u> rather than <u>showed</u> in the first item). Experiment 2 employed the first phrase within the square brackets; Experiment 3 used the second phrase; and Experiment 4 used the third phrase. All these experiments did not use the phrase in the braces before the target. Experiment 5 used none of the phrases in the square brackets, but used the phrase in the braces. Experiment 6 used the final phrase in the square brackets and the phrase in the braces.

1. [On Friday/As Anne claimed/The report claimed that], the racing driver showed (the torn overall/the helpful mechanic). {The rumours alleged that}the patient showed.
2. [Last Sunday/As Tom knew/The film revealed that], the cricket player showed (the ball/ the umpire). {The documents revealed that} the car mechanic showed.
3. [This morning/As Bill said/The video revealed that], the youngster showed (the colourful toy/the kind teacher). {The programme alleged that} the private detective showed.
4. [After breakfast/As Lisa heard/The paper reported that], the grandmother handed (the big present/the little girl). {The headline claimed that} the tennis fan handed.
5. [This evening/As James claimed/The programme alleged], the barman handed (the cocktail/the customer). {The report claimed that} the postman handed.
6. [Yesterday morning/As Craig admitted/The report disclosed that], the check-out assistant handed (the bag/the shopper). {The report revealed that} the junior surgeon handed.
7. [During the voyage/As Sarah complained/The headline declared that], the captain gave (the spare lifejacket/the old sailor). {The report stated that} the bus driver gave.
8. [At lunchtime/As Jo knew/The photographs revealed that], the mother gave (the expensive toy/the hungry baby). {The advert announced that} the florist gave.
9. Last Thursday/As Neil said/The rumours alleged that], the lecturer gave (the big book/ the old professor). {The programme claimed that} the shopkeeper gave.
10. [On Tuesday/As John claimed/The report stated that], the secretary sent (the invoice/ the manager). {The rumours alleged that} the boyfriend sent.
11. [After the accident/As Cathy admitted/The documents revealed that], the woman sent (the insurance claim/the insurance company). {The article disclosed that} the fan sent.
12. [This morning/As Paul heard/The paper alleged that], the blackmailer sent (the photos/ the politician). {The paper reported that} the lonely sailor sent.
13. [After the party/As Simon complained/The headline alleged that], the fashion designer lent (the red jacket/the tall model). {The paper reported that} the climber lent.
14. [On Sunday/As Dave knew/The report claimed that], the neighbour lent (the lawnmower/the man). {The headline declared that} the actor lent.
15. [At lunchtime/As Sue said/The film revealed that], the receptionist lent (the spare key/ the new trainee). {The letters alleged that} the hairdresser lent.
16. [In April/As Ruth claimed/The documents disclosed that], the millionaire loaned (the valuable painting/the struggling artist). {The film revealed that} the teenager loaned.
17. [During the holiday/As Roger admitted/The video revealed that], the swimmer loaned (the towel/the diver). {The documents stated that} the carpenter loaned.
18. [On Saturday/As Mike complained/The paper claimed that], the student loaned (the money/the friend). {The programmed alleged that} the little girl loaned.

Item list for Experiments 7 and 8

1. [The report claimed that], the racing driver showed (the torn overall/the helpful mechanic).[The rumours alleged that] the patient showed.
2. [The film revealed that], the cricket player showed (the ball/the umpire). [The documents revealed that] the car mechanic showed.
3. [The video revealed that], the youngster showed (the colourful toy/the kind teacher). [The programmed alleged that] the private detective showed.
4. [The programme mentioned that] the journalist showed (the pictures/the editor). [The headline declared that] the spy showed.
5. [The paper reported that], the grandmother handed (the big present/the little girl). [The headline claimed that] the tennis fan handed.
6. [The programme alleged], the barman handed (the cocktail/the customer). [The report claimed that] the postman handed.
7. [The report disclosed that], the check-out assistant handed (the bag/the shopper). [The report revealed that] the junior surgeon handed.
8. [The paper reported that] the dinner lady handed (the chips/the schoolchild). [The film revealed that] the hostess handed.
9. [The headline declared that], the captain gave (the spare lifejacket/the old sailor). [The report stated that] the bus driver gave.
10. [The photographs revealed that], the mother gave (the expensive toy/the hungry baby). [The advert announced that] the florist gave.
11. [The rumours alleged that], the lecturer gave (the big book/the old professor). [The programme claimed that] the shopkeeper gave.
12. [The report stated that] the headmaster gave the (severe punishment/the troublesome pupils). [The video revealed that] the pharmacist gave.
13. [The report stated that], the secretary sent (the invoice/the manager). [The rumours alleged that] the boyfriend sent.
14. [The documents revealed that], the woman sent (the insurance claim/the insurance company). [The article disclosed that] the fan sent.
15. [The paper alleged that], the blackmailer sent (the photos/the politician). [The paper reported that] the lonely sailor sent.
16. [The rumours alleged that] the generous aunt sent (the cheque/the nephew). [The paper reported that] the famous writer sent.
17. [The headline alleged that], the fashion designer lent (the red jacket/the tall model). [The paper reported that] the climber lent.
18. [The report claimed that], the neighbour lent (the lawnmower/the man). [The headline declared that] the actor lent.
19. [The film revealed that], the receptionist lent (the spare key/the new trainee). [The letters alleged that] the hairdresser lent.
20. [The newspaper reported that] the motorist lent (the spare tyre/the stranded walker). [The documents stated that] the farmer lent.
21. [The documents disclosed that], the millionaire loaned (the valuable painting/the struggling artist). [The film revealed that] the teenager loaned.
22. [The video revealed that], the swimmer loaned (the towel/the diver). [The documents stated that] the carpenter loaned.
23. [The paper claimed that], the student loaned (the money/the friend). [The programme alleged that] the little girl loaned.
24. [The headline declared that] the father loaned (the car/the daughter). [The paper reported that] the gardener loaned.

LANGUAGE AND COGNITIVE PROCESSES
2006, 21 (7–8), 1011–1029

 Psychology Press
Taylor & Francis Group

The functions of structural priming

Victor S. Ferreira

University of California, San Diego, CA, USA

Kathryn Bock

University of Illinois at Urbana-Champaign, Urbana-Champaign, IL, USA

Structural priming refers to speakers' tendency to produce sentences with previously heard or produced syntactic structures. We review arguments and evidence for three common accounts of the functions of structural priming. One is that structural priming enhances fluency. Only some (reaction time and fluency measure) evidence supports this view. A second account argues that structural priming stems from implicit learning of how features of meaning are linked to syntactic configurations. We describe evidence suggesting that structural priming exhibits effects characteristic of both learning and implicitness. A third account claims that structural priming is an aspect of coordination or *alignment* among interlocutors. Consistent with this, some evidence shows that structural priming involves a shorter-term component that is broadly sensitive to repeated bindings of wide-ranging types of knowledge. Together, these observations suggest that structural priming is likely a multifaceted force that reflects implicit learning and, possibly independently, alignment among interlocutors.

People tend to repeat themselves. They say things that they've heard themselves say before, and that they've heard others say before. They repeat specific words (Kubovy, 1977), sounds (Dell, Burger, & Svec, 1997), and the general framing or mental model of the subject under discussion (Garrod & Anderson, 1987; Garrod & Pickering, 2004). In short, though

Correspondence should be addressed to Victor S. Ferreira, Department of Psychology 0109, University of California, San Diego, La Jolla, CA, 92093-0109, USA.
E-mail: ferreira@psy.ucsd.edu

Preparation of this paper was supported in part by National Institute of Health grants R01 MH-64733, R01 HD21011, and R01 MH66089, and National Science Foundation grant BCS 0213270.

http://www.psypress.com/lcp   DOI: 10.1080/016909600824609

linguistic performance is quintessentially creative, it can also be surprisingly recapitulative.

Among all forms of repetition, one that has received much scrutiny in recent years is here termed *structural priming* (sometimes called *syntactic priming*). Structural priming refers to speakers' tendency to use current utterances that are similar in general form to sentences they have previously experienced. For example, speakers who previously produced (Bock, 1986) or heard (Bock, Dell, Chang, & Onishi, in press; Branigan, Pickering, & Cleland, 2000a) a *prepositional dative* structure like *The governess made [a pot of tea] [for the princess]* are likely to describe a subsequent picture with another prepositional dative like *The woman is showing [the dress] [to the man].* In contrast, speakers who previously heard or produced a double-object structure like *The governess made [the princess] [a pot of tea]* are likely to describe a subsequent picture with another double-object like *The woman is showing [the man] [the dress].* Structural priming is evident in naturalistic (Bock et al., in press; Gries, 2005; Szmrecsanyi, 2004, 2005; Weiner & Labov, 1983) as well as experimental (e.g., Bock, 1986) settings, and in utterances produced to communicate (e.g., Branigan et al., 2000a) or to support memory (e.g., Bock, 1986). Structural priming appears in the production of different kinds of structures, including transitives and datives (actives vs. passives or prepositional datives vs. double objects; e.g., Bock, 1986), the mention of the optional *that* (Ferreira, 2003a), particle placement (Konopka & Bock, 2005), different noun-phrase structures (Cleland & Pickering, 2003), and from one level of syntactic embedding to another (Branigan, Pickering, McLean, & Stewart, 2006). Structural priming has been observed in English (e.g., Bock, 1986), Dutch (e.g., Hartsuiker & Kolk, 1998), and German (e.g., Loebell & Bock, 2003; Scheepers, 2003). In sum, structural priming is a wide-ranging phenomenon, that manifests in different settings, different languages, and with different linguistic structures.

Most work on structural priming has aimed to establish its representational underpinning, and this work has led to the consensus that structural priming occurs because speakers tend to repeat syntactic structures from utterance to utterance. This conclusion follows from studies showing that the repetition of structure is not dependent on the repetition of different aspects of the contents of previous utterances. For example, structural priming is observed even when an initial *prime* sentence and a subsequent *target* sentence share no open-class words at all (nouns, verbs, adjectives; Bock, 1986), though the effect is larger when sentences do share open-class words (Pickering & Branigan, 1998). Structural priming is also observed between sentences that have similar syntactic structures but are semantically distinct, though it is not observed between sentences that have different syntactic structures but are similar in terms of prosody or superficial appearance (Bock & Loebell, 1990). Furthermore, structural priming is insensitive to whether prime and target sentences have similar or distinct inflectional or closed-class lexical content (Bock, 1989; Ferreira, 2003a; Pickering & Branigan, 1998). Speakers tend to repeat thematic (Chang, Bock, & Goldberg, 2003) and semantic assignments from sentence to sentence, such that when they produce sentences with an inanimate grammatical subject, they are likely to do so again (Bock, Loebell, & Morey, 1992; Griffin & Weinstein-Tull, 2003); however, speakers also repeat syntactic structures over and above these semantic-assignment priming effects (Bock et al., 1992).

Another question about structural priming that has received less attention and for which answers are not yet clear is a functional one: What is structural priming for? How might syntactic repetition or persistence serve linguistic processing or communication? Recent work has seen the emergence of three different ways of characterising the function of structural priming. One view is that priming enhances the fluency of communication by promoting faster speech onsets (Corley & Scheepers, 2002; Smith & Wheeldon, 2001) or more fluent formulation of utterances (Bock & Loebell, 1990). Another view describes structural priming as a shorter-term reflection of the longer-term process of learning how the syntactic constructions in a speaker's language map onto the features of meaning that they express (e.g., Bock & Griffin, 2000; Chang, Dell, Bock, & Griffin, 2000). A third view characterises structural priming as a link in a larger chain that promotes efficient and ultimately successful communication between interlocutors (Pickering & Garrod, 2004). Though fundamentally different, these accounts are in fact not mutually exclusive, a point to which we return at the end of this paper.

STRUCTURAL PRIMING AS A VEHICLE OF FLUENCY

The Law of Exercise is one of the oldest principles of psychology. A typical consequence of practicing a skill is increased fluency, ease, or efficiency in performance, and it is simple to imagine that structural priming is a manifestation of this basic principle. Smith and Wheeldon (2001) explicitly proposed that priming serves to decrease speakers' processing effort, and thereby to make speaking easier, faster, and more fluent. In line with this, they showed that structurally primed noun-phrase structures were begun more rapidly than unprimed structures (see also Corley & Scheepers, 2002). Along similar lines, Bock and Loebell (1990) observed that when passive structures were the most frequently produced structures in an experimental session, they were produced more fluently than corresponding active sentences, despite the latter's greater overall frequency in the language.

Against this hypothesis about the functional utility of priming, however, is the observation that increased fluency due to priming is short-lived (Wheeldon & Smith, 2003), whereas priming itself is at least sometimes surprisingly long-lived (see below). Moreover, Szmrecsanyi (2004, 2005) presents corpus analyses showing that speakers are actually *less* likely to use primed structures when messages are more complex, counter to the expectation that momentarily easier structures should be more likely to be deployed. This effect might be due to syntactic interference from the material that creates the greater complexity, though experimental work suggests that material in and around primed constructions does not systematically influence degree of priming (Bock, 1986; Branigan et al., 2006; Fox Tree & Meijer, 1999). Together, these observations suggest that additional accounts of syntactic priming are needed. We turn to two others in what follows.

STRUCTURAL PRIMING AS IMPLICIT LEARNING

In general, *implicit learning* refers to the incidental tuning or adjustment of the tendencies of a processing system as a function of experience. Most often, implicit learning reflects the modification of relatively superficial perceptual or motor processes. The *stem completion* task illustrates implicit learning (Roediger & Blaxton, 1987; Tulving, Schacter, & Stark, 1982). In this task, participants read a list of words (e.g., *motel*). Sometime later, they are provided with 'stems' – a list of the first few letters of words (e.g., *mot*) – and are asked to complete the stems with the first words that come to mind. People are consistently likely to complete stems with words they originally read even when the same words are unlikely to be used by control participants (who tend to use higher frequency completions such as *mother*). Awareness of or *explicit* memory for the originally studied words is unnecessary for the phenomenon to arise. These results suggest that readers' experience with words tunes the process of lexical access toward more efficient retrieval of those particular words; when the stem-completion task engages the lexical-retrieval process again, the tuned words are more likely to be retrieved and so be provided as responses.

Structural priming too might reflect the operation of an implicit-learning process. Here, the relevant processes are components of *grammatical encoding*, the processes that link features of ideas to be expressed (often termed *messages*) to syntactic configurations or constructions in the grammar of a language. That is, when comprehenders encounter linguistic expressions, one thing they must do is determine how the syntactic structures of those linguistic expressions map onto 'who did what to whom'

– how the subject, verb, direct object, indirect object, and so forth in the sentence map onto the relationships among the entities, actions, and modifiers that are identified by the (open-class) lexical content of the expression. Analogously, when producers create linguistic expressions, they must determine how the relational content of their message-level representations can be expressed in terms of grammatical subjects, direct objects, indirect objects, modifiers, adjuncts, and so forth, and in what order. Structural priming, then, might reflect tuning of this aspect of grammatical encoding: Comprehending or producing a linguistic expression causes speakers to link certain syntactic configurations in certain orders to relational structures in their message representations. Having done so once, the grammatical-encoding process is tuned to compute those linkings of message structures and syntactic configurations again (Bock et al., in press).

This idea of structural priming as implicit learning is somewhat counterintuitive. Relational knowledge represented at the message level and syntactic knowledge represented at grammatical encoding seem to be open-ended representations that are computed on the fly based on the current utterance being processed. How could the linking of such dynamic structures be subject to experience-based tuning?

One solution to this puzzle lies in imparting at least some additional structure to the relevant message-relational and syntactic levels. At the message-relational level, representational schemes such as those using event semantics (Chang, Dell, & Bock, 2006) or thematic roles (Fillmore, 1968; Jackendoff, 1972) might structure speakers' message-level representations of who did what to whom. At the syntactic level, aspects of the notion of syntactic construction or families of syntactic structures could similarly classify an otherwise open-ended syntactic vocabulary into phrasal categories consistent with structural representations in contemporary syntactic theories that call on context-sensitive grammars. Defined in this way, message-level role features that organise relational knowledge could be consistently mapped to syntactic constructions that organise syntactic knowledge. These mappings, which are semantically broad and multiply determined, but are also structurally strongly constrained, could then be subject to experience-based tuning.

One proposal along these lines comes from Chang (2002; see also Chang et al., 2006; Chang et al., 2000) in the form of models that explain structural priming in terms of error-based learning (Rumelhart, Hinton, & Williams, 1986). Learning occurs as the models come to represent the connections between abstract relational features of meaning and the word sequences that tend to convey those features. The models include a 'dual-path' architecture that creates a division of labour between the meaning representations and a sequencing system. The sequencing system in turn learns (via a simple recurrent network) to create dynamic structural frames for expressing words. This learning yields an ability to create structured sequences of words that are in important respects separable from specific meanings and can work independently of them. When the model is presented with input or produces meaningful output, the sequencing system undergoes error-based learning that causes changes in processing that yield a combination of meaning-independent and meaning-sensitive effects of structural priming.

Structural priming as learning

Some current structural-priming results are consistent with this implicit-learning interpretation. Most relevant is evidence suggesting that structural priming reflects a form of learning because (a) it can cause relatively long-lasting changes to performance, and (b) it is sensitive to speakers' current state of knowledge. The clearest evidence of the longevity of structural priming comes from Bock and Griffin (2000). They had speakers repeat auditory prime sentences that either were alternating dative forms (prepositional datives vs. double-object datives, like *The governess made [a pot of tea] [for the princess]* vs. *The governess made [the princess] [a pot of tea]*) or were alternating transitive forms (passives vs. actives, like *One of the fans was punched by the referee* vs. *The referee punched one of the fans*). Then speakers repeated some number of auditory filler sentences that were neutral structures – intransitive structures like *Bob jogs every morning* or predicate-adjective structures like *Brandon and Brenda are similar*. Finally, speakers described target pictures that after dative primes could elicit dative (prepositional or double-object) descriptions, and that after transitive primes could elicit transitive (passive or active) descriptions.

Most importantly, Bock and Griffin (2000) manipulated whether speakers heard and repeated 0, 1, 2, 4, or 10 neutral sentences between the prime sentence and the target description. Note that 10 intervening neutral sentences constitutes a substantial interruption, both in terms of time (a minute or more) and in terms of processing events (with each neutral event involving hearing a sentence, repeating it back, and judging whether the sentence had been heard in the experiment before). Nonetheless, Bock and Griffin found that structural priming was about as robust when 10 neutral sentences intervened between prime repetition and target description as it was when no neutral sentences intervened between prime repetition and target description. Bock et al. (in press) observed this pattern again, even when participants only heard and did not repeat the prime sentences (see also Bock & Kroch, 1989). So, structural priming has an important characteristic of implicit learning: It can be an enduring effect that survives across extensive amounts of intervening time and processing material (though see below for discussion of evidence suggesting that priming can sometimes be more short-lived). Developmental data, including evidence of priming in young children, are likewise consistent with this conception (Brooks & Tomasello, 1999; Huttenlocher, Vasilyeva, Cymerman, & Levine, 2002; Huttenlocher, Vasilyeva, & Shimpi, 2004).

Another set of observations pointing to the possibility that structural priming reflects a form of learning comes from the *inverse-preference* effect. In general, learning ought to be sensitive to the learner's current state of knowledge, such that when something is poorly known, it should be subject to greater learning, whereas when something is already well known, it should be subject to less learning. Formally, such asymmetries are the basis of computational accounts of the above-described error-based learning mechanisms (Chang, 2002; Chang et al., 2000; Chang et al., 2006; Rumelhart et al., 1986).

A number of observations in the literature suggest that structural priming exhibits an inverse-preference pattern (Bock, 1986; Bock & Griffin, 2000; Ferreira, 2003; Hartsuiker & Kolk, 1998; Hartsuiker, Kolk, & Huiskamp, 1999; Scheepers, 2003). Most of these have shown that structures that were in general less preferred or less common exhibited greater structural priming relative to a neutral baseline, whereas structures that were in general more preferred or more common exhibited less structural priming relative to a neutral baseline. Further evidence suggests that even the same structure exhibits greater syntactic persistence when it is produced in a context in which it is less preferred, compared to a context in which it is more preferred (Ferreira, 2003b). Other observations suggest that such inverse-preference effects too might be enduring. Specifically, Hartsuiker and Westenberg (2000) had Dutch speakers produce sentences with subordinate clauses, which in Dutch can be produced either with a participle-final or an auxiliary-final word order. Initial baseline measurements revealed that the participle-final word order was preferred to the auxiliary-final word order. Priming manipulations then revealed that relative to baseline, the more-preferred participle-final primes increased participle-final target production only weakly, whereas the less-preferred auxiliary-final primes decreased participle-final target production more strongly. When Hartsuiker and Westenberg assessed speakers' baseline preferences at the end of the experiment, after speakers had produced approximately equal numbers of each kind of prime structure, they found that speakers' baseline preferences reversed: the auxiliary-final word order was numerically preferred to the participle-final word order. This suggests that in the course of the experiment, the less-preferred auxiliary-final order accumulated more long-term priming than the more-preferred participle-final order.

Note that the sensitivity of learning to a structure's overall preference in the language addresses a potential cost of structural-priming-as-implicit-learning (Ferreira, 2003b). Specifically, the possibility that learning occurs every time a sentence is processed raises the concern that syntactic knowledge could become crystallised and inflexible, especially in light of baseline differences between structures. For example, active structures heavily outnumber passives in everyday language use, which might cause actives to effectively become overlearned and thus be used every time a speaker aims to express a transitive relational structure. However, the inverse-preference effect counteracts any such tendency: Because passive structures seemingly undergo more learning per processing event than actives (as a function of their degree of preference), inverse preference balances the more frequent learning that the active accrues.

Implicit versus explicit contributions to structural priming

The evidence reviewed thus far suggests that structural priming can be long-lived and is sensitive to the knowledge state of the primed syntactic structures. Together, these observations point to the conclusion that structural priming reflects learning. However, what is still uncertain is the degree to which structural priming is a form of *implicit* learning versus *explicit* learning (for a review of these forms of learning, see Squire, 1992). As noted above, implicit learning reflects the relatively specific tuning of a mechanism's processing tendencies – in this case, the mechanism responsible for linking the relational structures of speakers' messages to features of syntactic constructions. A different possibility is that structural priming partially or completely reflects explicit learning. By an explicit-learning account, structural priming might involve the encoding of utterances as 'facts' in long-term memory, complete with their conceptual, thematic, syntactic, lexical, and prosodic characteristics, all bound into a single episodic instance. This might be comparable to how other declarative knowledge is learned, for example, historical facts, or where one parked his or her car in the morning. Indeed, knowledge acquired through explicit learning could exhibit the features of learning that were attributed to structural priming in the previous section – explicit memories can be long-lived, and unusual explicit memories might be easier to remember than ordinary explicit memories.

In fact, based on current implicit-learning evidence, it is not obvious that structural priming could be an implicit-learning effect at all. This is because the signature effects of implicit learning are largely restricted to representational domains that are perceptual or motor in nature, such as stem completion (described above) and mirror drawing (where subjects trace shapes while viewing their actions in a mirror; see Milner, Corkin, and Teuber, 1968). Syntactic structure is neither as perceptual nor as motor in nature as these other representational domains, and so it is not obvious that structural priming, even if it is long-lived and is sensitive to a speaker's state of syntactic knowledge, could be a consequence of implicit learning of the kind revealed by tasks such as stem completion and mirror drawing. Another reservation is that implicit or procedural learning has been characterised as less relational than explicit, declarative learning (Cohen & Eichenbaum, 1993). Because syntax is nothing if not relational, this suggests that a nonrelational form of memory (implicit memory) may not be computationally capable of supporting structural priming. (Note that the conjecture that structural priming reflects implicit learning is different from the claim that syntactic processing in general might be implicit. Even if syntactic processing is implicit, it implies neither that such implicit processing leaves an enduring memory trace, nor that structural priming itself reflects sensitivity to any such memory trace.)

Until recently, just two observations spoke to possible implicit versus explicit memory contributions to structural priming. Both come from data reported in Bock et al. (1992). The first evaluated the supposition that if structural priming is implicit, there should be no relationship between speakers' explicit memory for prime sentences and the degree to which those prime sentences cause structural priming. Bock et al. (1992) assessed this prediction by determining whether primes that speakers explicitly remembered (as assessed by a multiple-choice recognition-memory test) caused more structural priming, and complementarily, whether primes that caused structural priming were better remembered. They observed no relationship between structural priming and explicit memory. Across the entire experiment, 29% of all prime sentences caused structural priming. If this priming were influenced by explicit memory, then prime sentences that were explicitly remembered should have been more effective primes, but they were not: 29% of the prime sentences that speakers explicitly remembered also caused structural priming. Complementarily, across the entire experiment, speakers explicitly remembered 66% of all prime sentences. If structural priming influenced explicit memory, then sentences that successfully caused priming should have been better remembered, but they were not: Speakers explicitly remembered 67% of the sentences that caused priming.

Another way to assess implicit versus explicit contributions to structural priming is to determine whether degree of priming is sensitive to task instructions that encourage subjects to explicitly remember syntactic structure. In the Bock et al. (1992) structural priming procedure, two groups of speakers were tested in a running-recognition memory procedure, whereby speakers are asked after each sentence whether they had heard that sentence before in the session. One group was instructed to pay close attention to the wording of sentences, because they needed to distinguish whether current sentences were different from previous sentences even if they had (roughly) the same meaning (i.e., even if they were syntactic alternations). In essence, these instructions asked speakers to (explicitly) remember the syntactic structures of the presented sentences. The second group was instructed to remember meaning and not wording, so that syntactic structure was (as in everyday language use) only incidentally remembered. Bock et al. found that the subjects instructed to remember syntax showed greater structural priming (about a 12% difference) than subjects instructed to remember meaning (about a 5% difference). This suggests that structural priming is sensitive to explicit memory for syntax, which in turn is consistent with the possibility that structural priming might be due to explicit-memory functioning.

Less equivocal evidence that structural priming is an implicit-memory phenomenon comes in data from Ferreira, Bock, Wilson, and Cohen (2005). They assessed structural priming in a group of patients with *anterograde amnesia*. Anterograde amnesia is a memory condition that causes a severely impaired ability to encode new knowledge into explicit memory. At the same time, anterograde amnesia leaves implicit learning nearly intact. For example, if someone with anterograde amnesia is shown a list of words, later recognition memory ('indicate whether this word was on the previous list') or recall ('say all of the words from the previous list') performance will be much worse than that of a matched control. But when tested in a stem-completion task, the words from the previous list are as likely to emerge as completions as when a matched control is tested in the same task. Anterograde amnesia thus provides a powerful way to assess whether structural priming is based on implicit memory.

Ferreira et al. (2005) tested speakers with anterograde amnesia and matched control speakers in a structural priming paradigm similar to the one used by Bock and Griffin (2000). The procedure assessed both structural priming from and explicit memory for a set of prime sentences. Results showed that speakers with anterograde amnesia exhibited about the same amount of structural priming (an 8% effect) as matched controls (a 7% effect). Despite these comparable structural priming levels, speakers with anterograde amnesia exhibited a marked recognition memory impairment. Specifically, when speakers with anterograde amnesia discriminated prime sentences from a set of semantically and/or syntactically distinct foils, they showed a discriminability (d') score of 0.9, whereas control speakers showed a discriminability score of 1.8. Thus, the same prime sentences that caused about equivalent structural priming in speakers with anterograde amnesia and control speakers led to significantly poorer recognition memory in speakers with anterograde amnesia than in control speakers. In fact, when the structural priming and recognition memory measures of the speakers with anterograde amnesia were separately standardised with respect to control performance, speakers with anterograde amnesia exhibited impaired recognition memory (a z-score of -1.8) but normal structural priming (a z-score of 0.1). This points to a dissociation between these forms of memory.

The observation of intact structural priming in amnesic patients despite their impaired explicit memory strongly suggests that at least a component of the structural priming effect reflects implicit learning. This agrees with the evidence described above showing a dissociation between implicit and explicit memory for sentences (Bock et al., 1992). The contrary observation, that of greater structural priming observed when speakers were told to attend to the wordings of sentences (Bock et al., 1992) might either reflect an attentional effect (the message-to-syntax links that are subject to implicit learning might have been subject to greater strengthening due to heightened attention to syntax irrespective of explicit learning), or an additional explicit-memory contribution to structural priming (in fact, the possibility that structural priming might be multifaceted in this manner will be addressed further below). Evidence that at least a component of the structural priming effect reflects the operation of implicit memory, when combined with the evidence described in the previous section suggesting that structural priming has properties of learning in general (it is long-lived and is sensitive to the state of speakers' syntactic knowledge), suggests that structural priming has both features of implicit learning – it's implicit, and it's learning.

STRUCTURAL PRIMING AS ALIGNMENT

Recently, Pickering and Garrod (Garrod & Pickering, 2004; Pickering & Garrod, 2004) more formally developed a notion initially suggested by Branigan et al. (2000a), that structural priming might implement an important dialogue function. Branigan et al.'s initial observation was that not only is structural priming evident in dialogue – from 'prime' sentences that a speaker hears from an interlocutor to 'target' sentences that the speaker says back to his or her interlocutor – but the numerical size of the priming effect is substantially larger than the structural priming effects that have been revealed in standard (memory-based isolated production) structural-priming paradigms (Bock, 1986; Bock & Griffin, 2000; Ferreira et al., 2005). Pickering and Garrod synthesised this general idea into the construct of *alignment*. The claim is that during dialogue, interlocutors strive to align their representations of the current situation at hand (their *situation models*). Representations in situation models, in turn, are systematically related to the lexical and syntactic devices that interlocutors use to describe them. This implies that if interlocutors align on lexical and syntactic levels, using the same words and structures to describe comparable aspects of the situation, alignment at the situation model is more likely as a result. In short, structural priming may directly reflect communication among interlocutors, by revealing the correspondence of their respective representations of (ultimately) the situation at hand.

The implicit learning and alignment views of structural priming are often placed in opposition to one another. However, the two accounts are not mutually exclusive. In fact, what could be taken as the central claims of the two views are strikingly complementary: Structural priming as implicit learning claims that when speakers link a relational structure (represented in a message) to a particular syntactic configuration, the tendency to link those two again becomes stronger (i.e., there is learning); priming is one manifestation of that strengthening. Structural priming as alignment claims (or can be taken to claim) that the links between syntactic configurations and the relational structures represented in situation models allow primed (aligned) syntactic configurations to promote priming (alignment) of relational structures (represented in situation models). Drawing a correspondence between messages and situation models, we see that both explanations for structural priming rely on the notion that representations between distinct levels (messages/situation models and syntax) are strengthened as a function of use. The implicit learning account formalised by Chang et al. (2006) emphasises that such strengthening reflects the gradual acquisition of the relevant knowledge, whereas the alignment account emphasises that a consequence of such strengthening, the binding of representations, can promote communication among interlocutors.

In fact, it is straightforward to posit an evolution (in a nongenetic sense) from structural-priming-as-implicit-learning to structural-priming-as-alignment and vice versa. This evolution emphasises the development and use of knowledge relationships that form the bedrock of *bootstrapping* accounts of language acquisition, both syntactic bootstrapping (Landau & Gleitman, 1985) and semantic bootstrapping (Pinker, 1989). The general idea is that as we accumulate linguistic experience, implicit learning mechanisms strengthen the knowledge relationships between relational structures represented in our messages/situation models and the syntactic configurations made available to us through our grammar. This is how we learn message-to-syntax relationships. With the strengthening of a message-to-syntax link comes increased use of that link – persistence due to priming. This implies that priming in the form of repetition of a particular syntactic configuration can be used to infer the presence of a particular message structure in the interlocutor who exhibits the priming. This inference is presumably tacit, and according to Pickering and Garrod (2004), automatic. Thus, if interlocutors become sensitive to repetition within a particular dialogue context (a 'situation', in the sense of the situation model used by Pickering and Garrod), the repeated structure or material can support communication of one aspect of the subject matter at hand, namely the relational meanings under discussion.

From this evolution, it is a small step to a more independent structural-priming-as-alignment mechanism. Consider how we develop nonsyntactic strategies that communicate effectively, say, using particular patterns of intonation that capture attention, or using particular patterns of gesture that convey scalar properties. Presumably, such strategies develop because we are (tacitly) sensitive to the systematic relationships between particular behaviours (intonation, gesture) and their communicative consequences (capturing attention, conveying scalar properties). Eventually, the sensitivity to these systematic relationships becomes instantiated as a (tacit) strategy, whereby we use the behaviours themselves to achieve the communicative effects. So too might we be sensitive to the relationship between priming (i.e., the seeming overrepresentation of a linguistic feature in a particular context) and the prevalence of the corresponding message structures (a relationship which, according to the structural-priming-as-implicit-learning account, should not only exist, but ought to be systematic as well). This sensitivity begets a tacit strategy whereby priming between interlocutors can be used as a device to better infer relational meaning and thereby achieve more successful communication. Viewed in this way, structural-priming-as-implicit-learning may play a critical role in structural-priming-as-alignment by explaining why representations of meaning and representations of syntactic form might be systematically related to one another in the first place. Indeed, this kind of account can be seen in Pickering and Garrod's (2004) explanation for *routinisation*, a longer-term (e.g., learning-based) representation and use of lexical and phrasal devices that carry relatively specific meanings (see also Kuiper, 1996).

This latter 'small step' carries an important implication: If structural-priming-as-alignment has its own at least partially independent processing mechanism, then structural priming might have multiple underlying cognitive bases. In particular, it may be that structural priming has both a longer-term manifestation, critical to its function as a reflection of implicit learning, and a shorter-term manifestation, critical to its function in alignment. Interestingly, a number of observations in the structural priming literature point to the possibility that structural priming has multiple cognitive bases. Suggestive evidence is reviewed next.

The multiplicity of structural priming

Though Bock and Griffin (2000) presented evidence that structural priming can be long-lived, other observations show that priming can be quite transient. For example, Levelt and Kelter (1982) showed that a priming-like pattern in spoken production, involving the repetition of words and structures, disappeared after a single clause. Similarly, Branigan, Pickering, and Cleland (1999) found that with written production, processing even one intervening neutral sentence causes structural priming to diminish. However, Branigan, Pickering, Stewart, and McLean (2000b) showed that under similar circumstances with spoken production, structural priming was robust over longer intervals. Exactly what conditions cause structural priming to be shorter- or longer-lived is presently unclear; for present purposes, what is important is that these different time courses point to a complex structural priming effect with more than one cognitive basis.

A second set of observations that points to the multiplicity of structural priming is the evidence from production-latency investigations reviewed above. That is, a number of reports have shown that on trials where speakers exhibit structural priming, they begin their utterances more quickly than on trials where they do not exhibit structural priming (Corley & Scheepers, 2002; Smith & Wheeldon, 2001). As noted above, however, such production-latency effects of structural priming are markedly short-lived: Wheeldon and Smith (2003) observed that when one neutral trial intervened between prime and target sentences, the production-latency benefit is eliminated. They argue that because the production-latency effect is more short-lived than the structure-choice effect, that the effects likely have different cognitive bases, one shorter term (which could underlie alignment effects) and the other longer term (which could underlie implicit-learning effects).

Also relevant is that nonsyntactic factors appear to influence the likelihood of syntactic repetition. That is, the magnitude of structural priming is affected by whether speakers repeat content words from prime to target sentences (Pickering & Branigan, 1998), or even whether the content words in prime and target sentences are semantically similar to one another (Cleland & Pickering, 2003). The order of adjectives in speakers' utterances (e.g., 'stripy orange circle' vs. 'orange stripy circle') is also subject to persistence (Haywood, Pickering, & Branigan, 2003), even though the syntactic differences between such structures is not obvious. And the magnitude of structural priming can be independently boosted by whether speakers are able to repeat semantic or thematic assignments between prime and target sentences (Bock et al., 1992; Chang et al., 2003).

Conceivably, a basic syntactic repetition effect may reflect the operation of a longer-lived, implicit learning mechanism, whereas in the shorter term, the binding of specific contents (lexical, semantic, or thematic) and positions in specific structures triggers the repetition of structure. Because these shorter-term effects involve multiple cognitive dimensions, it is reasonable to suppose that they rely more heavily on explicit-memory processes. Consequently, the influences that trigger the shorter-term effect should have a shorter time course, dissipating over intervening events. Konopka and Bock (2005) observed a pattern of this kind with respect to the influence of open-class lexical repetition between prime and target sentences. Like Pickering and Branigan (1998), they obtained larger structural-priming effects when prime and target sentences shared main verbs. This lexically enhanced priming was observed when no neutral trials intervened between prime and target sentences. However, when neutral trials separated the prime and target sentences, the levels of structural priming were the same regardless of whether the verbs repeated.

This suggests that multiple mechanisms can contribute to structural priming. Shorter-term effects may be broadly sensitive to disparate kinds of repetition that occur between prime and target sentences, whereas longer-term effects may more specifically reflect structural learning. This follows from the proposed functional taxonomy: Dynamic, shorter-term effects, sensitive to the kinds of repetition that flag coordination among interlocutors, are suitably flexible supports for alignment; repetitions of the relational mapping from message structures to syntactic configurations reflect a longer-term learning of message-to-syntax relationships that support communication more broadly.

SUMMARY AND CONCLUSIONS

The evidence reviewed here suggests the following: Structural priming has characteristics of learning in general, in that it can be long-lived (Bock & Griffin, 2000) and shows evidence of sensitivity to the state of a speaker's knowledge of the learning domain (e.g., Ferreira, 2003b; Hartsuiker & Westenberg, 2000). Structural priming also appears to be due to implicit learning, being as robust in speakers with anterograde amnesia as it is in matched controls, despite the profound recognition memory impairments of the amnesic speakers for the very same prime sentences. More speculatively, structural priming may consist of several component effects, one based on shorter-term memory that appears at short prime-target lags and the other based on longer-term memory that appears at long prime-target lags. This possibility is suggested by a variety of evidence in the structural priming literature showing that in general, structural priming is a multifaceted effect.

This evidence makes a convincing case that structural priming reflects implicit learning, exhibiting the characteristics of other implicit learning effects (for a complete presentation of the ways in which structural priming looks like implicit learning, see Bock & Griffin, 2000). Such implicit learning can be seen as a mechanism by which speakers come to connect and strengthen their knowledge that specific relational structures encoded in message representations can be expressed by specific syntactic configurations in their grammar. The evidence is also consistent with the claim that structural priming supports normal communicative functions, whereby some of the bindings that enter into priming are exploited to allow interlocutors to more confidently infer the representation of particular message structures during dialogue. The possibility that structural priming has several processing bases, some that are short-lived and underlie alignment effects and others with longer-term consequences, is tentatively suggested by the different time-courses of lexically enhanced and lexically independent structural priming.

In sum, the issues discussed in this paper help shed light on why language users might be so surprisingly recapitulative: The repetition of linguistic features – the features of everyday conversational interaction – may reflect the workings of basic learning processes, and at the same time provide important communicative benefits. It is this effective learning and communicative facility that ultimately allows the creative linguistic capacity in humans to be successfully learned, and then effectively used.

REFERENCES

Bock, J. K. (1986). Syntactic persistence in language production. *Cognitive Psychology, 18,* 355–387.

Bock, J. K. (1989). Closed-class immanence in sentence production. *Cognition, 31,* 163–186.

Bock, J. K., Dell, G. S., Chang, F., & Onishi, K. H. (in press). Persistence structural priming from language comprehension to language production. *Cognition.*

Bock, J. K., & Griffin, Z. M. (2000). The persistence of structural priming: Transient activation or implicit learning? *Journal of Experimental Psychology: General, 129* (2), 177–192.

Bock, J. K., & Kroch, A. S. (1989). The isolability of syntactic processing. In G. N. Carlson & M. K. Tanenhaus (Eds.), *Linguistic structure in language processing* (pp. 157–196). Dordrecht: Kluwer.

Bock, J. K., & Loebell, H. (1990). Framing sentences. *Cognition, 35,* 1–39.

Bock, J. K., Loebell, H., & Morey, R. (1992). From conceptual roles to structural relations: Bridging the syntactic cleft. *Psychological Review, 99,* 150–171.

Branigan, H. P., Pickering, M. J., & Cleland, A. A. (1999). Syntactic priming in written production: Evidence for rapid decay. *Psychonomic Bulletin and Review, 6* (4), 635–640.

Branigan, H. P., Pickering, M. J., & Cleland, A. A. (2000a). Syntactic co-ordination in dialogue. *Cognition, 75*(2), B13–B25.

Branigan, H. P., Pickering, M. J., McLean, J. F., & Stewart, A. J. (2006). The role of global and local syntactic structure in language production: Evidence from syntactic priming. *Language and Cognitive Processes, 21,* 974–1010.

Branigan, H. P., Pickering, M. J., Stewart, A. J., & McLean, J. F. (2000b). Syntactic priming in spoken production: Linguistic and temporal interference. *Memory and Cognition, 28* (*8*), 1297–1302.

Brooks, P. J., & Tomasello, M. (1999). Young children learn to produce passives with nonce verbs. *Developmental Psychology, 35* (*5*), 29–44.

Chang, F. (2002). Symbolically speaking: A connectionist model of sentence production. *Cognitive Science, 26*, 609–651.

Chang, F., Bock, J. K., & Goldberg, A. (2003). Can thematic roles leave traces of their places? *Cognition, 90*, 29–49.

Chang, F., Dell, G. S., & Bock, J. K. (2006). Becoming syntactic. *Psychological Review, 113*, 234–272.

Chang, F., Dell, G. S., Bock, J. K., & Griffin, Z. M. (2000). Structural priming as implicit learning: A comparison of models of sentence production. *Journal of Psycholinguistic Research, 29* (*2*), 217–229.

Cleland, A. A., & Pickering, M. J. (2003). The use of lexical and syntactic information in language production: Evidence from the priming of noun-phrase structure. *Journal of Memory and Language, 49* (*2*), 214–230.

Cohen, N. J., & Eichenbaum, H. (1993). *Memory, amnesia, and the hippocampal system.* Cambridge, MA: MIT Press.

Corley, M., & Scheepers, C. (2002). Syntactic priming in English sentence production: Categorical and latency evidence from an internet-based study. *Psychonomic Bulletin and Review, 9* (*1*), 126–131.

Dell, G. S., Burger, L. K., & Svec, W. R. (1997). Language production and serial order: A functional analysis and a model. *Psychological Review, 104* (*1*), 123–147.

Ferreira, V. S. (2003a). The persistence of optional complementizer production: Why saying "that" is not saying "that" at all. *Journal of Memory and Language, 48* (*2*), 379–398.

Ferreira, V. S. (2003b). *The processing basis of syntactic persistence: We repeat what we learn.* Paper presented at the 44th Annual Meeting of the Psychonomic Society, Vancouver, Canada.

Ferreira, V. S., Bock, J. K., Wilson, M., & Cohen, N. J. (2005). *Structural persistence in anterograde amnesia: Evidence for implicit learning.* Paper presented at the 46th Annual Meeting of the Psychonomic Society, Toronto, Canada.

Fillmore, C. J. (1968). The case for case. In E. Bach & R. T. Harms (Eds.), *Universals in linguistic theory* (pp. 1–88). New York: Holt, Rinehart and Winston.

Fox Tree, J. E., & Meijer, P. J. A. (1999). Building syntactic structure in speaking. *Journal of Psycholinguistic Research, 28* (*1*), 71–92.

Garrod, S., & Anderson, A. (1987). Saying what you mean in dialogue: A study in a conceptual and semantic co-ordination. *Cognition, 27*, 181–218.

Garrod, S., & Pickering, M. J. (2004). Why is conversation so easy? *Trends in Cognitive Sciences, 8* (*1*), 8–11.

Gries, S. (2005). Syntactic priming: A corpus-based approach. *Journal of Psycholinguistic Research, 34*, 365–399.

Griffin, Z. M., & Weinstein-Tull, J. (2003). Conceptual structure modulates structural priming in the production of complex sentences. *Journal of Memory and Language, 49* (*4*), 537–555.

Hartsuiker, R. J., & Kolk, H. H. J. (1998). Syntactic persistence in Dutch. *Language and Speech, 41* (*2*), 143–184.

Hartsuiker, R. J., Kolk, H. H. J., & Huiskamp, P. (1999). Priming word order in sentence production. *Quarterly Journal of Experimental Psychology, 52A*, 129–147.

Hartsuiker, R. J., & Westenberg, C. (2000). Word order priming in written and spoken sentence production. *Cognition, 75* (*2*), B27–B39.

Haywood, S., Pickering, M. J., & Branigan, H. P. (2003, March). *Priming and audience design: Evidence for the effect of different processes on language production in dialogue.* Paper presented at the 16th Annual CUNY Conference on Human Sentence Processing, Cambridge, MA.

Huttenlocher, J., Vasilyeva, M., Cymerman, E., & Levine, S. (2002). Language input and child syntax. *Cognitive Psychology, 45*(3), 337–374.

Huttenlocher, J., Vasilyeva, M., & Shimpi, P. (2004). Syntactic priming in young children. *Journal of Memory and Language, 50*(2), 182–195.

Jackendoff, R. S. (1972). *Semantic interpretation in generative grammar.* Cambridge, MA: MIT Press.

Konopka, B., & Bock, J. K. (2005, April). *Helping syntax out: What do words do?* Paper presented at the 18th Annual CUNY Conference on Human Sentence Processing, Tucson, AZ.

Kubovy, M. (1977). Response availability and the apparent spontaneity of numerical choices. *Journal of Experimental Psychology: Human Perception and Performance, 3,* 359–364.

Kuiper, K. (1996). *Smooth talkers: The linguistic performance of auctioneers and sportscasters.* Mahwah, NJ: Lawrence Erlbaum Associates Inc.

Landau, B., & Gleitman, L. R. (1985). *Language and experience: Evidence from the blind child.* Cambridge, MA: Harvard University Press.

Levelt, W. J. M., & Kelter, S. (1982). Surface form and memory in question answering. *Cognitive Psychology, 14,* 78–106.

Loebell, H., & Bock, K. (2003). Structural priming across languages. *Linguistics, 41*(5), 791–824.

Milner, B., Corkin, S., & Teuber, H. L. (1968). Further analysis of the hippocampal amnesic syndrome: 14-year follow-up study of H. M. *Neuropsychologia, 6* (3), 215–234.

Pickering, M. J., & Branigan, H. P. (1998). The representation of verbs: Evidence from syntactic priming in language production. *Journal of Memory and Language, 39* (4), 633–651.

Pickering, M. J., & Garrod, S. (2004). Toward a mechanistic psychology of dialogue. *Behavioral and Brain Sciences, 27* (2), 169–226.

Pinker, S. (1989). *Learnability and cognition: The acquisition of argument structure.* Cambridge, MA: MIT Press.

Roediger, H. L., & Blaxton, T. A. (1987). Effects of varying modality, surface features, and retention interval on priming in word-fragment completion. *Memory and Cognition, 15* (5), 379–388.

Rumelhart, D. E., Hinton, G. E., & Williams, R. J. (1986). Learning internal representations by error propagation. In D. E. Rumelhart & J. L. McClelland (Eds.), *Parallel distributed processing: Explorations in the microstructure of cognition.* Cambridge, MA: MIT Press.

Scheepers, C. (2003). Syntactic priming of relative clause attachments: Persistence of structural configuration in sentence production. *Cognition, 89* (3), 179–205.

Smith, M., & Wheeldon, L. (2001). Syntactic priming in spoken sentence production: An online study. *Cognition, 78* (2), 123–164.

Squire, L. R. (1992). Memory and the hippocampus: A synthesis from findings with rats, monkeys, and humans. *Psychological Review, 99* (2), 195–231.

Szmrecsanyi, B. (2004). *Persistence phenomena in the grammar of spoken English.* Unpublished Ph.D. dissertation, Albert-Ludwigs-Universität Freiburg, Freiburg, Germany.

Szmrecsanyi, B. (2005). Language users as creatures of habit: A corpus-based analysis of persistence in spoken English. *Corpus Linguistics and Linguistic Theory, 1,* 113–149.

Tulving, E., Schacter, D. L., & Stark, H. A. (1982). Priming effects in word-fragment completion are independent of recognition memory. *Journal of Experimental Psychology: Learning, Memory, and Cognition, 8*, 336–342.

Weiner, E. J., & Labov, W. (1983). Constraints on the agentless passive. *Journal of Linguistics, 19*, 29–58.

Wheeldon, L. R., & Smith, M. C. (2003). Phrase structure priming: A short-lived effect. *Language and Cognitive Processes, 18* (*4*), 431–442.

Language and Cognitive Processes
Special Issue Subject Index

For Product Safety Concerns and Information please contact our EU
representative GPSR@taylorandfrancis.com Taylor & Francis Verlag GmbH,
Kaufingerstraße 24, 80331 München, Germany

Batch number: 08153805

Printed by Printforce, the Netherlands